Secretary Stimson

Secretary Stimson

A STUDY IN STATECRAFT

With a new Introduction by the Author

Richard N. Current

Archon Books, 1970

ISBN: 0 208 00966 3
Library of Congress Catalog Card Number: 71-114419

74661

PRINTED IN THE UNITED STATES OF AMERICA

To
J. W. B., Jr.

Contents

INTRODUCTION TO THE 1970 EDITION

This book first appeared in the spring of 1954, when the Eisenhower administration was about to commit the United States to the support of South Vietnam. The book's protagonist, Henry L. Stimson, had then been dead for four years. Yet these pages have something to say, at least by indirection, about the Vietnam involvement. The policy that led to the involvement and that continues to sustain it is the practical expression of an idea, and the idea owes a great deal to Stimson. Though he did not originate the concept, he revitalized it and gave it respectability and authority.

The idea in question has no single, satisfactory label, but it has often been called "collective security." This term is rather hard to define, its connotations depending somewhat on the user and the circumstances. Essential to any definition, however, is the element of *cooperation among nations to enforce peace.* The concept assumes a rather clear-cut distinction between good and bad, law-abiding and law-breaking, or "peace-loving" and "aggressor" countries. It implies an obligation, on the part of the peace lovers, to "punish" the aggressors and thus, presumably, to deter other potential evildoers from their wicked ways. That is to say, it entails upon certain nations the duty of policing the world and making the others behave. Its logical consequence is war to end or prevent war.

Though the phrase "collective security" did not come into circulation until the 1930's, the concept itself had been developed earlier by a number of statesmen and publicists, including prominent Americans. Even before World War I, Theodore Roosevelt had proposed the "establishment of some form of international police power," this to be exercised by "some combination between those great nations which sincerely desire peace." Roosevelt presented his plan in the homely and familiar American terms of the vigilance committee and the posse, as if international politics were comparable to the struggle between bad men and law-abiding citizens in the Wild West.

After the outbreak of World War I, Woodrow Wilson made himself the foremost of the idea's growing number of advocates. There must be, President Wilson said in 1916, "a universal alliance to maintain freedom of the seas and to prevent any war begun either a) contrary to treaty covenants or b) without warning and full inquiry,—a virtual guarantee of territorial integrity and political independence." At that time Wilson apparently had no intention of taking the United States into the war, no intention of trying for a crushing defeat of Germany. As late as January 22, 1917, he explained that the new international arrangement must be based upon a compromise peace, a "peace without victors," since "only a peace between equals can last."

When, only six weeks later, Wilson led the United States into the war, his idea of an association of the nations underwent a profound, though subtle, change. In his war message (April 2, 1917) he spoke of what amounted to a *partial* league rather than a "universal alliance." According to his new conception, the postwar organization was to include only the "free peoples," only the democratic and peace-loving nations, only those who could be trusted to "keep faith" and observe the "covenants." And the organization was to be based on no "peace between equals." The way to end wars and make the world safe for democracy, it now appeared, was first of all to smash the troublemakers, the autocracies that reportedly had inflicted war upon innocent humanity.

Afterwards, in rejecting Wilson's League of Nations, the United States Senate repudiated the notion that this country ought to pledge itself "to go to war whenever war may be necessary" for maintaining the integrity or independence of any and all the League members. Whatever the real opinion of the American people in 1919 and 1920, the great majority soon lost interest in the idea of enforcing peace. Only a few continued to hope that the United States would somehow associate itself with the League as a peace-enforcement agency.

These few convinced themselves that the United States, without actually joining the League, had finally associated itself with it when, in 1928, the American government sponsored the Pact of Paris, or Kellogg Pact. This treaty, which practically every nation in the world eventually signed, bound the signatories to "renounce" war as an "instrument of national policy" and to seek solutions for their disputes only "by pacific means." The treaty contained no provisions for its enforcement, and its negotiator, Secretary of State Frank B. Kellogg, made perfectly clear that, regardless of its terms, all the parties remained free to do as they pleased so long as they said they were acting in self-defense. Nevertheless, the League's friends in the United States contended, in the words of one of them, that the treaty linked their government with the League as a "guardian of peace."

The first high government official to find in the Kellogg Pact a call to collective security was Kellogg's successor in the State Department, Henry L. Stimson. Years earlier, Stimson had joined with other prominent Republicans to wreck Wilson's hopes for American membership in the League of Nations. By 1932, however, taking Japan's conquest of Manchuria as a personal affront, he was casting about for means to punish the Japanese. He now asserted that the Kellogg Pact had opened a wholly new era in international relations. Hereafter, according to him, war was "an illegal thing" and if any signer of the pact should attempt it, none of the rest of the signatories would have the option of neutrality: all must combine in putting down the alleged aggressor. In his effort to base American policy on these assumptions, Stimson as Secretary of State ran into difficulty because of the opposition of President Herbert Hoover and because of the hesitancy of the League powers themselves. Stimson found President Franklin D. Roosevelt somewhat more sympathetic and, after joining the Roosevelt administration as Secretary of War in 1940, had a part in the toughening of policy against Japan.

World War II brought about a reversal of public opinion on the question of enforcing peace. Opinion polls in 1942 and 1943 indicated that a large majority of Americans were now ready for the United States to take its place in a world organization with an "international police force." Many of them were becoming convinced that the war had resulted from a "great betrayal"—the refusal of the United States to live up to Wilson's ideals and join his League. These people rejoiced when, in 1945, the Senate almost unanimously approved of American membership in the United Nations. They nevertheless had a lingering sense of guilt because of the country's previous failure and its presumed responsibility for the recent holocaust. Very likely this guilt feeling helped to account for the extreme, fanatical devotion that Americans in subsequent years continued to give to the idea of collective security, regardless of the particular form or forms that the idea was to take in actual practice.

Once the UN was launched, it of course provided no such big-power cooperation for policing the world as had been hoped for. The assumption on which the UN as a peace-keeping organization was based—the assumption of unity among the victorious powers—proved illusory from the outset. The prospect, already grim, grew worse when the Russians began to share the secrets of atomic fission and fusion.

Instead of relying on the UN, the American government turned to developing a system of alliances: the Rio Pact, NATO, SEATO, and all the rest. Official spokesmen justified these under the UN charter's provisions regarding "regional" and "self-defense" arrangements, even though the alliances obviously were directed against a fellow UN member. "The steps we take to strengthen our collective security," Secretary of State Dean Acheson assured the General Assembly (September 20, 1950), "are not only essential to the survival of the United Nations but will contribute positively toward its development."

The idea of peace enforcement underlay the military intervention in Korea, with the formal approval of the UN, and then the intervention in Vietnam, without such approval. Referring to Vietnam, Secretary of State John Foster Dulles rephrased the idea in 1954. "Under the conditions of today," he declared, "the imposition on Southeast Asia of the political system of Communist Russia and its Chinese Communist ally, by whatever means, must be a grave threat to the whole free community. The United States feels that that possibility should not be passively accepted but should be met by united action. This might involve serious risks. But these risks are far less than those that will face us in a few years from now if we do not be resolute today." Secretary of State Dean Rusk continued the Dulles policy and expounded it in similar terms. "The principle of collective security for defense is as old as the history of nations," Rusk stated in a 1961 address to the SEATO council. "We cannot imagine the survival of our own free institutions if areas of the world distant from our own shores are to be subjugated by force or penetration. We cannot hope for peace for ourselves if insatiable appetite is unrestrained elsewhere."

That continued to be the official line as the Vietnam war dragged on to become the longest in American history, to leave a toll of American dead exceeding 40,000 and wounded exceeding 260,000, to strain the national economy with inflationary war spending, and to rend the whole society with dissension over the necessity, the justice, and even the sanity of the government's course. In announcing his determination to keep on supporting the South Vietnamese generals' regime, President Richard M. Nixon on November 3, 1969, restated the familiar doctrine of peace through war. "Our defeat and humiliation in South Vietnam would without question promote recklessness in the councils of those great powers who have not yet abandoned their goals of world conquest," Nixon averred. "This would spark violence wherever our commitments help maintain peace—in the Middle East, in Berlin, eventually even in the Western Hemisphere."

Thus, during the two decades since Stimson's death (in 1950), during the administrations of five Presidents (Truman, Eisenhower, Kennedy, Johnson, Nixon), the United States has persisted in carrying on what might fairly be called a Stimsonian policy. "To Secretary of State Dean Acheson," as James Reston wrote in 1951, "Mr. Stimson was much more than an illustrious predecessor. He was a personal hero, carefully studied and perhaps unconsciously followed." Acheson, like Stimson, was "determined to punish the aggressors in Korea and China as much as possible." In the same spirit, whether consciously following Stimson's example or not, Acheson's successors have been determined to "punish the aggressors" in Vietnam.

The idea of collective security, in the form in which Woodrow Wilson originally presented it, has an undeniable charm. Just imagine a world in which all the nations join together—as members of a "universal alliance"—to enforce the law and preserve the peace! For that matter, imagine a world in which the nations even agree on what the law is and who the violators or "aggressors" are! But that dream, of course, has yet to come true. Wilson himself soon turned to a more modest and more exclusive vision, embracing only selected, victorious countries and excluding the rest. Even this vision was realized quite imperfectly in the League of Nations and in the United Nations. Recognizing the imperfections of the UN as a peace-enforcement agency, the American government turned to a system of partial alliances, while invoking the UN charter to give the appearance of international constitutionality to them. When the allies refused to go along with the "commitments" that the American government claimed for one of the alliances—as Great Britain and France refused to do in the case of SEATO and Vietnam —the United States went it alone except for Australia, New Zealand, and a few small mercenary client countries. Collective security had become less and less collective, if not also less and less secure.

Yet, all the while, the advocates of collective security continued to talk of enforcing law and morality, punishing aggressors, and thereby assuring future peace. Theirs is the Stimson style.

"Prof. Current's book is timely," ran an editorial in the *Cleveland Plain Dealer* of April 6, 1954, ". . . in view of the fact that the problems facing the United States in Indochina are quite similar to those with which Secretary Stimson struggled." Another editorial, in the New York *Sunday News* of May 25, 1954, referred to President Eisenhower's recent assurances that there would be no unconstitutional involvement in the Indo-China war, Vice President Nixon's blurting "off the record" that the United States might send troops to Indo-China if the French should pull out, and Secretary Dulles' hints that he himself favored a "keep-'em guessing" policy. "We have a strong hunch," the *Sunday News* commented, "that Dulles could profit considerably from a fairly close reading of a new book: 'Secretary Stimson: A Study in Statecraft,' by Richard N. Current."

Though a few of the academic reviewers also saw in the book some relevance to contemporary events, on the whole they gave it a rather mixed reception. One of the more favorable reviewers, William A. Williams (then of the University of Oregon), remarked: "It is unpopular—as a survey of the reviews of Current's book will attest—to challenge the idea that America is duty bound to liberate the world." Except for Williams and one or two others, such as William L. Neumann (Goucher) and Jeannette P. Nichols (Pennsylvania), the experts in diplomatic and military history who reviewed the book found in it more to condemn than to praise.

The dean of American diplomatic historians, Samuel Flagg Bemis (Yale), characterized it as an "ironical, provocative, and clever book, brilliantly written." Probably he did not intend all those adjectives in a complimentary sense. Anyhow, he disagreed on three of five issues that apparently seemed to him the most important. He argued, by way of dissent, that (1) "Japan did not go to war because of the Stimson Doctrine or any last-minute embargoes in 1941. She went to war because, as captured Japanese archives show, the European conflict seemed to her war lords to present the opportunity of a nation's lifetime to conquer an opulent empire in Greater Eastern Asia, including India, Australia, New Zealand and the archipelagoes of the Pacific." (2) "Stimson's casual thought of maneuvering the Japanese into firing the first shot in war with the United States" was irrelevant—which indicates that the reviewer did not read carefully if at all the pertinent pages of the book, for it nowhere supports the view that Stimson (or Roosevelt) thought literally of maneuvering the Japanese into firing on this country or its possessions. Bemis agreed with the author on (3) Stimson's "inadequate vigilance in guarding against a surprise attack at Pearl Harbor" and his "trying to evade his share of responsibility for the disaster," and (4) the inadequacy of his "justification of the use of the atom bomb." But Bemis took exception again in regard to (5) "Stimson's labors to give authority to a new doctrine of international law which affirms the use of force as a means of deterring or bringing to a righteous peace an outlaw so declared by collective judgment"—a doctrine which "has captured the opinions of mankind throughout a large portion of the free world" and which "may mean the preservation of freedom as we know it."

A number of other critics concurred with Bemis on the causes of the war between Japan and the United States. One of these critics, George Albert Lanyi (Oberlin), repeating almost word for word a portion of the Bemis review, said the reason for the Japanese decision to attack Pearl Harbor was "neither the Stimson doctrine nor our last-minute economic embargoes" but rather the conclusion on the part of the "rulers of Japan" that the time was ripe for conquering a vast new empire. Robert H. Ferrell (Indiana) added: "The fact that we entered the war in 1941 had little to do with the effect of the Stimson Doctrine upon the Japanese; it had long been forgotten in Tokyo."

Ferrell could have arrived at this dictum only by confining himself to a very narrow squint at the Stimson Doctrine and seeing no more in it than the words of the nonrecognition note as dispatched to Japan at the beginning of 1932. As for the contention of Bemis and Lanyi that American policy up to December 7, 1941, had absolutely nothing to do with the Pearl Harbor attack—this is hardly borne out either by common sense or by the evidence, including that in the "captured Japanese archives." Some of the Japanese officials had plans of conquest, of course, but others doubted the feasibility of the plans: the Tokyo government as well as the Washington government contained relatively dove-like elements along with extremely hawkish ones. There is good reason to doubt whether the hawks could have prevailed in Japan if the hawks had not also prevailed in the United States. In any case, there is no reason to believe that the Japanese would have attacked Pearl Harbor if the Americans had refrained from imposing the 1941 embargo or had agreed to relax it.

"When one reads Professor Current's list of reasons for the [postwar] 'empty places' in the Far East [p. 240], one notes at least one omission," wrote Gordon Craig (Princeton). "Were not the Japanese, in their blind ambition, also responsible for the fate which overtook them?" Of course they were. But the question is not quite so pertinent as Craig represented it; he overlooked the brief reference to it in the book [pp. 242–243]. Alexander DeConde (Duke) made the same criticism and the same oversight when he complained: "The deeds of the Axis powers in bringing on World War II are given too little consideration." The Craig and DeConde strictures reflect a point of view much like that of the Johnson and Nixon administrations with respect to Vietnam: the decision for peace or war is up to the other side; we ourselves have no choice.

The issue of collective security drew fire not only from Bemis but also from other critics, most of whom appeared to share, in one degree or another, Stimson's feeling that peace and international morality are the products of military force. "One feels," Ferrell remarked, "that Mr. Current is rephrasing Herbert Hoover's well-known point of view— that America has a destiny of its own and cannot hope to reshape the misshapen European and Far Eastern nations, and therefore we had better stay out of foreign wars." That sentence hardly needs comment, except to note its implication that the United States *can* and *should* "reshape the misshapen" nations of the world and ought to get into foreign wars in order to do so.

Craig asked: "Would it not be more reasonable to say that the war and what followed it were less the result of the

Stimson type of diplomacy, with its insistence that treaties are meant to be observed and that breaches of international law and morality must be punished by collective action, than the result of a failure on the part of the democracies to apply Stimson's principles soon enough?" To insist that treaties be observed and that breaches of international law and morality be punished requires the use of military force. If it means anything, it means war. So Craig's question might be rephrased this way: Could we not have avoided war in the 1940's by going to war in the 1930's? Or this way: Can we not prevent future wars by fighting now instead of waiting? Either way, the question is unanswerable, if not downright absurd. Yet the logic of our Vietnam venture is based upon an affirmative answer to it.

Some of the reviewers seemed to think that the book condoned lawlessness and immorality when it questioned the notion of "law and morality," imposed by force, as a prime objective of American foreign policy and suggested "balance and stability" as a preferable aim (p. 247). "Others may believe that law and morality form the most solid basis for balance and stability," said Ruhl J. Bartlett (Fletcher School). This might be true if there existed a real international community with some kind of world government and with legal and moral rules that were more or less universally accepted and applied. The point intended was that, in a world of separate and sovereign states, which have yielded none of their sovereignty to any international organization, it is not legal and moral but only legalistic and moralistic for one nation or one group of nations to try and impose *their* conceptions of law and morality on others. The attempt, as in Vietnam, clearly presents the gruesome paradox of enforcing morality by killing or maiming women, old men, and children and leaving countless civilians homeless and impoverished. That it leads to calm or stability in international affairs is somewhat less obvious.

As much or more concerned about the Stimson personage than about the public issues, certain reviewers expressed regret at what they considered an exercise in sheer denigration. Ferrell called it an "effort to cut Stimson down to size" and thought it indicated that, lamentably, some Americans were incapable of appreciating the true greatness of their wartime leaders. The most upset was Mark S. Watson, who had had some acquaintance with Stimson while preparing an official history of the War Department's role in World War II. Watson put much more indignation than substance into his review of *Secretary Stimson*. "Were that wise and forceful old statesman alive, it would astonish him (as it will his continuing admirers) to see how faulty his decisions often were"—in the opinion of the author, an upstart outsider. "Those who at close range saw the aging but indomitable Stimson at work in that period [World War II] will for the most part be distressed at the picture of him which emerges from these pages." Watson recommended the "solid guidance" of Stimson's own memoirs as against the unfair questions and the "innuendo" of this book. About the only paragraph in it he could approve was the concluding one, in which "Current aptly quotes Stimson twice," the final quotation being this: "We are forced to act in the world as it is, and not in the world as we wish it were, or as we would like it to become." That quotation, in the context, was intended to be somewhat ironic as an implied criticism of Stimson himself, but apparently the point was too subtle for the reviewer.

Another reviewer, H. Bradford Westerfield (now of Yale), noted the "thrusts of sarcasm and more subtle irony," but objected: "This technique . . . enables Mr. Current to avoid taking any clearly defined, consistent position of his own from which to make his appraisal of Stimson's statesmanship." An "isolationist and even a pacifist position is implied in many of the criticisms," though not in all of them. "Episode by episode, the author shifts his line of attack to wherever Colonel Stimson looks to him most vulnerable." Lanyi said of the author: "He seems to demand from political leaders both a doctrinal 'inner consistency' and a gift of omniscience." Ferrell accused him of a "highly selective use of quotation," and DeConde charged him with utilizing "only a part of the pertinent available sources."

In the belief of several of the critics, the book was defective because of the author's all-too-evident personal bias—his "effort not to be prejudiced in favor of his subject," as Watson put it; his "inimicality toward Stimson," in DeConde's words; or his "hostile predisposition," according to L. Ethan Ellis (Rutgers). Such a book, DeConde said, could hardly present a "well-proportioned portrait" or a "well balanced view of Stimson." While apparently conceding the justice of the Stimson picture as drawn, William H. Harbaugh (Connecticut) found fault with the author on other grounds. "Stimson was the product of the complex forces of his times, not merely of his own social and intellectual arrogance," Harbaugh wrote. "And it is in the failure to treat those forces in both depth and breadth that Professor Current falls short."

The book was not conceived, however, as a study in depth and breadth of Stimson and his times, nor was it designed to present a balanced view or a rounded portrait of the man. Rather, it was intended, as the foreword points out, to "raise questions" about "certain controversial phases of his career." These phases either had been neglected or had been treated in a self-serving, ex parte manner by Stimson and his collaborator, McGeorge Bundy, in the Stimson memoirs, *On Active Service in Peace and War* (1948)—the volume that Stimson's admirer Watson endorsed as a more than adequate record of the man's career. That book, too, made a highly selective use of quotations and utilized only a part of the available sources. It, too, was biased, and strongly so, despite its magisterial air of impartial authority. *Secretary Stimson* was written to question that account, to administer at least a small dose of antidote, and to present a partial and tentative statement of the other side of the case.

If the author seemed to concentrate on some of the less admirable aspects of the man's character, that was a reaction and perhaps an overreaction to Stimson's smugness and self-righteousness and to his own and his admirer's claims, in his behalf, of near infallibility. But the author was much more concerned with issues than with personality, and if he disliked Stimson, he did so mainly because of what the man stood for. To some reviewers' insinuation that the author selected evidence to fit preconceived ideas, he can only reply that the reverse was actually the case. He began his research with a conviction that Stimson (along with F. D. Roosevelt) had, as frequently charged, deliberately provoked or invited the Japanese to attack at Pearl Harbor. The mass of evidence itself convinced the author of the falsity of the charge and gave him the clue as to what Stimson really had meant by his phrase "how we should maneuver them into the position of firing the first shot."

As for the standards for judging political leaders, the author certainly demanded or expected no "gift of omniscience," and if he pointed out that on occasion Stimson lacked the gift, the purpose was only to refute the claim of near omniscience that his admirers made for him and that he made for himself. (The matter of the historian's "hindsight" and the statesman's "foresight" is touched upon in the book, p. 244.) As for the consistency of the author's position, the reader is left to make his own judgment, but the author pleads nolo contendere to the charge of "isolationist" if that term be taken not in its literal but in its usual sense as designating those who, in John Bassett Moore's words, "do not believe in war as the prime, or natural and appropriate, creator of peace." He also confesses to being a "pacifist" if this means one who opposes wars that are fought supposedly to prevent future wars but who does not necessarily rule out the use of military force in all possible contingencies.

"The author accepted the risk of those who write close to the event, before the documentation necessary to a full appraisal has become available," Ellis charitably remarked. And Nichols predicted: "In the far future, historians may perhaps approximate that cool detachment presently unattainable and conclude that Stimson was as much the creature of his environment as the creator of it." Perhaps.

If more of the "documentation necessary to a full appraisal" had been available when the book was written, the appraisal probably would not have been very different in its main outlines, but in some respects it could have been confirmed, sharpened, or extended. For example, the powers of diplomatic analysis and prediction on which Stimson prided himself are proved no better than average, to say the most for them, in portions of his correspondence and diary that were not yet open to scholars at the time when research for the book was done. (Notes from the F. D. Roosevelt papers and from the Stimson diary in the 1940's have been supplied by Professor M. S. Venkataramani, director of American Studies at the Indian School of International Studies, New Delhi.)

A few illustrations of Stimsonian foresight: In a letter to Roosevelt, November 15, 1937, Stimson admonished that there must be no concession, "no surrender of principle," to Japan. But he recommended appeasement or at least temporizing in the case of Germany. "In Europe, where war has not yet broken out and where the national interests are so many and complex," he explained, "a temporary solution of expediency may be essential in order to gain time for a proper solution ultimately. Time in Europe is running in favor of an ultimately sane and sound adjustment." On June 17, 1941, five days before the Germans invaded the Soviet Union, he put down his thoughts in his diary: "Germany is bringing every bit of her gigantic pressure to bear on Russia to get some enormous advantages at the threat of war and at present, from all the dispatches, it seems to be nip and tuck whether Russia will fight or surrender. Of course, I think the chances are that she will surrender." Regarding a discussion with Secretaries Cordell Hull and Frank Knox, he noted on June 2, 1942: "All of us agreed that of course the first job was to win the war and there will be, after the war is over, a long period in which the victor democracies will have to, by force of arms, hold the two restless powers in check, Germany and Japan."

If the diary for the World War II years had been accessible when *Secretary Stimson* was written, this book could have given an account of a subject it neglected—Stimson and the Negro. The account, once more, would have questioned the version given in Stimson's apologia, *On Active Service.* In those memoirs, Stimson and Bundy present a man who as War Secretary was free from prejudice and eager for black progress inside and outside the army but sensibly aware of the complexities of the race problem. Some theater commanders abroad were reluctant to accept Negro troops. "But fair-minded soldiers agreed that the Army must make full use of what Stimson called 'the great asset of the colored men of the nation.'" Thus the memoirs imply that Stimson took the lead in advocating the full use of this asset. He only opposed those black and white reformers who held "radical and impractical" ideas and who made "deliberate use of the war emergency to stir unrest and force new policies for which the Negroes themselves were unprepared." But the diary itself, without the editing and the glossing that Stimson and Bundy gave it in their book, reveals a man of "abolitionist" professions and racialist convictions, convictions as strong as or stronger than those of most of his white contemporaries. After taking over the War Department, Stimson approved and continued the set policy of keeping black soldiers in segregated regiments. Expressing the views of the great majority of Negro Americans, Negro leaders objected to this policy, and the Republican party platform of 1940 included a plank promising an end to discrimination in the army. Before the election, Roosevelt countered with a few fairly high military appointments for Negroes, one of whom he designated as an assistant to the Secretary of War. Stimson accepted the appointment without enthusiasm, noting in his diary (October 22, 1940): "The Negroes are taking advantage of this period just before election to try to get everything they can in the way of recognition from the Army." His new black civilian aide was William H. Hastie, a graduate (like Stimson) of the Harvard Law School, dean of the Howard University Law School, and an NAACP leader.

The War Secretary and his new assistant were soon at odds. Hastie represented those black Americans who objected to the army's segregating blacks, hesitating to draft them, assigning them to service rather than combat duties, and excluding them from all but a few low-ranking officer positions. But Stimson had no desire to meet any of these objections. He viewed the Negro as more a nuisance to be avoided than as an asset to be fully and fairly utilized.

Stimson was especially opposed to seeing blacks put into positions of command. "Leadership is not imbedded in the negro race yet," he told his diary (September 30, 1940), "and to try to make commissioned officers to lead men into battle—colored men—is only to work disaster to both. Colored troops do very well under white officers but every time we try to lift them a little bit beyond where they can go, disaster and confusion follows. In the draft we are preparing to give the negroes a fair shot in every service . . . even to aviation where I doubt very much if they will not produce disaster there." Stimson thought that World War I had taught a lesson when President Wilson was pressured into accepting a few Negro officers "and the poor fellows made perfect fools of themselves." When President Roosevelt also yielded to pressure and decided to increase the number of Negro officers, Stimson confessed to his diary (January 12, 1942): "I am very skeptical about the possible efficiency of such officers but, as it has been determined that we shall have them, I propose that we shall educate them to the highest possible standards and make the best we can of them." In the training and assignment of black officers, however, he declined to go one step farther than he had to.

And he refused to budge in the face of demands for lessening discrimination in the army. Such demands only offended and outraged him. In the campaign for equal treatment, one of the most prominent whites was Mrs. Franklin D. Roosevelt, and another was Archibald MacLeish, the Librarian of Congress. When Stimson learned that MacLeish was about to give a lecture on army discrimination, he got together with MacLeish and gave him a lecture of his own (January 24, 1942):

"I told him how I had been brought up in an abolitionist family; my father fought in the Civil War, and all my instincts were in favor of justice to the Negro. But I pointed out how this crime of our forefathers had produced a problem which was almost impossible of solution in this country and that I myself could see no theoretical or logical solution to it at war times like these, but that we should merely exercise utmost patience and care in individual cases. I told him of my experience and study of the incompetency of colored troops except under white officers, and the disastrous consequences to the country and themselves which they were opening if they went to battle otherwise, although we were doing

our best to train colored officers. I pointed out that what
these foolish leaders of the colored race are seeking is at
bottom social equality, and I pointed out the basic impossibility of social equality because of the impossibility of race
mixture by marriage. He listened in silence and thanked me,
but I am not sure how far he is convinced. But I am quite
certain that he has been put up to this latest by Mrs. Roosevelt's intrusive and impulsive folly, as this is only the latest
of similar troubles that I have had on that same question
by reason of her activities."

Thus Stimson characteristically asserted his devotion to
high principle—his abolitionist background, his instincts of
justice for the Negro—while actually taking a prejudiced
and reactionary stand. In the drive for equal rights, he could
see nothing but the meddling of misguided do-gooders or,
even worse, the sinister activity of enemy provocateurs. "We
have direct evidence through MAGIC [the decoding of Japanese radio messages]," he noted (March 19, 1942), "that the
Japanese and the Germans are conducting a systematic campaign among the American Negroes stirring up their demands for equal representation and [we have direct evi-
dence] showing that a good many of their [the Negroes']
leaders have actually been receiving pay from the Japanese
ambassador to Mexico."

In early 1943 Hastie resigned as Stimson's civilian aide
and issued a protest against the army's persisting discriminatory policies. (Stimson and Bundy did not even mention
Hastie in *On Active Service*.) By this time a serious manpower shortage was developing, and Stimson was beginning
to think of conscripting labor for war plants. Meanwhile he
continued to refrain from making full use of black manpower in the army. Only after a War Department committee
had urged that something be done to relieve the dangerous
discontent among Negroes did he reluctantly agree to committing black troops to combat. "We have got to use the

colored race to help us in this fight," he finally told the General Staff, as he recorded in his diary (January 27, 1944). The upshot was the sending of the black Ninety-second Division into action in Italy early in 1945. This division apparently did not distinguish itself, though other Negro units performed extremely well on various occasions. Two explanations have been offered for the poor performance of some elements of the Ninety-second Division. One explanation was the low morale, which resulted from widespread resentment because of the segregation of the troops and because of the discrimination in favor of the division's white officers. The other explanation was the natural incompetence of black soldiers. This second view was, of course, the one that Stimson took. In his diary (February 21, 1945) he noted with apparent satisfaction a conversation in which General George C. Marshall told him that troops of the Ninety-second had run from battle.

The story of Stimson and the Negro in World War II can now be followed in two scholarly studies: Ulysses G. Lee, Jr., *The United States Army in World War II: Special Studies: The Employment of Negro Troops* (1966); and Richard M. Dalfiume, *Desegregation of the U. S. Armed Forces: Fighting on Two Fronts, 1939–1953* (1969). As Dalfiume observes, "The example of Secretary of War Stimson indicates to what extent racist assumptions existed within the Army and dictated its Negro policy."

In the sixteen years since *Secretary Stimson* was originally published, a number of other studies, some of them much more thorough than this one, have been made of Stimson and the events in which he had a part. Yet it perhaps remains debatable whether we yet have a balanced and well rounded account, written from a detached point of view, of the man and his career.

There is, of course, Elting E. Morison's Parkman Prize winning biography, *Turmoil and Tradition: A Study of the Life and Times of Henry L. Stimson* (1960), a charmingly written account which makes its subject come alive as an understandable, if not always likeable, human being. In Morison's pages we discover Stimson, to begin with, as "a sober little boy, sallow, weak-limbed, hating physical exercise above all things." For a long time, it appears, "he labored under an ill-defined impression that his father in some strange way held him accountable for the death of his mother." And the father was a person of "a certain detachment, a kind of disinterested, even chilling calculation." No wonder the boy became the man he did, humorless, imperious, and self-conscious about his own and others' honor. No wonder he grew up to be as strenuous an advocate of "the strenuous life" as was his friend Theodore Roosevelt. Besides its revelations concerning Stimson's personal life and personality, the Morison biography contributes information and insights regarding his legal career and, in public office, his administrative work. The book tells, for example, how he dealt with office organization and routine and, more particularly, how he put efficiency into the War Department after taking it over in 1940.

As an authorized biographer, Morison had the advantage of free access to all the man's memorabilia. But in selecting evidence from this material the biographer was careful to conceal facts that might reflect upon his hero. For example, he says nothing at all about Stimson's objections to the use of black officers in the army, and from all the diary entries on this question he quotes only a fragment of the one in which Stimson recorded his effort to dissuade MacLeish from speaking out against discrimination. "When he heard that Archibald MacLeish of the Office of Facts and Figures was going to give a speech about alleged discrimination in the Army, he spent an hour with MacLeish, 'pointing out' how 'this crime of our forefathers had produced a problem which was almost impossible of solution in this country and that I myself could see no theoretical or logical solution to it at war times like these. . . ." There the biographer cuts off the quotation. But he utilizes another part of that same entry to demonstrate Stimson's "knowledge of the past and his sense of history": "in dealing with the assimilation of colored troops he started from his father in the Civil War." Thus Morison leaves the reader to infer that family tradition had led Stimson to favor something he actually opposed, namely, the "assimilation of colored troops."

Morison's biography, like Stimson's memoirs, catches and reflects the spirit of the times only in the sense in which that spirit moved Stimson and like-minded men. The book does less than justice to dissenting views. It relates, taking for granted his superior wisdom, that in the 1930's Stimson went about "correcting the deep-seated error on which our policy was based—the setting of peace above righteousness." It offers the excuse that at least he "thought he was right" in what he did or left undone in preparing Pearl Harbor against attack and in assigning blame for what ensued. Regarding the decision to drop the atomic bombs, it assures us of his realization that power, even the power of nuclear explosives, does not corrupt when "directed toward wholesome uses by responsible men." It gives the impression that Stimson and those who agreed with him were moral giants, while with the possible exception of Herbert Hoover those who disagreed with him were rather petty creatures. Thus William R. Castle, Hoover's Assistant Secretary of State who seldom saw eye to eye with Stimson, is summarily disposed of as "an insecure little man."

On the whole, Morison in *Turmoil and Tradition* allows us to view Stimson only as he viewed himself and as his admiring friends viewed him. The few mild criticisms are safely grounded on the subject's own assumptions; these assumptions themselves are never examined. In short, the book presents no really critical evaluation of the man or of his career. But, then, the author obviously had no such object in mind. His purpose was to praise, even to adore, and this he does extremely well, capping it with a final encomium written in a pseudo-Biblical style: "Wherefore he had been able to withstand in the evil days, and, having done all, to stand. After all the doings he had left all the words—justice, duty, honor, trust—as he had found them—solid, quite solid. And his hands were steady until the going down of the sun."

In recounting Stimson's role as a policy maker, the Morison biography is competent though not especially rewarding to those familiar with the already existing literature. Morison relied heavily on recent monographs, among them Robert H. Ferrell's *American Diplomacy in the Great Depression: Hoover-Stimson Foreign Policy, 1929–1933* (1957; 1969). Ferrell's study is based on thorough research in published and unpublished sources and on a careful reading of the more important secondary writings. It is written in a concise, lively, and lucid style. Its thesis may be stated thus: American diplomacy from 1929 to 1933 "succeeded or failed in its grand purpose, the preservation of peace, because of the combination in each diplomatic instance of four factors." First and most important, the Great Depression "palsied the hands of American statesmen." Second, the existing "diplomatic assumptions and policies of the United States," notably the assumption of continuing international equilibrium and the policy of moral suasion, were inadequate to the needs of the time, if not downright fallacious. Third, the human element, the character of American policy makers with their "personal abilities or lack thereof," was on the whole remarkably good despite Stimson's excessively lawyerlike way of looking at foreign affairs. Fourth, there was "the problem of the events themselves," and these were baffling in their complexity and inherent difficulty.

This interpretation has many virtues, including charity as

well as clarity. Certainly it is much more charitable toward
Hoover's Secretary of State than is the account in *Secretary
Stimson*. Ferrell takes issue with this book when he discusses
the response of the President and the Secretary to the Far
Eastern crisis. Ferrell questions the seriousness of the policy
differences between the two men. He also questions the
existence of two distinct versions of nonrecognition, a Hoover Doctrine and a Stimson Doctrine. "In reality," he says,
"the two men agreed far more than they disagreed, and it
was only in the latter 1930's that they began to differ radically over issues of foreign policy." The curious reader may
compare the evidence and argument given in *Secretary Stimson* (pp. 83–113, 118–128) with that presented in *American Diplomacy in the Great Depression* (p. 169 n. and *passim*). Ferrell gives a similar and equally generous interpretation of Stimson's policies in *The American Secretaries of
State and Their Diplomacy*, Vol. XI (1963).

The most scholarly, thorough, and fully documented account of Stimson's response to the Far Eastern crisis is Armin
Rappaport's *Henry L. Stimson and Japan, 1931–33* (1963).
Rappaport expresses admiration for Stimson's unbounded
"courage, nobility, and strength of character" and is sympathetic with his aims in the Far East. Nevertheless, Rappaport
proceeds to amass the evidence for a staggering indictment,
which is all the more convincing because of his precise and
cautious presentation. According to Rappaport, Stimson was
a legalist who "did not seem to realize that in international
affairs there was no clear-cut, categoric right or wrong." He
was a moralist who too often followed his own emotions
rather than the dictates of national interest or even of common sense. In 1932 he proceeded to threaten and thus to
antagonize Japan. "Soon, . . . his moral sensibilities outraged,
he elected to give vent to his ire by brandishing the pistol,
which, unhappily, was not loaded, thereby transgressing the
cardinal maxim of the statesman and placing his country in

jeopardy." His policy proved itself, by 1933, to be utterly barren. "All Stimson really handed on to his successor was the implacable enmity of the Japanese."

For brief and rather tentative discussions of a theme that is basic to Stimson's career, see Richard N. Current, "The United States and Collective Security: Notes on the History of an Idea," in Alexander DeConde, ed., *Isolation and Security* (1957), and "Consequences of the Kellogg Pact," in George L. Anderson, ed., *Issues and Conflicts in Twentieth Century American Diplomacy* (1959).

For a profound and exhaustive and yet highly readable study of the same theme—a study that cannot be too highly recommended—see Roland N. Stromberg, *Collective Security and American Foreign Policy: From the League of Nations to NATO* (1963). Stromberg concludes with an analysis of the fallacies and failures of the peace-enforcement idea. One of the fallacies is "that there is some sort of final, permanent, basic 'agreement' possible in world affairs. Thus, we find Secretary Stimson holding, back in 1945, that the great powers should *first* 'thresh out' the 'underlying issues,' agreeing on their major lines of policy for the postwar world, and *then* create the United Nations—otherwise they would quarrel within the United Nations." Other fallacies include the following: the assumption that "all or most wars are the products of deliberate acts of aggression by states that may be considered hardened criminals ('bandit nations')"; the notion that "aggression" has been or can be objectively defined and that specific cases can be readily identified (as Samuel Taylor Coleridge put it long ago: "What two nations were ever at war, and did not obstinately charge the aggression, each on the other?"); and the expectation that the "good" powers can preserve world peace by acting as a "vigilantes committee, or self-appointed lynch gang." Such fallacies have gained a semblance of truth from "myths about the road to World War II," myths which made collective security "the most fashionable of ideologies . . . because of a belief that its application could have prevented that war." Among the myths was "an almost entirely legendary version of the Manchurian Affair," according to which "collective security could have easily set all to rights." Stromberg cites a valuable work that was overlooked by the author of *Secretary Stimson*: Reginald Bassett, *Democracy and Foreign Policy: A Case History of the Sino-Japanese Dispute, 1931–1933* (1952).

On other phases of diplomatic history in which Stimson played some part, and especially on the coming and the conclusion of the war with Japan, the books and articles appearing since 1954 are far too numerous to be discussed or even listed here. A few of the most important are the following:

On Pearl Harbor: Louis Morton, "Japan's Decision for War," in K. R. Greenfield, ed., *Command Decisions* (1959), shows the limited aims of the Japanese, who sought retention of their conquests and their dominance in the Far East, not a total victory over the United States. D. J. Lu, *From the Marco Polo Bridge to Pearl Harbor: Japan's Entry into World War II* (1961), stresses the differences among Japanese policy makers and the reluctance of many of them to risk an American war. R. J. C. Butow, *Tojo and the Coming of the War* (1961), written from Japanese sources, maintains that the more bellicose leaders could have been restrained, if at all, only by a last-minute compromise with the United States. Roberta Wohlstetter, *Pearl Harbor: Warning and Decision* (1962), puts blame for the inadequate defense not on individuals in the American government but on the system—or, rather, lack of system—in handling intelligence information.

On the dropping of the atom bomb: R. J. C. Butow, *Japan's Decision to Surrender* (1954), based on Japanese sources, argues convincingly that militarists in the Japanese government might have delayed for some time an end to the hostilities if the bomb had not been used. R. C. Batchelder, *The Irreversible Decision, 1939–1950* (1962), justifies the dropping of the first bomb, on Hiroshima, but not the second one, on Nagasaki. Gar Alperovitz, *Atomic Diplomacy: Hiroshima and Potsdam: The Use of the Atomic Bomb and the American Confrontation with Soviet Power* (1965), emphasizes predominance over the Soviet Union rather than victory over Japan as the prime motive. Herbert Feis, *The Atomic Bomb and the End of World War II* (a 1966 revision of a 1961 work entitled *Japan Subdued*), disagrees with Alperovitz. Feis concedes that Japan could probably have been brought to eventual defeat without use of the bomb, but he follows Stimson and Truman in concluding that the main reason for using it was to hasten the end and thus to save lives. The United States could be "fairly criticized," according to Feis, only for failing to make clear, before the final ultimatum, the nature of the new weapon.

On this issue, as well as on others in which Stimson was to a greater or lesser degree involved, the experts have yet, as of 1970, to reach a full and final consensus. *Secretary Stimson* is now being republished in the hope that it still has something to say in the ongoing debate, something of relevance for citizens who are concerned about the trends of American foreign policy today.

Richard N. Current
Greensboro, North Carolina
January 1970

Foreword

This is not a biography of Henry L. Stimson but an account of his role in the making of American policy, his part in the creation of the world crisis with which we live today. Concentrating on certain controversial phases of his career, it is intended more to raise questions than to give final answers, many of which are not yet available and some of which may never be.

In writing it I have been aided by many people who did not always agree with me but nevertheless gave graciously and unstintingly of their time and attention. Mr. McGeorge Bundy, co-author of Stimson's memoirs and trustee of the Stimson papers, permitted me to use and to quote the Stimson diary, available on microfilm in the Yale University Library, and he made me the beneficiary of a challenging and stimulating personal correspondence. The Yale librarians were also most courteous and helpful.

Mr. Herbert Hoover gave me the benefit of a pleasurable conversation with him. Mr. William R. Castle received me most hospitably in his home and opened the riches of his private diary to me.

Mr. William L. Neumann carefully read and criticized my manuscript, corrected a number of errors, and called my attention to many items of information I otherwise would have overlooked. Professors Frank Freidel, Arthur E. Bestor, Jr., Kenneth M. Stampp, William B. Hesseltine, and Fred H. Harrington offered me much valuable advice, and doubtless I would have done better to take even more

of it than I did. From the beginning, Mr. Harry Elmer
Barnes provided stimulus and encouragement that kept me
going, and he presented insights that I found most helpful,
but I came to some conclusions quite different from his
own.

To Professor F. C. Dietz, head of the history department
at the University of Illinois, to the Graduate Research
Board of the University, and to my successive research assistants, John Cooley and John Tevebaugh, I owe a tremendous debt for aid in the hidden drudgery which a study
of this kind necessarily entails. My wife, Rose M. Bonar,
not only indulged me cheerfully in my preoccupation with
the project but also did most of my typing.

I wish to re-emphasize the fact that the mention of my
creditors in this enterprise is not meant to constitute an endorsement, on their part, of my finished product. They disagree with each other and with me on many issues. For any
errors of fact or inference in the pages that follow, I alone
am to blame.

R. N. C.

Secretary Stimson

1 The Shape of His Greatness

He had been a "tower of strength," said General George C. Marshall. A "pillar of strength and integrity," declared the *New York Times*. "It was then, when it was finished, that the U. S. could best see the shape of his greatness," elaborated *Time* magazine. "It stood like a high column, reaching up through half a century, each year mortared tightly to the next by integrity, wisdom and selflessness." [1]
A tower . . . a pillar . . . a high column.

Henry Lewis Stimson, at his death on October 20, 1950, closed what was indeed a remarkable career. He had held high office of some kind under no fewer than seven Presidents. Under Theodore Roosevelt he was United States attorney for the southern district of New York. In Taft's Cabinet he was Secretary of War. He was a colonel of artillery in the Army of which Wilson was Commander-in-Chief. For Coolidge he went to Nicaragua as a special executive agent and to the Philippines as governor general. He was Hoover's Secretary of State. Under Franklin D. Roosevelt he was War Secretary a second time, and he continued in office for a while under Truman.

But his distinction lay not merely in the length and variety of his office holding. He influenced high policy. He made and helped to make decisions which literally shook the earth. The shape of his greatness was reflected in the shape of world

[1] *New York Times*, October 21, 22, 1950; *Time*, October 30, 1950.

3

affairs and American foreign policy at the middle of the twentieth century.

He authored the Stimson Doctrine. This has been ranked with the original Open Door notes of John Hay as one of the great pronouncements of American policy in the Far East. It held that the United States should refuse to recognize territorial or other changes made in violation of American treaty rights. But there was more to it than nonrecognition, as Stimson saw it. His doctrine implied the use of economic pressure and, if necessary, of military and naval force. During the Manchurian crisis of 1931–33, when he first proclaimed it, he could not carry out all its implications because of the resistance of President Hoover. Later he conveyed the idea to President Roosevelt, and in 1940 and 1941 it was applied with successive embargoes against Japan. The Japanese response came on December 7, 1941.

He helped to plan diplomatic moves and Pacific defenses during the months preceding the Japanese attack. The phrase "how we should maneuver them into the position of firing the first shot" was his. The "war warning" to the Army command in Hawaii—a message which was so interpreted as to leave American planes at the mercy of the sudden foe—was also his. Both immediately and remotely he had much to do with the entry of the United States into the second World War.

And he had much to do with mobilizing the victory. Before the war he pressed for and got a peacetime draft, after years of campaigning for compulsory military training. During the war he made "military necessity" the overriding consideration in all questions of production and procurement, manpower and labor, censorship and civil rights. The wartime "relocation" of Americans with Japanese ancestors was in the last analysis his responsibility. In large degree he determined how the war was to be fought on the home front, though he had little say on matters of military strategy itself—with one very notable exception.

That was the decision to use the atom bomb against Japan. He was President Roosevelt's and later President Truman's chief adviser on atomic policy. He had assisted notably in the development of fissionable weapons by securing the cooperation of Congress and the Army in the Manhattan project. While he did not originate the war aim of "unconditional surrender," he justified its enforcement by means of the atomic blasts.

He, more than any other one man, gave authority to new doctrines of international law that denied the rights and duties of neutrality and affirmed the use of violence as a means to righteous peace. His writings were quoted to justify the trial and execution of enemy leaders as war criminals after their defeat. His assumptions—the indivisibility of world peace, the possibility of maintaining it by force—still underlay the conduct of America's foreign affairs at the time of his death.

Born September 21, 1867, Stimson was turning sixty when, in 1927, he began the career that was to give him a place in history books, and he was going on eighty when, in 1945, he left his last public office. At an age when most men think of retiring, he was in a very real sense just starting out.

Always proud of his physical fitness, he did not look his years. He was a confirmed horseman and sportsman, who in youth climbed peaks and shot big game in the Rocky Mountains and in old age still rode and hunted, though no longer for grizzlies. His outdoor habits kept his body trim, his shoulders square. Gray was appearing, however, in the black hair and mustache that used to set off his gray-blue eyes and gleaming white teeth. And the aura of vigorous good health about him was more than a bit misleading. He never could stand hard and steady work indoors for any length of time, but every now and then had to refresh himself with some outdoor sport. As he grew older his infirmities, signalled by high blood pressure and lumbago, gave him increasing trouble. Not that he became by any means a dotard or a dodderer, but when Republicans disparaged the "tired old men" of F. D. R.'s wartime administration, he showed extreme sensitivity about his advancing age and declining energy.

On his face was an habitual look of "bored martyrdom," or so an unsympathetic newsman said, and his friends agreed at least that he was by nature cold, reserved, austere, shy. Yet they testified that in the woods or on the golf links or before a cozy fireplace he could be genial and even entertaining, though they did not suggest that he was distinguished by a sense of humor. He had no capacity for laughing at himself. He was dignity incarnate, a devotee of punctilio and protocol. As a member of Hoover's administration, he used to parade with a retinue of servants past saluting guards to the White House tennis courts, and as a member of F. D. R.'s he made a good deal of gold-braid ceremony out of his daily arrivals at the war office. Cold though he might seem, he had a hot temper which could flare up in startling ways. "There is no blinking the fact," a subordinate was once moved to say, "that Stimson is an unlovable character, a very hard man to work under."

His intimates conceded that he had a one-track mind. In courts of law his "tenacity of purpose," visible in his firm lips and hard-set jaw, disconcerted his opponents. In ordinary conversation it sometimes disconcerted his friends. He stuck firmly to one theme at a time and did not hide his annoyance when someone else interjected what he believed to be a trivial or irrelevant thought. In formal speech he talked slowly and paused often, as if weighing the great significance of every phrase. "It is difficult to be cynical or flippant," an admirer said, "when you listen to his sincere, convincing words."

Once he had made a decision, he knew it was ethically right as well as pragmatically correct. He never doubted himself. His conscience was demanding, yet he could satisfy it. Morally fastidious, he eschewed all gossip and dirty stories, scorned the vulgar and the cheap. Doubtless he was incorruptible so far as money or favor had power to corrupt. As a friendly commentator said, "Stimson's character sticks out all over him—his fairness, his determination, his sense of honor." To those less friendly it seemed that a line could hardly be drawn where rectitude left off and self-righteousness began.[2]

He lived according to the inspiration of his family name. He was born a Stimson, with all which that implied, and it implied a great deal. The family had been represented in King Phillip's War, in the Revolution, in the Civil War, in almost every American conflict. One Stimson after another had achieved at least a local eminence in business or the professions or politics. Though not so well known as some other illustrious families of New York—the Schuylers or the Livingstons, the Fishes or the Roosevelts—the ancestors of Henry L. Stimson were nevertheless impressive folk. They bequeathed to him a sense of kinship with the great, a soldierly tradition, and a consciousness that he was born to govern.

Worthy scions of the line, his father and his uncle taught

---

[2] On Stimson's character and personality see Henry F. Pringle, "Henry L. Stimson: A Portrait," in the *Outlook and Independent,* 151: 409–11, 437–38 (March 13, 1929), for a detached view; Drew Pearson and Robert S. Allen, *Washington Merry-Go-Round* (New York, 1931), 103–36, for an unsympathetic and sometimes hostile treatment; and Claude M. Fuess's sketch in the *Atlantic Monthly,* 168: 335–42 (September, 1941), for an uncritical and flattering appraisal. These accounts have been supplemented by information from one or two of Stimson's acquaintances, who prefer not to be identified.

him other things, too, mostly by their own examples. His father, Lewis Atterbury Stimson, once a banker, salted away a fortune early in life, then devoted himself to the study and practice of medicine. His career demonstrated to his son that there was more to life than making money. So did the career of the uncle, the Reverend Henry Albert Stimson, a liberal Congregationalist who preached a gospel of social reform. He gave his nephew something of an idealistic and humanitarian bent.

Henry L. Stimson was the last of his own line. Though he was happily married from the age of twenty-five, he and his wife remained without children, either by birth or by adoption. Some of his acquaintances used to speculate about what effect, if any, his childlessness might have had upon his personality and his career. It might at least have confirmed his unbending ways, heightened his feeling of ancestral destiny, and intensified his attachment to the children of his alma mater.

He was graduated from Phillips Academy at Andover, Yale College, and the Harvard Law School. Though loyal to all of them, he was much the fondest of Yale. As a scholar he did well, well enough to make Phi Beta Kappa as an undergraduate and an editorship of the *Harvard Law Review* as a law student. What impressed him most, however, was not the work of the classroom but the spirit of the New Haven campus, where he qualified for Skull and Bones, the inner circle of Yale good-fellowship. He never lost that college spirit. Throughout his life he acted as if he took almost literally the collegiate motto "For God, for Country, and for Yale."

His academic record—and still more his social position—helped him to get his first job. Next door to his father in New York lived John C. Carter, a prominent member of both society and the bar. A word from Dr. Stimson to Mr. Carter would give the young law graduate access to the best legal firms in the city. Not long after passing his bar examination he joined the firm of Root & Clarke, in 1893.

The senior partner, Elihu Root, was to teach Stimson far more than any of his professors did. Root's career set a pattern for Stimson's own. Already a flourishing corporation counsel and a rising Republican politician, Root later served as United States Senator, Secretary of War, and Secretary of State. He concocted a unique mixture of conservatism and idealism, imperialism and internationalism. Eventually, as an elder statesman, he helped to prevent American membership in the League of Nations while he fathered and advocated membership in a League adjunct, the World Court. Stimson was to carry on the work by adapting some of Root's ideas—though not all of them—to the crises of a later generation.

The new clerk rose rapidly in Root's law office. After a dozen years his annual fees amounted to about $20,000. He stayed on, except for leaves to hold public office, and prospered with the firm as its business grew and its personnel changed. After 1927 the partnership was known as Winthrop, Stimson, Putnam & Roberts. By that time, having invested shrewdly during the frenzied finance of the 'twenties, he had become, even by his own standards, a "rich man." [3]

He was also a country gentleman. His fine old-fashioned house at "Highhold," his Long Island estate, dominated the top of a hill from which he could see both the ocean and the Sound. When he became Secretary of State he reproduced this spacious and rural air as nearly as he could in Washing-

---

[3] Stimson presented a brief summary of his private and professional life in his memoirs: Henry L. Stimson and McGeorge Bundy, *On Active Service in Peace and War* (New York, 1948), xi–xxii. He left an account of his acquaintance with T. R. in a typewritten document dated 1913 and entitled "Previous Relations with Colonel Roosevelt," available on microfilm in the Yale University Library. See also the sources cited in the preceding footnote and the obituary in the *New York Times*, October 21, 1950.

ton. He cashed in some of his high-priced stocks, soon to fall in the stock-market crash, and bought the fabulous estate of "Woodley," with its Southern colonial mansion, which Van Buren and other Presidents had used as a summer home. Here he could enjoy comfort and quiet and a view at least across the valley of Rock Creek. In both houses the furnishings were rather formal, in keeping with his and Mrs. Stimson's tastes. When, in 1933, he visited the Franklin D. Roosevelt home at Hyde Park, he immediately reflected to himself that the disorderly array inside would not please his wife.[4]

Another Roosevelt—the incomparable T. R.—was until his death in 1919 a neighbor of Stimson's on Long Island. From Oyster Bay to Highhold was a distance of only eight miles, nothing at all for two such indefatigable equestrians as Theodore Roosevelt and his friend. Stimson first met him in 1894, their common interests having brought them together in New York under the auspices of the Boone-Crockett Club, an organization of gentlemanly sportsmen. From the outset Stimson admired with all his heart the country's foremost exponent of the strenuous life, who believed in aggressive self-assertion for the nation as well as the individual, and whose slogan was "walk softly and carry a big stick." Theodore Roosevelt influenced him more profoundly than did any other person, even including Elihu Root.

Like T. R., Stimson accepted war as a not altogether disagreeable fact of international life. To him the highest virtues were soldierly ones. Among his dearest memories were those of his army experience in the first World War, and he grew almost tearfully sentimental whenever he joined with veteran artillerymen to sing "As the caissons go rolling

---

[4] Stimson, "Memorandum of Conversation with Franklin D. Roosevelt, Monday, January 9 [1933], at Hyde Park," on microfilm in the Yale University Library.

along." [5] Even in civilian pursuits he always thought of
himself as a soldier, "on active service," and in matters of
law and government he prided himself on what he called his
"combat psychology." True, he decried "Prussianism." To
many of his countrymen Prussianism connoted a mentality
that put inordinate value on military ways and military
men. It was marked by such chivalric touches as the scarred
cheeks of saber-duelling young officers. All this differed in
detail from his own warrior-like ideals and gentlemanly
code, but just how it differed in principle, Stimson never
made clear.

His sense of soldierly duty reflected his philosophy of
noblesse oblige. He took as his model the English squire,
who because of advantages of birth and breeding owed to
less favored humanity an obligation of generosity and
service. At Highhold he used to sponsor a Thanksgiving
frolic, when—for the one day—the bars of class were down,
and debutantes competed with stable boys in horseback
races while chauffeurs and tradespeople communed with
the elite of the countryside. "It's a lot of trouble," he admitted, "but we like to keep it up because it is good for the
community." In the same spirit he gladly sacrificed himself
to the cares of public office. As he told his Yale classmates at
their twentieth reunion, the career of a lawyer did not quite
satisfy him, for it was directed too much to making money
and not enough to doing good.[6] By an extension of this kind
of good will, he came to accept firmly and frankly Rudyard
Kipling's precept of the "white man's burden," or benevolent
imperialism.

As a public man, he did not fit neatly into any of the
categories that students of political personality have de-

[5] Edward T. Folliard and William Costello, "Secretary of War Stimson," in the *American Mercury*, 59: 275 (September, 1944).
[6] Pringle, in the *Outlook and Independent*, 151: 437; *On Active Service*,
16–17.

vised, such as the administrative, the agitating, or the theoretical type (the constructions of Professor Harold Lasswell).[7] He was essentially an "administrator," and an able
one, but he was also something of an "agitator," in the sense
of relying on verbal formulae for reforming the world, and
he was a bit of a "theorist," who tried to construct a logical
and coherent rationale of policy, at least in foreign affairs.
Certainly he was no politician of the back-slapping, vote-
getting kind. He could not mingle cheerfully with the sweat-
ing crowd, nor were voters much attracted to him, as when
he ran for governor of New York in 1910. The only elective
position he ever held was that of delegate to the state's constitutional convention of 1915.

So far as political principles went, he avowed he was a
"progressive conservative," and he may well have been one.
In the day of Theodore Roosevelt's Square Deal he was an
active and ardent trust-buster, but he showed less enthusiasm
for the social and economic reforms of Woodrow Wilson's
New Freedom. Still, when many of his friends were condemning the income tax as socialistic, he gave it his approval,
though recommending that it be broadened so as to include
low incomes. And when, during the postwar red scare, the
New York Assembly refused to seat a number of duly
elected Socialists, he dared to speak out in protest. Yet the
quondam trust-buster, as a wealthy Wall Street lawyer in
the 'twenties, defended a combination of cement-makers
against an antitrust suit, took the side of a coal operators'
organization against their striking miners, and opposed the
prosecution of a big construction company for alleged wartime frauds in the building of army camps. In the 'thirties
he vociferously denounced some aspects of Franklin D.
Roosevelt's New Deal.

His progressivism could be summed up as little more than
a belief in powerful and efficient government. It was the

[7] H. D. Lasswell, *Psychopathology and Politics* (Chicago, 1930).

progressivism of Alexander Hamilton. Stressing the concept of the leader, of leadership, Stimson endorsed the strong man as President. "Poor old Jefferson," he once wrote; how ridiculous his "fear of any strong Executive"! [8] He shared none of Jefferson's—or Lincoln's—faith in the common people. Aloof, he viewed them as from Olympus, the home of the gods.

His fame was late in flowering. The atmosphere of the critical and questioning depression decade hardly favored its growth. It burst into full bloom after the coming of the war years.

As Hoover's Secretary of State, he suffered from a generally bad press, which was partly his own fault. Suspicious and resentful of prying newsmen, he let them know as little as possible of what he was trying to do, and some of them baited him by writing up sinister rumors of his intentions. He especially disliked exposing his mind to the free-for-all of the daily press conference. A day came when the interrogations, pertinent and impertinent, seemed utterly intolerable to him. Thereafter, except for routine handouts, he dispensed his news privately at luncheons in his Woodley mansion, to which he invited only those journalists he thought he could trust.

Whatever his troubles with reporters, he presented his case to the public very cogently whenever he turned his own hand to articles and books. In his story of his 1927 mission to Nicaragua, published serially in the *Saturday Evening Post* and then in book form, he convincingly argued that peace had been the fruit of his policy, even though the

[8] *New York Times*, April 16, 25, 30, June 22, 23, October 5, 1923; January 31, 1924; January 25, 1925; *On Active Service*, 61, 107–109. Stimson elaborated on his conception of the strong President in testimony given at Washington, September 30, 1919, recommending an executive budget. Sixty-sixth Congress, First Session, *Supplement to Hearings before the Select Committee on the Budget of the House of Representatives on the Establishment of a National Budget System* (Washington, 1919), 618–48.

United States marines were still fighting in Nicaragua. In his book *The Far Eastern Crisis* (1936) he managed to write authoritatively about the nonrecognition doctrine without so much as hinting at any disagreement between himself and President Hoover, though they disagreed profoundly. Afterward, when the State Department's official selections of documents appeared in the *Foreign Relations* series, diplomatic historians were perplexed, as one of them confessed, "in trying to reconcile the documented record with Stimson's personal interpretation as found in his book." [9] It is perhaps unfair, though, to apply the canons of historical criticism to these writings of his. As lawyer's briefs, they were well done and above reproach.

Scholars of widely differing points of view disapproved his policies as Secretary of State. One of them was A. Whitney Griswold, then a professor and later the president of Stimson's own Yale. Stimson "had based his efforts on premises many of which were unfounded in fact or history," Professor Griswold declared in 1938. "He had tried to achieve an old objective by certain new methods, and he had failed." His misguided leadership had "left the United States to bear the brunt of a Japanese antagonism" which European statesmen had been happy to avoid. Another academic critic, Sara R. Smith, a protégé of Professor James T. Shotwell at Columbia University, believed that Stimson had not gone far enough in the direction in which Griswold thought he had gone too far. Miss Smith contended that if Stimson had taken a stronger stand against the Japanese, they could have been pressured into yielding. Or, if not, they still could have been stopped by force, and, according to her, "war in 1931 would have been preferable to war in 1941." [10]

[9] Richard W. Van Alstyne, in the *Pacific Historical Review*, 18: 505-506 (November, 1949).
[10] A. Whitney Griswold, *The Far Eastern Policy of the United States* (New York, 1938), 437-38; Sara R. Smith, *The Manchurian Crisis, 1931-1932: A Tragedy in International Relations* (New York, 1948), 225.

At any rate, war in 1941 brought Stimson new opportunities both in the making of policy and in the winning of public opinion. In war time, secrecy and censorship became virtues, and patriotism demanded ungrudging support for the Secretary of War. Stimson now got a very good press. Even Drew Pearson, once the most shrewish of his journalist critics, began to trumpet his character and ability. And the experienced propagandist George Creel, head of the government's Committee on Public Information during the previous war, prepared a fine piece of press-agentry for him in 1943. Creel presented him as a most outstanding public servant who had made the Army the most modern in the world. "Why, then, haven't people been told about this super duper?" The answer, said Creel, was simple. "Henry Stimson lacks oomph and is entirely without the publicity sense that furnishes the press with good hot stuff." His work was too efficient, too good. "No quarrels, no blunders, no bellows." Hence no news.[11]

After the war, to give a cue to future historians, Stimson produced a thick volume of memoirs. He explained: "This book is intended to be a 'pilot biography'—written while my memory of important events is still alive—in order to forestall possible biographies written without the careful aid of my papers or myself." In retrospect it seemed to him that "foolish nations and inadequate statesmen" had brought the horrors of war upon themselves, and he regarded himself as, perhaps, one of those who had not always been quite up to the needs of the hour. He had in mind his opposition to Wilson's League of Nations and his early hesitancy to smite the Japanese. Reviewers hailed his *apologia* with superlatives. Gerald W. Johnson, for one, averred: "Neither pride, nor fear, nor partisan rancor, nor ambition, could deter Stimson from admitting the truth, first to himself and

[11] Drew Pearson and Robert S. Allen, "Washington Merry-Go-Round," in the Champaign-Urbana *Daily Illini*, April 30, 1941; February 24, 1942; George Creel, "Secretary of War," in *Collier's*, 112: 17 ff. (August 7, 1943).

then to others." [12] But in other postwar books there appeared hints that the sins he confessed might not have been the ones he was most guilty of.

True, almost all the harvest of now-it-can-be-told writings mentioned him only to praise him. Vannevar Bush, the atomic scientist, dedicated his *Modern Arms and Free Men* to him. Some memoirists, however, expressed doubt about the wisdom and justice of some of the policies he helped to make, as for example the decision to drop the atom bombs. "It is my opinion that the use of this barbarous weapon at Hiroshima and Nagasaki was of no material assistance in our war against Japan," wrote Admiral William D. Leahy. "My own feeling was that in being the first to use it, we had adopted an ethical standard common to the barbarians of the Dark Ages." And Herbert Hoover in his memoirs, dryly noting that his "able Secretary was at times more of a warrior than a diplomat," indicated his conviction that Stimson's way with Japan was not the way of peace.

Historians, amateur and professional, did not all take the cue that Stimson had provided. Decrying what they viewed as Roosevelt-Stimson policies, Charles A. Beard and other "revisionists" even implied that Roosevelt and Stimson had plotted to expose Pearl Harbor to attack and then had made scapegoats of the officers in command there. On the other hand, at least one staunch friend of the administration, John Gunther, concluded, with reference to the Pearl Harbor disaster: "Stimson does not by any means exonerate himself or the War Department." And the best informed writer on the diplomacy of that time, Herbert Feis, himself a former adviser of Stimson's, raised the question whether his ideas of economic pressure in 1940–41 were well conceived. Again, regarding the mass evacuation and incarceration of Japanese-Americans, the most thorough student of the subject, Morton Grodzins, declared that while the Japanese-Americans were the immediate victims, the process by which

[12] *On Active Service*, xi; *New York Times*, October 18, 1948.

the decision was made "betrayed all Americans." Except for the "revisionists," these writers did not criticize Stimson himself.

Nor did George Kennan, the State Department expert who authored the rationale of the Truman administration's program of Soviet containment. Appraising the past fifty years of American diplomacy, Kennan in 1950 denounced as mischievous a long list of the concepts and practices to which Stimson had devoted his career. According to Kennan, the United States should never have taken up the "white man's burden," kept the Philippines, or pursued the will-o'-the-wisp of the Open Door in China. We should not have tried "to achieve our foreign policy objectives by inducing other governments to sign up to professions of high moral and legal principles." We should not have assumed a "legalistic-moralistic" attitude toward problems of foreign affairs. Thus Kennan, yet he hastened to say he would be "most unhappy" if any of his observations should be considered as "a mark of disrespect" for such men as Stimson. We should remember, Kennan urged, what Gibbon said of a great Byzantine general: "His imperfections flowed from the contagion of the times; his virtues were his own." [13]

And so, it seems, a consensus on the statecraft of Stimson is yet to be arrived at. Meanwhile certain phases of his career may bear re-examination, as a preliminary step toward appraisal of its meaning and merit.

[13] Vannevar Bush, *Modern Arms and Free Men: A Discussion of the Role of Science in Preserving Democracy* (New York, 1949); William D. Leahy, *I Was There: The Personal Story of the Chief of Staff to Presidents Roosevelt and Truman Based on His Notes and Diaries Made at the Time* (New York, 1950), 441; *The Memoirs of Herbert Hoover*, Vol. 2: *The Cabinet and the Presidency, 1920–1933* (New York, 1952), 366; Charles A. Beard, *President Roosevelt and the Coming of the War, 1941: A Study in Appearances and Realities* (New Haven, 1948), 517–69; John Gunther, *Roosevelt in Retrospect: A Profile in History* (New York, 1950), 322 n; Herbert Feis, *The Road to Pearl Harbor: The Coming of the War between the United States and Japan* (Princeton, 1950), 49–50; Morton Grodzins, *Americans Betrayed: Politics and the Japanese Evacuation* (Chicago, 1949), 374; George F. Kennan, *American Diplomacy, 1900–1950* (Chicago, 1951), 18–19, 37, 44–52, 92, 95, 100–101.

2 *The Yale Man's Burden*

The creek was high that chilly March afternoon as a lone horseman, trim and erect, jogged along in Washington's Rock Creek Park. He was a New York lawyer, taking an outing while on an errand in the Capital. His mind on his legal business, he did not notice the two riders on the other side of the stream until one of them called to him. Then he recognized his friends Theodore Roosevelt and Elihu Root. When Root invited him over, he only smiled. The creek was high.

So Root straightened up in his saddle and barked: "Sergeant Stimson, the President of the United States through the Secretary of War orders you to report immediately!"

With no hesitation at all this time, Sergeant Stimson of the New York National Guard spurred his horse into the water, struggled through the current, and finally made it up the opposite bank, where he reined in before the President.

"Dee-lighted!" exclaimed T. R. with his toothy grin. "I didn't think you would be so foolish. But I'm delighted. Now go right home, take a drink, and change your clothes." [1]

In 1906 President Roosevelt offered Stimson his first government job, as United States attorney for the southern district of New York. Though his new salary would be only half of his current income, he snatched at

[1] Henry F. Pringle, "Henry L. Stimson: A Portrait," in the *Outlook and Independent*, 151: 410 (March 13, 1929). Pringle says that Root was "fond of telling this story on his young protégé."

the opportunity for public service. It was, as he afterward said, a case of love at first sight. He liked the work and he worked hard, putting energy and efficiency into what had been a rather sleepy and disorganized office. Indeed, the President never had a more loyal and eager aide. T. R. was in a trust-busting mood, and his new attorney, in whose district trusts abounded, set to busting them right and left. He forced the American Sugar Refining Corporation to pay up several millions in customs duties it had evaded. He got convictions or admissions of guilt in suits he brought against the New York Central, the Great Northern, the Rock Island, and other railroads on charges of rebating. He sent the Wall Street swindler Charles W. Morse to the penitentiary and made the New York publisher James Gordon Bennett pay a fine for putting indecent "personals" in his *Herald*. The forces of public righteousness had a field day.

And then, in the middle of it, certain of the citizenry dared to suggest that the President himself was guilty of evil-doing. They criticized Roosevelt for the way he "took Panama." The worst of it was that his way was quite unnecessary. The United States had offered Colombia ten million dollars (plus a modest annuity) for the privilege of cutting a canal across the isthmus. But the United States promised forty million to the new Panama Canal Company for the charter rights which Colombia had earlier granted to the old company of Ferdinand de Lesseps and which were now about to expire. Forty million to this corporation and only ten to the Colombian government itself! The Colombians balked. If Roosevelt had been willing to give Colombia more and the company less, he need not have had to help stage a Panamanian revolution in order to acquire the canal zone.

Why Roosevelt acted as he did was—and is—something of a mystery. It might be called the mystery of the missing forty million. Who got the money? It was paid to the firm of J. P. Morgan, ostensibly for transfer to a large number of anonymous French stockholders. But the New York *World* and then the Indianapolis *News* and a few other papers told a different story. They asserted that a small group of Americans, including a brother-in-law of Roosevelt's, had bought up a majority of the company's stock, and most of the forty million had gone to them.

Roosevelt fairly screamed. In a message to Congress he denounced the story as a libel upon the United States government (with which he obviously identified himself). He swore that his government would prosecute the libelers to the hilt.

As a federal attorney, Stimson needed no prodding to carry out the President's will, but he faced the problem of establishing federal jurisdiction in the case. Soon he thought he had found a way. First, he dug up an old statute designed to protect the nation's harbor defenses and other fortifications from "malicious injury." Next, he decided that the *World's* story had been "published" on federal property because twenty-nine copies of the paper had been circulated at West Point. And then he took the unprecedented view that the government could prosecute the case in "a number of distinct and independent jurisdictions" at the same time. On this reasoning he secured an indictment for criminal libel in New York, and other indictments were obtained in Washington and Indianapolis, though none of the individuals named in the newspaper stories had begun a libel suit in his own behalf.

Stimson's novel theories menaced the freedom of the press, or so the *World* maintained in one editorial after another. The publishers pointed out that the United States possessed thousands of fortifications and harbor defenses, and no newspaper could afford to defend itself in many of these jurisdictions at once. Nevertheless, the publishers swore that they would not be muzzled, even if they had to go to jail. Agreeing with them, the United States attorney in Indianapolis resigned rather than prosecute the local *News*. Stimson's principles, he said, were "dangerous, striking at the very foundation of our form of government." So he could not "honestly and conscientiously insist to the court that such is the law or that such construction could be put upon it." Stimson himself had no misgivings.

Unimpressed by his line of argument, however, the judges of the Circuit Court and finally those of the Supreme Court decided that they had no jurisdiction in the case. The remedy, if any, must be sought in the state courts. Neither Roosevelt nor Stimson tried to bring action there, and their fiasco was soon forgotten.[2]

Their intimacy increased. During his three years as district attorney, Stimson often went to Washington to confer with Roosevelt about the government's lawsuits. He came to be listed as one of that select group of white-flanneled Presidential playfellows known as the "tennis Cabinet." After he and Roosevelt were both out of office, they continued to see much of each other, until the ex-President departed for his African safari.

Back from his travels, Roosevelt began to preach the "new nationalism," and Stimson cheered him on. In a harangue at Osawatomie, Kansas, in 1910, Roosevelt proposed among other startling things the popular recall of judges. This struck many shuddering Republicans as demagoguery of the worst sort, but Stimson sent Roosevelt his congratulations, saying that the "richer and more intelligent" citizens must take the lead in reform so as to save the country from those—presumably the poorer and more stupid—who might otherwise resort to violence. A little later Roosevelt

[2] Henry L. Stimson and McGeorge Bundy, *On Active Service in Peace and War* (New York, 1948), 4–14, narrate at some length the trust-busting and other crusading activities of District Attorney Stimson but do not so much as mention the government's libel case. This, however, is adequately treated by Pringle, in the *Outlook and Independent*, 151: 411.

confided to a California friend about the situation in New York: "Among all the people who are prominent here, Harry Stimson is the only man who is anywhere near as radical as I am, the only man, for instance, who approved my Osawatomie speech."

Roosevelt, for political reasons of his own, wanted Stimson to run for governor in 1910. Some of Stimson's friends warned him that it was not a Republican year, but Elihu Root prevailed upon him to make the race. He ran a poor second, lagging behind the rest of the losing ticket. His only real political strength lay in his being Roosevelt's man, and yet it was also a weakness to be vulnerable, as he was, to taunts of "Teddie's boy."

If he could not be elected to office, he could be appointed again. In 1911 President Taft offered him a place in his Cabinet as Secretary of War. Taft had gone into the White House as Roosevelt's hand-picked successor, but he was now losing Roosevelt's friendship and support, and he had cause to fear that T. R. might challenge his renomination in 1912. Perhaps he could forestall the danger if he could draw a good Roosevelt man into his own administration. Before accepting the offer, Stimson inquired of Roosevelt, and Roosevelt gave his consent.

The new War Secretary liked Taft, a fellow Yale alumnus, and he loved the War office, even though it was in those peaceful days much the least influential of the Cabinet jobs. The life was pleasant. Mornings the vigorous Secretary rode in Rock Creek Park and often went to his desk still accoutred with boots and breeches and crop. There was little work to be done. The Army numbered only about four thousand officers and seventy thousand enlisted men, most of them scattered over the country at obsolete military posts. Stimson and his chief of staff, Major General Leonard Wood (who, rather than T. R., had actually commanded the Rough Riders in the Spanish-American War), did accomplish important reforms. They regrouped the tiny forces into a more efficient pattern and streamlined the internal organization of the War Department.[3]

While Taft's Secretary of War, Stimson continued to look at Roosevelt as his model and mentor. The two Long Island neighbors frequently discussed affairs of state on their horseback jaunts. Or Roosevelt sent notes to Stimson, like this one: "Nothing could have a healthier or more steadying influence, by the way, than the visit of a warship with the Secretary of War to Havana and San Domingo. These countries can remain independent always only if they will not be too foolish, will not contract debts they cannot pay, and will not indulge in revolutions; and it is a good thing for them, and tends to promote sobriety, to see the power of the United States tangibly expressed before their eyes." Stimson was glad to do them good, and he did, in Roosevelt's way. He also tried to stiffen up Taft's policy with Rooseveltian vigor when a Mexican revolution caused disturbances along the border. He thought the United States would be justified in "violating the sovereignty of Mexican soil to the extent that it was necessary to protect American lives," but he did not convince President Taft.

Yet things were going happily enough for him until an estrangement developed between Taft and Roosevelt. Stimson did his best to prevent a complete break, and when it came, at the end of 1911, he faced the dilemma of choosing between his chief and his friend. He observed afterward that "there was no real issue of political principle between the two men." Root, however, said at the time that "Theodore" had "gone off on a perfectly wild program" and that Stimson and himself could not "possibly go with Roosevelt

[3] *On Active Service*, 22, 25–29; Philip C. Jessup, *Elihu Root* (2 vols., New York, 1938), 2: 162, 170–71; Pringle, in the *Outlook and Independent*, 151: 409–10.

in his new departure." [4] The Roosevelt program was then no wilder than a year before, when Stimson had applauded it. Anyhow, he chose in 1912 to go with Taft—and Root. His decision meant the temporary sacrifice of one of his most prized possessions, the friendship of Theodore Roosevelt.

If William Howard Taft served as a catalyst to separate Stimson and Roosevelt, Woodrow Wilson provoked a reaction that brought the two together again. They could and did join in deploring Wilson's hesitancy to take the United States into the first World War. And after the war Stimson and Roosevelt and Root, all three, combined to frustrate Wilson's plan for taking the United States into the League of Nations.

Siding with England and France from 1914 on, Stimson contemned President Wilson's advice to Americans to remain neutral in thought as well as deed. He thought they should hate the enemy—"Prussianism." From his recent experience in the War Department he knew as well as anybody that the Army was not of a size or shape to fight, and he considered Wilson much too slow in doing anything about it. So did Roosevelt, who began to characterize the President as a pacifistic mollycoddle. One day in 1915 Roosevelt and Stimson dined together and renewed their friendship in a common cause, Preparedness.

To rouse the people to a warlike attitude, Stimson went up and down the land speaking under the auspices of such propaganda groups as the New York Mayor's Committee on National Defense, the National Civic Federation's Committee on Military and Naval Preparedness, and the National Security League. He was careful to propose not actually

[4] Stimson, typewritten reminiscence, 1913, "Previous Relations with Colonel Roosevelt," on microfilm in the Yale University Library; Root to Robert Bacon, March 9, 1912, quoted in Henry F. Pringle, *Theodore Roosevelt: A Biography* (New York, 1931), 560.

going to war but only getting everybody, male and female, ready for it—the men by universal military training, the women by other means, beginning with a "military census." At the same time he opposed giving the vote to women, for fear they might use it to defeat preparation for war. He declared: "Participation in the decision of such questions by woman, who is not only wholly ignorant of the methods of force, but whose very nature shrinks from the thought of it, cannot but be a source of peril to the government which permits it."

While he called upon others to prepare, Stimson also girded himself, enrolling along with flabbier men than he in the voluntary officers' training camp at Plattsburg, New York. From youth he had wanted to experience the life of a fighting soldier, as so many of his ancestors had done. When the Spanish-American War began he signed up with the National Guard, only to be left behind with his troop while another sailed off to the field of conquest in Puerto Rico. For nine years he rode proudly in peace with his dashing cavalry, while he rose to the rank of lieutenant. Would he have his chance to see real action before he was too old to fight? He was nearing fifty when, at last, war against Germany was declared.

His first desire, until the government turned down the whole romantic idea, was to go abroad with a volunteer division of latter-day Rough Riders which Roosevelt aspired to lead. Then he thought of the regular Army, but it would hardly do for a one-time War Secretary to serve as a mere lieutenant. So he studied awhile at the War College in Washington, paid a personal visit to the incumbent Secretary of War, Newton D. Baker, and shortly obtained a promotion and an artillery command. Though overseas nine months, he saw only three weeks of actual fighting, then was sent home for another promotion and the command of a newly formed regiment. After the armistice he was mustered out as a colonel.[5]

He thoroughly enjoyed his experience in France. In a magazine article published in 1919 he wrote enthusiastically of what he called the "joy of war." War seemed to him a "game of wits," spiced by a "pleasant uncertainty," ennobled by touches of "glamor" and gallantry. "It reminded me of nothing so much as a good grizzly-bear hunt in my younger days," Stimson said. His artillery post was in a "quiet sector" in the Vosges Mountains. "Under the branches of the firs camp-life went on with all the enjoyable surroundings of an outing in the Adirondacks." Life there was especially glamorous for Stimson whenever he "came in contact with the officers of our gallant allies," the French, who would "spread out under the pines a delicious repast, admirably served, with cooking of a kind. to which the American army was a stranger."

And when at last a call to action came, the excitement made life even more enjoyable. Stimson gave the order that sent off what he always believed was the first shell fired against the Germans by the United States Army. He took delight in the roar of the barrage that followed. Long afterward, in old age, he was still to recall how "wonderfully happy" he felt throughout the next three weeks,[6] until he had to leave.

Though Stimson joyed in the Wilsonian war, he looked with mixed feelings upon the Wilsonian peace. Wilson believed that, the war to end war having been fought to a successful conclusion, the nations of the world should dis-

[5] *On Active Service*, 83–90, 92–93, 99–100; Stimson to Miss Alice Hill Chittenden, president of the Association Opposed to Woman Suffrage, May 24, 1915, in the *New York Times*, June 12, 1915; and news of Stimson's preparedness activities in the same paper, June 15, July 11, 1915; February 18, 1916; January 23, February 3, March 19, 22, 25, April 2, 16, 1917.

[6] Henry L. Stimson, "Artillery in a Quiet Sector," *Scribner's Magazine*, 65: 709–16 (June, 1919); *On Active Service*, 97–98.

card neutrality as an outworn concept and should consider
an attack on any of them as an attack on all. This idea he
embodied in the covenant of the League of Nations, in
article ten, by which each member undertook to preserve
the integrity of the others against aggression. Wilson viewed
article ten as the very heart of the League, and on this point
he steadfastly refused to compromise.

Before the covenant had been drafted, Stimson discussed
with Root the question whether it should include a guarantee
against aggression. Root said "he was opposed to any proposal that we should agree, as a nation, to go to war on the
order of someone else, such as the decision of a league." Aggression could not be defined as a crime, he thought, until
there had been "a change made in the fundamental conception of international law."

As soon as the draft of the covenant appeared in the
newspapers, Stimson and Root spent the morning together
(February 15, 1919) to examine the document. At once
Root found serious fault with it. His "main objection
seemed to be that the instrument rested on the strength of
covenants rather than upon an establishment of international
law." Here the famous publicist, drawing a distinction between treaties and the law of nations, implied that the one
could not augment the other. To Stimson the point appeared to be a vital one. He declared in an open letter: "The
time is surely coming when in international law an act of
aggression by one nation upon the other will be regarded as
an offense against the community of nations." Aggression,
in other words, would someday be a crime, but that day was
not yet, and article ten was not the proper means to hasten
it.

Here, then, was a legal and theoretical issue between Wilson and Stimson (following Root): Should aggression be
made a crime by treaty, now, as Wilson urged, or should it
be made a crime by the development of international law

in some other (unspecified) way and at some other (unspecified) time? But the practical issue, in view of Wilson's stubborn stand on article ten, was different: Should the United States join the League as Wilson wanted it—or no League at all? And there was a political issue: Should the Republicans allow a Democratic President to reap the popularity, if not the blessedness, of a successful peacemaker?

For partisan and personal reasons, Theodore Roosevelt (until his death in early 1919) and Henry Cabot Lodge and other Republican stalwarts were determined to defeat any plan that Wilson might bring back from Versailles. They needed on their side a voice as exalted as Wilson's own. So they looked to Root, an elder statesman who, if anyone, could address the people with all the force of vast experience and wise detachment. The problem was to induce him to speak out.

Stimson provided the link between the party's strategists and the party's voice of high and disinterested authority. At their behest he saw Root and begged him to make a public statement, then called on him a second time along with Will H. Hays, chairman of the Republican National Committee. Root finally gave in.

His blast demolished article ten. The most he could say for it was that it should remain in force no more than a few years. "If perpetual," he wrote, "it would be an attempt to preserve for all time unchanged the distribution of power and territory made in accordance with the views and exigencies of the Allies at this present juncture of affairs." It would be not only "futile" but "mischievous" as well. "Change and growth are the law of life, and no nation can impose its will in regard to the growth of nations and the distribution of power, upon succeeding generations." [7]

[7] Stimson, "Memorandum of Talk with E. R. [Elihu Root] . . . ," December 22, 1918, and Stimson diary, February 15, 1919, and December 3, 1919, on microfilm in the Yale University Library; Jessup, *Root*, 2: 383, 388–95; *On Active Service*, 91, 101–107.

This statement of Root's, which Stimson himself had elicited, condemned as fallacious the idea of enforcing peace, on the grounds that the attempt would only result in a futile war for the *status quo*. The great irony of Stimson's career is the fact that he was eventually to become the world's foremost exponent of the very concept his legal mentor thus denounced.

Stimson again joined in condemnation of Wilson's League when, at the height of the Presidential campaign of 1920, he along with Root signed a statement of thirty-one eminent Republicans declaring that the issue for voters was between Wilson's covenant with its article ten, on the one hand, and on the other a Republican substitute purged of that noxious commitment. "To bring America into an effective league," Stimson and the thirty others solemnly asserted, "we can look only to the Republican Party and its candidate." After the election President Harding did nothing, of course, to "bring America into an effective league." Neither did Stimson. In the early nineteen-twenties his one contribution to the cause of world peace was his crusade, resumed after the war to end war, for compulsory military training.[8]

In 1927 President Coolidge recalled Stimson from his profitable law business and sent him forth to take up the imperial burden, first in Nicaragua and then in the Philippines.

In Nicaragua there was civil war, the outs against the ins, the Liberals against the Conservatives. The warring factions had held off for more than a dozen years, as long as the legation guard of a hundred American marines remained in the capital. In 1925, less than a month after the marines left the country, a revolt began. Though refusing to deal with the Conservative leader who first proclaimed himself president, the Coolidge administration did recognize his right-hand man, Adolfo Díaz. The Mexican government

[8] *New York Times*, December 11, 1919; October 15, 1920.

gave its support to a man from the other camp, Dr. Juan B. Sacasa, the Liberal candidate. And the war went on.

It became a fretful problem to Coolidge and his Secretary of State, Frank B. Kellogg. When Coolidge sent marines back into Nicaragua, liberals in the United States denounced him as a highhanded warmaker, and he had to protest: "We are not making war on Nicaragua any more than a policeman on the street is making war on passers-by." The nervous Kellogg feared that Bolsheviks, by way of Mexico, were undermining American interests in Nicaragua. Finally Coolidge and Kellogg decided to send a trouble shooter to the scene. Stimson, with Root's recommendation, was a logical choice. Recently he had advised the State Department in its efforts to settle the Tacna-Arica dispute between Chile and Peru. He eagerly accepted the call to serve again.[9]

Before he sailed he got from Coolidge the impression that he was to have a completely free hand as the President's personal agent. But Kellogg told the American minister in Managua that the trip was intended merely to effect an exchange of views between the State Department and its representatives already on the ground. When Stimson reached Managua he found these instructions in a telegram: "The Stimson mission should not be characterized in any sense as an act of mediation." But he had not journeyed all the way to the Nicaraguan wilds just to act as the State Department's messenger boy. Nor did he.

He made up his mind to mediate, to bring the leaders of the warring factions together to talk peace. And he decided that, to succeed in this, he would have to commit the United States to supervising the next presidential election in Nicaragua. "Believe," he reported, "that such action by the

[9] Samuel F. Bemis, *The Latin American Policy of the United States: An Historical Interpretation* (New York, 1943), 212-13; *On Active Service*, 110; *New York Times*, April 26, 1927, quoting Coolidge.

United Sates would appeal far more strongly to both American and Latin American public sentiment than naked military intervention in support of Díaz and against Liberals which may otherwise quite probably become necessary to bring about early pacification of the country." According to his plan, both sides were to cease firing, disarm, and observe a general amnesty. Díaz would bring leading Liberals into his cabinet and would remain in office until the end of his term. The reconstituted government would organize a nonpartisan constabulary, under American officers, and this force together with the American marines would police the next elections.

Stimson quickly induced the Conservative president, Díaz, to accept these terms, then sent them to the rival president, Dr. Sacasa. "If Sacasa refuses to settle," he cabled home, "I fear only alternative will be between leaving country to such anarchy [as continued war would bring] and a forcible disarmament of the insurgents by the marines." From Sacasa he got a reply which indicated a willingness to agree on every point except one, the continuance of Díaz in office.

Preparing for the worst, Stimson called for naval reinforcements and for permission to threaten Sacasa that the marines might be used to attack and disarm the insurgents. "Whatever effect on Sacasa," he explained, "believe it would greatly affect many of his more practical military associates." With the power of the Navy behind him, he met on an American destroyer three delegates whom Sacasa had sent to enter into preliminary and "unofficial" talks with him.[10]

He found the Sacasa men conciliatory but unwilling to commit themselves without the approval of the commander

[10] Henry L. Stimson, *American Policy in Nicaragua* (New York, 1927), 42–43; U. S. Department of State, *Papers Relating to the Foreign Relations of the United States, 1927* (3 vols., Washington, 1942), 3: 318–33.

of the Liberal army, General José María Moncada. So Stimson arranged to go out and talk personally with the general. In the village of Tipitapa, on the border between Conservative and Liberal ground, he and Moncada sat down together in the shade of a blackthorn tree on the afternoon of May 4, 1927. Moncada spoke good English and he spoke it frankly. He did not like the idea of accepting Díaz as president, even for a day, but he could see the alternatives—yield, or face the overpowering force of the United States. He feared, however, that his officers and men might not see the dilemma as clearly as he did, himself. The better to persuade them to give up, he asked Stimson for a letter threatening forcible disarmament in so many words, and Stimson then and there wrote: " . . . the forces of the United States will be authorized to accept the custody of the arms of those willing to lay them down . . . and to disarm forcibly those who will not do so." Later in the afternoon Moncada told an Associated Press correspondent that, rather than take the field against the United States, he was ordering his troops to turn their weapons over to the American marines.[11]

A week and a half later, on May 15, Stimson telegraphed to Washington: "The civil war in Nicaragua is now definitely ended." Next day a news bulletin reported that Dr.

---

[11] Stimson, *American Policy in Nicaragua*, 77-79; *New York Times*, May 6, 8, 11, 1927. In his journal, at the time, Stimson described the Moncada meeting a little more tersely than he did later in his book. Moncada, he wrote, "Said Diaz issue had become a point of honor owing to the men who had died for it in battlefield and he could not accept a settlement with it. I told him it was also a point of honor to my chief & country & I could by yielding subject them to alleged admission of bad faith in recognizing Diaz. At one time he suggested that Diaz resign after 6 months. He said he w'd not fight U. S. if we insisted on the point. I said I am authorized to insist. He said if you will give me a letter I will try to persuade my men. I said I would. He said he did not want a single life to be lost between us on that issue." Ms. journal, entry for May 4, 1927, on microfilm in the Yale University Library.

Sacasa had denounced the Stimson-Moncada deal and that Nicaraguan forces had attacked a detachment of American marines, killing two of them and wounding two more. Stimson left for home, his mission accomplished, according to him. But the fighting continued. "When it comes to actual warfare, in which there are casualties in our marines, and a reported great slaughter among the Nicaraguans who attacked them," the *New York Times* editorialized, "it seems as if ill luck were malignantly pursuing the whole venture." [12]

Stimson himself told the American public a very different story in the *Saturday Evening Post* and in his book, *American Policy in Nicaragua* (1927). The intervention had been absolutely necessary, he argued. Just as Great Britain controlled her sea route to India, so the United States must make sure of the Panama Canal and its approaches, even if this meant enforcing "order" in the whole of the Caribbean area. Self-defense demanded it, and so did the Monroe Doctrine. Stimson quoted his old friend Theodore Roosevelt: "We cannot permanently adhere to the Monroe Doctrine unless we succeed in making it evident . . . that in as much as by this doctrine we prevent other nations from interfering on this side of the water, we shall ourselves in good faith try to help those of our sister republics which need such help toward peace and order."

The only alternatives Stimson could see for Nicaragua were these: continued "anarchy," or "naked military intervention" by the United States, or his own plan, which presumably was military intervention with its clothes on. There was, in fact, a fourth alternative: cooperation among all the Central American states in accordance with existing treaties, as practiced by President Harding's secretary of

[12] *New York Times*, May 17, 24, and editorial entitled "Bad Luck in Nicaragua," July 27, 1927.

state, Charles Evans Hughes. Cooperation of that kind in 1927 would have made "international police action" a more plausible fiction than it actually was.[13]

As Stimson saw it, the intervention was by no means an "act of selfish imperialism." True, it benefited the United States, but by a happy coincidence it benefited Nicaragua too. It blessed with peace and free elections a previously distracted land.[14]

The election of 1928 was indeed held according to the Stimson plan, and the Liberal candidate—General Moncada this time, not Dr. Sacasa—was counted in. "It is no disparagement of free elections or the *pax americana* in Nicaragua," commented Lawrence Dennis, formerly first secretary of the American legation in Managua, "to question whether these boons, by themselves, are worth to Nicaragua the life of one good American soldier." During the next few years more than a hundred American marines (not to mention some four thousand Nicaraguans) were to die in the pacification process.

Moncada was president. Moncada was at peace. But one of his former officers, Augusto César Sandino, kept up the fight. According to a *New York Times* correspondent, who got his information from Managua residents, Sandino had expected an invitation to meet Stimson at the time of the latter's Tipitapa conference with Moncada, and when he was overlooked he took it as a deliberate slight. According to Manuel Gomez, secretary of the All-America Anti-Imperialist League, Sandino felt outraged because Stimson at Tipitapa had persuaded Moncada to betray the

[13] During Stimson's negotiations with the Sacasa representatives, the foreign minister of Salvador did propose joint mediation by the Central American nations along with the United States in the Nicaraguan war. But Stimson told Kellogg that the Salvadorean foreign minister was "evidencing persistent desire to intrude," expressed concern lest this move hinder his own negotiations, and asked: "Can you take steps in Washington to head it off?" *Foreign Relations, 1927*, 3: 333-34.
[14] Stimson, *American Policy in Nicaragua*, 90-118.

Liberal cause by designating him as the next president. Whatever the truth in either of these accounts, Sandino's war was an awkward fact for Stimson to fit into his story of Nicaraguan peace. He nevertheless managed to explain the war away, by dismissing Sandino and his followers as "bandits" and "outlaws." It would seem, however, that if they had been mere bandits, they might have found safer and more profitable business than baiting the United States marines.[15]

Before the end of 1927 President Coolidge looked to Stimson for another pacification job. The President faced a problem in the Philippines, with the death of the governor general, Stimson's old associate Leonard Wood. When, as Wood's replacement, Stimson called at the White House for instructions, Coolidge told him he could draw them up for himself.[16] That was easy enough for Stimson, since he already held some strong convictions on Philippine affairs, and he could rely on the advice of Elihu Root, one of the original formulators of Republican policy with respect to the islands.

In the original definition of policy, in 1899, the Senate resolved that by the decision to hold the Philippines it was not "intended to permanently annex said islands," but rather to "prepare them for local self-government" and "in due time" to dispose of them in whatever way would best serve the interest of both the Filipino and the American

[15] Lawrence Dennis, "Revolution, Recognition, and Intervention," and "Nicaragua: In Again, Out Again," in *Foreign Affairs*, 9: 204–21, 496–500 (January, April, 1931); *New York Times*, January 4, 8, 11, March 23, 1928. Joseph O. Baylen, "Sandino: Patriot or Bandit?" in the *Hispanic American Historical Review*, 31: 405–406 (August, 1951), concludes that Moncada sought to use the power of the United States to destroy his most dangerous rival, Sandino; that "the charge of 'banditry' was an attempt to avoid recognition of Sandino as a revolutionary leader"; and that "if Sandino was really the ruthless outlaw that Stimson described," public opinion in Nicaragua would have been "more hostile to the 'bandit' than to the United States Marines."

[16] Stimson diary, February 8, 1928.

people. That was vague enough. And War Secretary Root's letter of instructions to High Commissioner Taft in 1900, despite its fine phrase about the "happiness, peace, and prosperity" of the island inhabitants, did not clarify the ultimate purpose of the United States. Nor did the Cooper Act of 1902, which authorized for the islands a government much like the governments of the royal colonies in America before the Revolution. Thereafter Republican administrations took seriously their self-given trusteeship and strove to protect the Filipinos from exploitation, improve their economic lot, educate them, and prepare them for a share in their own politics. But the Republicans never specified when, or whether, the Philippines were to be free.

The Democrats, after they came into power with Wilson, at last announced a definite aim, though not a definite date, in the Jones Act of 1916. Its preamble declared that the American people had not gone to war with Spain for "territorial aggrandizement," that their purpose had always been "to withdraw their sovereignty over the Philippine Islands and recognize their independence as soon as a stable government can be established therein," and that "for the speedy accomplishment of such purpose it is desirable to place in the hands of the people of the Philippines as large a control of their domestic affairs" as was consistent with the temporary sovereignty of the United States. The actual terms of the Jones Act did not quite live up to its preamble, but they did call for an elective two-house legislature with extensive powers, including the power of the Philippine Senate to confirm or reject almost all appointments by the governor general. Wilson's governor general, Francis Burton Harrison, who had gone to the islands with instructions to get them ready for freedom, proceeded according to the spirit rather than the letter of the new law. By appointing native politicians to office he "filipinized" the civil service, and by withholding his veto he allowed the Filipino legislators virtually a free hand.

When the Republicans returned to power in Washington, the Jones Act remained on the books, but it was applied so as to conform as nearly as possible with previous Republican policy. Harrison's successor, General Wood, went to the Philippines as joint head of an investigating commission before taking office. He was aghast at the evidence of governmental inefficiency and financial mismanagement he found. Harrison, in defense of his own administration, conceded that the spread of democracy in the islands might have cost something in inefficiency and waste, but he maintained: "if so, that disadvantage is more than offset by the gain in contentment of the people, the growth of respect and friendship for the United States, and the valuable lessons in self-government secured by the Filipinos." Unimpressed by these gains, Wood tried to undo most of what his predecessor had done. He refused to mix with the Filipinos, socially or politically, and surrounded himself with a "Cavalry Cabinet" of Army officers. Soon he and the native leaders were in a deadlock, and among the people he was as well hated as Harrison had been liked. Even the Republicans back home became embarrassed by his high and mighty attitude. President Coolidge sent out a commission headed by Carmi Thompson to investigate, and Thompson's report was, in the words of two dispassionate historians, "as sharp a condemnation of about as many of the major policies of General Wood as one could expect from a conservative, big-business Republican interested in retention of the Philippines." [17]

The experience of political self-expression under one

[17] Garel A. Grunder and William E. Livezey, *The Philippines and the United States* (Norman, Oklahoma, 1951), 45, 63, 80–82, 151–52, 155–56, 159, 161, 163–66, 168–81; Drew Pearson and Robert S. Allen, *Washington Merry-Go-Round* (New York, 1931), 116–17.

governor general—and then frustration under the next—whetted the desire of Filipinos for separate nationhood. Though Republicans generally denied that the island people really wanted independence, General Wood vetoed the Philippine legislature's proposal for a referendum on the question, and President Coolidge upheld his veto. An unofficial American visitor got the impression that the following groups in the islands opposed independence: the U. S. Army officers, the Catholic clergy, the American businessmen, and all the foreigners: the Spaniards, the British, and the Chinese, who controlled retail trade. "In fact," this observer concluded, "with the exception of a few of the Protestant missionaries, practically everybody in the Philippines, save the Filipinos, is against independence."

Another American, on a semiofficial visit to Manila in 1926, disagreed with that estimate of Filipino opinion and also with the more critical implications of the Thompson report on the regime of General Wood. This visitor was Stimson himself. He reported that a "comparatively small element of Mestizo politicians" was responsible for the independence agitation, and even they had nothing more in mind than "to catch unthinking votes for local purposes." The people, he said, were racially unfit to govern themselves. "The Malay race is generally characterized by a lack of the power of co-operation in governmental functions and by a lack of initiative." When given a chance, as during "the Harrison interlude," they had proved their incapacity. "The Malay tendency to backslide promptly made itself felt with disastrous consequences." Afterwards only the vigorous Governor General stood between "the material welfare of the Islands and that racial tendency towards backsliding." And Wood was putting things to rights. By his veto he was checking the childish impulses of the natives at Manila, and by his frequent tours of inspection he was extending "a fatherly guiding influence to the uttermost Islands of the Archipelago."

Stimson expressed his own decided opinions about what we should do with the Philippines. We must never let them go, and we must make that intention perfectly clear. We must announce and pursue a policy of developing them as "self-governing possessions or colonies whose citizens did not participate in our citizenship." That was the modern way of empire. "Along that general path the other group of English speaking peoples known as the British Empire is already travelling." We must learn the lesson of the British and their wards, then teach it to the Filipinos. "The primary thing is the creation of a stable and intelligent American opinion in regard to the Islands, and its application in a patient, consistent and steadfast colonial policy." [18]

In his inaugural address, March 1, 1928, Stimson asserted that the independence question was not for him to consider, for, he said, his duties as governor general would be strictly administrative. The fact is, however, that he utterly disagreed with the major premise of the Jones Act, under which the islands were supposed to be administered, and he immediately began to advance his own program of permanent empire.

Though he believed the Malays were racially his inferiors, he nevertheless treated them as gentlemen and ladies. Abolishing Wood's color line, he opened the doors of the executive mansion, Malacañan Palace, to native politicians and their wives. He welcomed Filipinos to his cabinet and used with them the methods of persuasion rather than command. His main project was, in his words, to "interest big,

[18] Grunder and Livezey, *The Philippines and the U. S.*, 180–81; Stephen P. Duggan, "The Future of the Philippines," in *Foreign Affairs*, 5: 114–31 (October, 1926); and Henry L. Stimson, "Future Philippine Policy under the Jones Act," in the same magazine, 5: 459–71 (April, 1927). Maximo M. Kalaw, "Why the Filipinos Expect Independence," in *Foreign Affairs*, 10: 304–15 (January, 1932), declared: "The verdict of the people, given through the ballot, has always been in favor of immediate independence."

highclass American business to go into the Islands" and engage in "sharing profits with the Filipinos." With the aid of local leaders he undertook to get the land and corporation laws changed so as to attract the beneficent kind of capital he desired. This, he thought, would make the people prosperous and contented. So it would contribute to his ultimate aim, which was to dispose of the independence movement by killing it with kindness.[19]

His predecessor Wood, harsh though Wood's administration was, had been willing at least to talk as if the islands someday would be free. Stimson would not even hint at independence, immediate or remote. Yet the people found him, after Wood, a refreshing relief. They liked him. So did the politicians, especially Manuel Quezón (who had recommended his appointment to Coolidge). The Quezóns, husband and wife, came to think of him almost as an uncle.

But Quezón never agreed with him on fundamentals. Once he told Stimson that if the United States should impose a tariff against the Philippines and at the same time hold them by force, it would "break his heart" and he would "go home and teach his boy to be a rebel." Stimson replied that, as for himself, he feared lest Congress, if it imposed the tariff, might yield to the Filipino demand for immediate independence. Then Quezón confessed: "If I could get a dominion government with free trade advantages, I would do so at the price of giving up all independence agitation for thirty years." Stimson said: "My dearest hope is that there shall be a permanent connection between the Philippine Islands and the United States." But this could "only come with the full consent and desire and probably the initiative of the Filipino people." It must be done not by "caveman methods" but "on a basis of honorable marriage where the

[19] Grunder and Livezey, *The Philippines and the U. S.*, 185, 187–88; Pearson and Allen, *Washington Merry-Go-Round*, 116–17; *On Active Service*, 146; Stimson diary, February 8, 1928.

Islands like a woman are persuaded that it is for their best interest to make the connection."

Quezón remained at heart a Philippine nationalist. "And the reason why I chose to follow and adopt the policy of the Nationalist Party for immediate, absolute, and complete independence," he explained in his autobiography, "was because I had always thought—and so think to this day—that it was easier to get freedom and liberty for the Filipino people through the road to independence which the average American understands than through the policy of Presidents Roosevelt and Taft, agreed to by Colonel Stimson, which, although known and practiced by the English in their relations with their white subjects, was entirely alien to the American mind." [20]

Yet Stimson might have made considerable progress toward his goal if pressure groups within the United States had not interfered. American sugar growers and refiners demanded tariffs and quotas to protect them from Philippine competition, whereas Stimson wanted to promote rather than restrict the exports from the islands to the United States. As governor general and later as Secretary of State he protested vehemently against the proposals of the American sugar lobby. If carried out, he said, they would be "inevitably interpreted as a betrayal of trust by the United States toward a dependent people." [21] Though he helped to postpone, he could not prevent the movement that led in time to a conditional grant of independence.

[20] Stimson diary, recording a conversation with Quezón, January 6, 1929; Manuel Quezón, *The Good Fight* (New York, 1946), 115, 140–41, 143–47. Quezón said he had a "high opinion" of Stimson as "a truly great man" who was "anxious about the fate of the Filipino people"—in spite of Stimson's opposition to independence, early or late. Another Filipino, Maximo M. Kalaw, in his appraisal of "Governor Stimson in the Philippines," in *Foreign Affairs*, 7: 372–83 (April, 1929), likewise disagreed with Stimson about independence but approved his administration of the islands.

[21] Stimson to the House Ways and Means Committee, in the *New York Times*, April 21, 1929.

He had the sympathy of Elihu Root. "The trouble is," Root believed, "people in the United States don't care anything about the Philippines." The American people, he feared, were not up to the high challenge of imperial rule. "Just so far as democracy exercises its powers, just so far is it incapable of governing colonies." [22] One must choose between democracy and imperialism, Root here implied. One must not expect both.

[22] Root to Jessup, September 30, 1930, in Jessup, *Root*, 1: 369-70.

3 Wrong-Horse Harry

"The stern daughter of the Voice of God has stood ever at his elbow," an admirer wrote of Henry L. Stimson as the new Secretary of State arrived home from the Philippines in the spring of 1929. "You saw him bow his head when the call came and sail away like a Roman proconsul."

The returning proconsul had not been in the State Department long before he realized that diplomacy was a more delicate and demanding business than imperial administration, even in the Philippines. He told an interviewer that a diplomat was like a man carrying a long ladder on a crowded street: if he swung one end aside to avoid hitting someone in front of him, he was almost sure to bang someone behind him with the other end.[1] Now he was swinging the ladder, himself.

The call had come from President Hoover, but Stimson was not his first choice for the job. Hoover would have preferred to keep Coolidge's Secretary of State, Frank B. Kellogg.[2] When Kellogg declined, Hoover yielded to the importunations of several prominent Republicans, among them, inevitably, Elihu Root. Not that the new President had anything against Stimson. He and Stimson deeply respected

[1] Drew Pearson and Robert S. Allen, *Washington Merry-Go-Round* (New York, 1931), 110; Anne O'Hare McCormick, "Hoover's Right Hand in a Great Task," in the *New York Times*, December 15, 1929.

[2] Mr. Hoover to the author, in a conversation in New York, December 28, 1951. On the appointment, see also the *New York Times*, January 25, 1929.

one another and, at first, they got along pretty well and agreed on most issues of foreign policy. But they were very different in spirit, and after a couple of years their differences began to tell.

Hoover was a man of simple tastes and unaffected manners, a man who believed in and practiced a gospel of hard and unremitting work. Stimson was a devotee of pomp and protocol, always attended by a personal military aide in the uniform of an Army captain, and he could not labor long without relaxation out of doors. Their mental habits were basically incompatible. Late in 1930, when he felt that Hoover was not pushing American membership in the World Court aggressively enough, Stimson noted in his diary that he had discussed "the President's peculiarities" with Root, the father of the World Court, at the latter's home near Clinton, New York. "I told him [Root] frankly that I thought that the President being a Quaker and an engineer did not understand the pyschology of combat the way Mr. Root and I did." [3]

By that time Stimson was beginning to doubt the adequacy of the President's ways for the high tasks of world statesmanship. Certainly the ills of the world were many and serious in these years from 1929 to 1931. There was hope and promise during the prosperous opening months of the Hoover administration, but this mood was badly shaken by the stock-market crash and the ensuing depression. In the Far East war over Manchuria threatened to involve China and Russia, if not eventually Japan. In Europe politicians talked of disarmament, security against aggressors, war debts and reparations, while skirting the edges of the central issue—to revise or to enforce the treaty of Versailles. In Latin America there was widespread ill-will against the

[3] Stimson diary, September 24, November 8, December 11, 1930, on microfilm in the Yale University Library.

United States, a legacy left over from such adventures as Stimson's own gunpoint truce in Nicaragua.

The times were out of joint, and with his stern sense of duty Stimson seemed to feel that he was born to set them right. He faced imposing handicaps. The world problems themselves were infinitely complex. The President stood in the way of a completely Stimsonian solution of them. Obstructionists, as it seemed to the Secretary, dominated the foreign relations committee of the Senate, notably William E. Borah and Hiram Johnson. The administration lost control of Congress after the elections of 1930. And the Secretary suffered, as will be seen, from his own confusions of thought.

July 24, 1929, was a red-letter day on the new Secretary's calendar. On that day he was to preside at a grand ceremony to proclaim, as in full and final effect, an agreement among the nations of the world to renounce war as an instrument of national policy and to settle their disputes by pacific means.

This remarkable pact—variously known by the names of Kellogg, Briand, Paris, and Peace—had originated in a proposal of the French foreign minister, Aristide Briand, to "outlaw" war between his country and the United States. Briand, busy as the architect of security for France, was completing a system of alliances with Belgium, Poland, Czechoslovakia, Rumania, and Yugoslavia to forestall a war of revenge by Germany, the historic foe. His proposed Franco-American antiwar pact read almost word for word like parts of his recent European treaties, such as the one with Rumania, which provided: "France and Rumania mutually undertake that they will in no case attack or invade each other or resort to war against each other." What he hoped to get from the United States was really a negative form of alliance to crown his security structure.

American pacifists, however, saw the scheme only as a

step toward the elimination of war, and they roused the public to demand that the Coolidge administration accept it. President Coolidge and Secretary Kellogg were caught in a dilemma. For a long time Kellogg did nothing except, privately, to curse the peace societies with his colorful profanity. At last he found a way out. To Briand he replied, in effect: This thing is very good, too good to keep to ourselves, so let's invite the whole world to join in. Then Briand was on the spot. The upshot was that France and more than fifty other nations signed the multilateral pact—with their fingers crossed. They reserved their rights of "self-defense," including the right to decide, each for itself, what action self-defense might require. All understood that the pact provided absolutely no "machinery" of enforcement. The United States Senate approved it as an innocuous and well-meant gesture, an "international kiss." [4]

But Stimson took it seriously, as he looked forward to the proclamation rites. Most inopportunely, there came reports from Manchuria which sounded suspiciously like war in the new warless world. China and Russia, both signatories of the pact, seemed about to come to blows.

To save the day, Stimson appealed to the Chinese and to the Russians with a reminder of their treaty obligation to arrange their differences by pacific means. The Russians protested that they should not be expected to arbitrate so long as the Chinese excluded them from the jointly owned Chinese Eastern Railway. The Japanese also objected, complaining that Stimson should have consulted them beforehand. They grew "uneasy at the sudden spectacle of America interfering in a sphere as important to Japan as is the Caribbean to the United States." Undertaking conciliation efforts of their own, they headed off Stimson by obtain-

---

[4] Robert H. Ferrell, *Peace in Their Time: The Origins of the Kellogg-Briand Pact* (New Haven, 1952), 70, 73, 138–39, 145, 164, 263–64. See also Drew Pearson and Constantine Brown, *The American Diplomatic Game* (New York, 1935), 9–50.

ing peace pledges from the Chinese and the Russians. On July 23, the day before the ceremony in Washington, newspapers reported: "Stimson feels that his main object has been achieved and the probability of war eliminated."

An assistant secretary in the State Department thus explained the meaning of Stimson's appeal to China and Russia: "One reason for this was to prevent declaration of war on the very day the pact is declared effective—tomorrow. It may have a definite good effect if the world can be made to believe that, through respect for the Pact, war was averted. This will not be true but that does not matter if the world believes it is true. It will make the Pact a real thing and something to be called forth in similar cases in the future."

Next day Stimson saw the pact of peace proclaimed, without a war declaration to mock him.[5]

And the following morning he took another step toward making a "real thing" of it. Summoning to his office the ambassadors of Great Britain, Italy, France, Germany, and Japan, he gravely read to them from a typewritten sheet, then handed out copies and dismissed the group. He was proposing a six-power commission to consult regarding ways of applying the peace pact to the Manchurian dispute. He was trying to do what none of the signers had intended —that is, to equip the thing with "machinery." But the invited powers, especially Germany and Japan, were unwilling, and he had to let the plan drop.

Several months later, in November, 1929, Russian cavalry crossed the Manchurian border, attacked and drove off the Chinese troops, then withdrew while a truce was arranged and peace negotiations began. At the critical moment Stimson was home at Highhold, on Long Island, for the Thanks-

---

[5] *New York Times*, July 22, 23, 24, 1929; diary of William R. Castle, July 23, 1929, in his possession in Washington, D. C.; Pearson and Brown, *American Diplomatic Game*, 50–54.

giving festivities. By the time he got back to Washington, events were far ahead of him. Finally, on December 1, he sent an appeal to all the signatories of the pact to bring their moral pressure to bear in Manchuria. "The efficacy of the Pact of Paris," he said, with no intention of irony, "depends on the sincerity of the governments which are party to it."

In appealing to Russia (by the devious route of the French ambassador in Washington, the Quay d'Orsay, and the French ambassador to Moscow—since the United States had not recognized the Soviet Union) Stimson left himself open to the sarcastic virtuosity of Maxim Litvinoff, the foreign commissar. To begin with, said Litvinoff, in a reply published to the world, the American Secretary is misinformed: there are no Russian troops on Chinese soil. In the second place, the Secretary is not contributing to peace but just the opposite: the effect, if any, of his *démarche* can only be to disturb the Russian-Chinese negotiations now being successfully concluded. Third, the Secretary himself is violating the treaty: "the Pact of Paris does not give any single state or group of states the function of protector of the Pact." And then the devastating jibe: "In conclusion, the Soviet Government cannot forbear expressing amazement that the Government of the United States, which by its own will has no official relations with the Soviet, deems it possible to apply to it with advice and counsel."

Recovering his aplomb after this unprecedented slap, Stimson issued a statement to the press, on December 4, in which he said with a straight face: "The present declaration of the authorities of Russia that they are now proceeding with direct negotiations which will make possible the settlement of the conflict is not the least significant evidence to show that the public opinion of the world is a live factor which can be promptly mobilized and which has become a factor of prime importance in the solution of prob-

lems and controversies which may arise between nations."
That is to say, he had mobilized world public opinion behind the pact of peace and, so doing, had averted war in
Manchuria! [6]
In the early months of 1930 a conference on naval disarmament was to meet in London. President Hoover, who
with Prime Minister Ramsay MacDonald had arranged for
the conference, earnestly wished to see the nations of the
world disarm, so as to give added meaning to their recent
declaration of universal concord in the Kellogg Pact. Stimson, however, set no great store by disarmament as such.
When asked whether he had not changed his mind about
compulsory military training, now that the United States
and the other powers had renounced war, he replied: No,
of course not. Yet he was going in person to London, and
he expected to accomplish a great deal of good, not through
disarmament but through a rapprochement of Great Britain
and the United States.

At London in 1930 five of the powers—Great Britain,
the United States, Japan, France, and Italy—were to try
to complete the work they had begun at Washington in
1922, when they had agreed on ratios (5-5-3-1.75-1.75)
limiting the over-all tonnage of their aircraft carriers and
battleships, but had failed to apply any limitations to
cruisers, destroyers, or submarines. The prospects now were
no better than they had been then. Japan demanded parity
with Great Britain and the United States, and Italy with

[6] *New York Times*, December 2, 3, 4, 5, 1929; Pearson and Brown, *American Diplomatic Game*, 54–64. President Hoover had proposed to Secretary
Kellogg (who remained in the Hoover cabinet for several weeks, until
Stimson arrived to take over the State Department) that an article be
added to the Kellogg Pact so as to put "teeth" into it by providing for a
conciliation commission and for the withdrawal of diplomatic recognition
from a recalcitrant party. *The Memoirs of Herbert Hoover*, Vol. 2: *The
Cabinet and the Presidency, 1920–1933* (New York, 1952), 335–36. There
was, of course, a difference between implementing the pact by amending
it, as Hoover proposed, and implementing it by the action of a few of the
signatories, as Simpson hoped to do.

France. And France insisted on a guarantee of her land frontiers.

Dim though the outlook was, Stimson beamed with optimism as he set sail for England. On the voyage he re-schooled his delegation thoroughly in the facts and figures of naval armament. But he was not prepared for the political as distinct from the technical phases of the subject. The question of the "freedom of the seas" was likely to arise with Great Britain. Would Stimson take a stand for neutral rights, or would he let the British navy enforce such blockades and embargoes as might be sanctioned by the League? The question of "security" was bound to come up with France. Would he commit his country to "consult" with European powers in case of threatened aggression? He did not have answers ready, nor was he much experienced in the kind of diplomacy that lay ahead. Negotiating with European statesmen was not quite the same as dealing with Moncada or Quezón.

At the conference France was the problem child. Japan could be appeased with a compromise, and was, while Stimson told the world he valued Japan as a "stabilizing influence" in the Far East. The Italians would have been satisfied with continued parity with France. But the French were adamant. No "consultative pact" for them, no naval agreement either!

In the course of the conference Stimson managed to stand on every side of the consultation issue. First, he stated that under no circumstances would the American delegation consider any kind of political agreement. Then, when the French delegate threatened to leave, he intimated that he might not be averse to discussing the subject. And when Briand arrived from Paris with a proposal for an Atlantic pact, Stimson seemed to be personally in favor of it. But he heard from Washington that any treaty containing the word "security" or "consultation" or the equivalent would be unacceptable at home. So he explained to newsmen that the United States, though favoring a consultative pact, could not herself become a party to it, because it would imply a moral obligation to use American armed forces against an aggressor.

On learning what Stimson had said, Briand announced that he was going back to Paris. "I do not know what Secretary Stimson means by talking about moral obligations toward France if the United States entered into a consultative pact," he fumed. "We do not ask Mr. Stimson to guarantee our security." And another thing: "When I originated the Kellogg Pact I intended it to be only a pledge between the United States and France, but Americans extended it to include the entire world. Now it might be said that all the world is obligated to help America settle her disputes."

Before long Stimson was persuaded, though not by the petulant Briand, to reverse himself again. The idea now was that Great Britain would guarantee the security of France: the United States would not have to. But the British must be sure that, in case their navy took action against an aggressor, the United States would not make trouble by insisting upon the freedom of the seas. So we would have to commit ourselves after all, at least to England. This formula pleased Stimson, and he indicated that he might be willing to accept it.

Washington wiseacres were dumfounded. "Up almost to the very eve of Secretary Stimson's surprising disclosure," a correspondent of the *New York Times* reported, "there was every reason to believe that the Hoover administration and the American delegation definitely had determined there should be no American participation in any international pact with a political slant." President Hoover himself, at his press conference, firmly repeated what he thought he had made clear before, that his government was not going to consider political guarantees of any kind.

So the French refused to sign the naval limitations treaty, and the Italians likewise refused. The others—British, Americans, and Japanese—did put ceilings on various categories of lesser warships, but left an escape for themselves by means of a so-called escalator clause. This provided that if any of the three should be menaced by the naval program of an outside power, then that signatory would be automatically released from its treaty obligations. And a Franco-Italian naval race was soon under way.

Yet Stimson viewed his London mission as a diplomatic success. True, the treaty did nothing effectively to limit the building of new warships, but that was all to the good: before long the erstwhile champion of naval limitations became one of the biggest of big-Navy men. To him the size and number of ships and guns had been only an incidental matter at the London conference anyway. "He had seen it throughout as a method of bringing the British and the Americans together," or so at least his memoirs were to say.[7]

In October, 1930, the government of Brazil had a formidable revolt on its hands, and both the government and the rebels looked to the United States for war supplies. All at once the American Secretary of State drew a line between the contending forces. He recommended and the President proclaimed an embargo on exports to the revolutionists alone. Forty-eight hours later the revolutionists were in power, the former government in collapse. Stimson's decision, whatever else might be said of it, had been poorly timed—too late to help the old regime, too soon to please the new.

Stimson never lacked explanations, nor did he on this oc-

[7] *New York Times*, 1930: January 31, March 27, May 20, June 3, 6, 7, 8, 11, 15, 20, July 3, 19; Pearson and Brown, *American Diplomatic Game*, 108–16, 120–21, 133, 146–51, 158–59, 169; Hoover, *Memoirs*, 2: 342–48; Henry L. Stimson and McGeorge Bundy, *On Active Service in Peace and War*, 164–74.

casion. In fact, he came out with two entirely different ones. On the day after the embargo, when American newspapers criticized it as both unprecedented and unwise, an act of taking sides in a South American domestic quarrel, he presented his justification in a State Department press release. He admitted that this was the first time the United States had acted thus in South America, but he pointed out that we had often done the same thing in Cuba, Central America, and China. Though of course discriminating between the legitimate government and the rebels, we were behaving with strict impartiality and in accord with the dictates of international law. "It is not a matter of choice on our part," he said. "We have no personal bias and are doing nothing but attempting to carry out the law of mankind." [8]

The next day, when first reports arrived of the sudden overturn in Brazil, he had a "rosy time," as he put it, at his press conference. "As I felt very confident of our position, however, and that it had been right and taken in accordance with grounds which were justifiable whatever the result, I stood my ground under a pretty heavy cross-examination and finally got the Press fairly well to understand the situation and around to my side."

Not long after that, to the bewilderment of the press, he completely shifted his ground and forgot about the requirements of international law. He had discovered a treaty which he thought would provide better justification for the inopportune embargo. This, the Havana convention of 1928, bearing the signatures of the United States, Brazil, and all the American republics, had to do with mutual rights and duties in the event of civil strife. Stimson said "it was one of the treaties which we were going to press in good time," but as yet it had not even been submitted to the Senate,

[8] *Papers Relating to the Foreign Relations of the United States, 1930,* 1: 437, 442–43.

and there was so much opposition to it that Senator Arthur H. Vandenberg warned against its submittal, lest it provoke a filibuster.

In Cabinet, when he ran against the charge that he had aroused Brazilian animosity against this country, Stimson fell back upon his new discovery, the unratified convention of Havana. "The temper of the Cabinet, however, was not very cheerful," he had to confess, "and when I told them about having found a treaty which compelled us to put on an embargo, there were some rather nasty remarks. Some of them didn't seem to realize that even without the treaty I had acted rightly, which was a good deal better than if I had acted wrong in the face of the treaty."

He was not done with explaining. The distinguished jurist John Bassett Moore delivered a lecture criticizing his policy, and he finally decided he must make a formal and authoritative reply to his critics one and all.

Months after the Brazilian revolution he expounded his elaborately prepared case in an address before the Council on Foreign Relations in New York. He quoted the language of the Havana convention itself: "The contracting parties bind themselves . . . to forbid the traffic in arms and war material, except when intended for the government, while the belligerency of the rebels has not been recognized, in which latter case the rules of neutrality shall be applied." There you are! These terms, he said, "made it compulsory for us to act as we did in placing the embargo." [9]

An alert and informed listener would have noticed some startling gaps in the speaker's reasoning. The terms of the Havana treaty did not literally compel the action which Stimson had taken. In the very words he quoted, an alternative was provided: we could have recognized the belliger-

[9] Stimson diary, October 24, 28, 29, November 7, December 6, 27, 1930; January 17, 1931; Stimson, "The United States and the Other American Republics," February 6, 1931, in *Foreign Affairs,* 9 (special supplement): xi–xii (April, 1931).

ency of the rebels and applied the rules of neutrality. Anyhow, the treaty was unratified and unknown to him at the time it supposedly compelled him to act.

The Brazilian episode earned him a new nickname among Washington correspondents. Earlier, as a dashing secretary of war, booted and spurred, he had been called Light-Horse Harry Stimson. Now he was known as Wrong-Horse Harry.[10]

As Hoover's Secretary of State, Stimson thoroughly reversed himself on Latin American affairs. President Hoover hoped to start a new era of friendly relations with our neighbors to the south. Before his inauguration he went on a goodwill tour, and after the crash of 1929 and the shrinkage of American exports he was more than ever determined to improve relations. His appointment of Stimson seemed at first to jeopardize this policy by stirring up old resentments among Latin Americans, some of whom excoriated the new Secretary, on the basis of his record in Nicaragua and the Philippines, as an agent of "yankee imperialism." Once in office, however, Stimson in effect repudiated much of his past as he loyally carried out the program of his chief.[11]

One step in Hoover's new departure was to redefine the Monroe Doctrine so as to restore it to its pristine purity. That meant removing from it the excrescence of the Roosevelt Corollary, which had made the whole doctrine most unpopular in Latin America. A State Department officer in the Kellogg period had prepared an interpretation of the Latin

[10] Pearson and Allen, *Washington Merry-Go-Round*, 121–22.

[11] For an able summary of the entire Hoover-Stimson program with respect to Latin America, only certain phases of which are treated here, see Alexander De Conde, *Herbert Hoover's Latin American Policy* (Stanford, 1951). De Conde observes (p. 46) that Hoover and Stimson "were in complete agreement on Latin American policy," and adds: "With Stimson as his chosen aide, Hoover proceeded to modify the Latin-American policy of his predecessor about as rapidly as one could. . . ." Of course, Stimson had been in complete agreement with Coolidge also—with that predecessor whose policy Hoover was now reversing.

American policy of the United States—the Clark Memorandum—which held that the Monroe Doctrine was one
thing and American intervention was quite another, and
that the two should be kept distinctly apart. It fell to Secretary of State Stimson to issue this Clark Memorandum, in
1930, as an expression of official dogma. Only a few years
before, he had sanctified his Nicaraguan errand with the
phrases of Theodore Roosevelt. Now he had to swallow
those words, and swallow them he did, with the best grace he
could. "The Monroe Doctrine was a declaration of the
United States versus Europe—not of the United States
versus Latin America," he explained in a public speech. In
faraway Ecuador a Guayaquil newspaper referred to the
Nicaraguan situation and then remarked that until the new
policy was proved in deeds no one should put any faith in
Secretary Stimson's words.[12]

The next step was to begin bringing home the American
troops occupying Caribbean countries. Even before the end
of 1929 Stimson had announced his intention of taking the
marines out of Nicaragua, while *La Prensa* was criticizing
his use of force there as inconsistent with his advocacy of the
Kellogg Pact. But he then protested that he could not yet
remove the troops, because—he said—the Nicaraguan
people themselves were strongly opposed to such a move.
Later he put forth a plan for a gradual withdrawal, the occupation to cease entirely after the supervision of the election of 1932. In the meantime, while reducing by stages the
size of the marine contingent, he tried to strengthen the
native constabulary and improve the roads so as to make it

[12] Samuel F. Bemis, *The Latin American Policy of the United States:
An Historical Interpretation* (New York, 1943), 221–23. (Bemis, it should
be noted, is an enthusiastic admirer of Stimson.) Kellogg originally suggested to Stimson that the Clark Memorandum be published. Stimson
forwarded this suggestion to Hoover, who at first thought the time was
not ripe. Stimson to Hoover, June 25, 1930, and Hoover to Stimson, June
26, 1930, in the Hoover papers, Stanford University, cited in De Conde,
Hoover's Latin American Policy, 49–50.

possible to eliminate Sandino. After a year's retirement in
Mexico the "bandit" took the field again, vowing to keep
up his guerilla warfare until all United States forces had
left the soil of Nicaragua.

In the spring of 1931, while the U. S. Senate was demanding immediate and complete withdrawal, some of Sandino's
incorrigibles challenged the authority of the United States
in a series of raids which severely damaged American property and destroyed the lives of several American citizens.
Secretary Stimson did nothing except advise the remaining
Americans to go at once to the coastal towns, where the
Navy could protect them or, if necessary, bring them home.
They "must not expect American forces to be sent inland to
their aid," the Secretary warned. The United States "cannot
undertake general protection of American citizens throughout that country with American forces." To do so, it now
seemed, "would lead to difficulties and commitments which
this government does not propose to undertake."

This did not sound at all like the Stimson of old. Why,
with lawlessness clearly breaking loose again, did he tamely
submit and simply tell Americans to leave? "It is charged
that the move indicates Washington's fear lest further
Americian intervention aggravate Latin America's antagonism toward the United States and injure our foreign
trade," said a prominent journal of opinion, the *Outlook
and Independent.* "More likely it indicates Mr. Stimson's
unwillingness to admit that his policy toward Nicaragua
won't work." That policy was supposed to be one of help-
ing President Moncada to set up a responsible government
and then taking out the marines. If Stimson had called upon
Moncada to protect American lives and property, Moncada
would soon have demonstrated that he did not have a capable and responsible government. On the other hand, if
Stimson had sent the marines into action, he would have
shown the futility of his own plan to withdraw them.

"Evidently it was to avoid both courses that he warned Americans to clear out of the country and let their property go to the devil."

Stimson privately blamed the newspaper and magazine criticisms on the New Orleans Banana Company, which he said was "spreading very ugly stories" for political reasons, and on the Standard Fruit Company, "the company that had been attacked by the bandits and who had been holloing the loudest for help." The criticisms did not faze him. He thought perhaps he had been unwise in making his announcement, at least "in the tone and in the form" he used, but he declared to his diary: "The more I think of it the more sure I am that I am right in regard to keeping the Marines from the center of Nicaragua."

In fact, he never could see anything wrong, any inconsistency or failure, in the whole of his Nicaraguan policy from beginning to end. According to his memoirs he had brought general peace to the country within a month of his arrival in 1927. He rounded out the good work by one of his last official acts as Secretary of State when, early in 1933, he approved the withdrawal of the last of the marines—on schedule. They left behind them a peaceful and independent land, he said. "It was a job well done." [13]

A third step in the Hoover administration's new attitude toward Latin America was the adoption of a different recognition policy. No longer would the United States insist upon constitutional legitimacy or political morality as a condition for recognizing new regimes. Instead, it would return to its old pre-Wilson custom of accepting *de facto* governments, regardless of how they had got into power. After discussing this change with one of his advisers, Stimson wrote: "The

[13] Lawrence Dennis, "Nicaragua: In Again, Out Again," in *Foreign Affairs*, 9: 496 (April, 1931); *New York Times*, November 23, 1929; February 7, 9, 14, April 19, 1931; "The Stimson Blunder," in the *Outlook and Independent*, 157: 581–82 (April 29, 1931); Stimson diary, April 16, 20, 21, 1931; *On Active Service*, 115–16.

American policy in regard to these matters had been un-
deviating until Woodrow Wilson came in and it was interesting to get a new view of the dangers which have come
from his curious character—a blend of high idealism with
absolute inability to foresee the reaction which his views
and efforts would produce on other people." [14] Stimson himself, in 1927, had dealt with Nicaragua in the Wilsonian
spirit which he now denounced. And if Wilson's nonrecognition policy was a curious blend of idealism and blindness,
full of dangers for the United States, one wonders what is
to be said of Stimson's own nonrecognition doctrine as later
applied to the Japanese regime in Manchuria.

The European issues of war debts and reparations, revision of the Versailles treaty, and "security" for France
came to a head in the spring and summer of 1931. Stimson's
views on these questions were not entirely clear, even to
himself. Personally he was inclined toward cooperation with
France, Great Britain, and the League, yet he was getting
tired of the feverish demands for cooperative action that
"so many of the peace people" were making on him. And
President Hoover, the Quaker and engineer, still lacked a
"combat psychology." Stimson was caught in the middle between the militant pacifists and the cautious President.

In this situation he equivocated. When a rumor arose that
he was "renewing the proposition for a consultative pact
for implementing the Kellogg Pact"—the proposition he had
made to the five ambassadors regarding the Manchurian
problem in 1929—Hoover telephoned him "rather excited
about it" and asked him to scotch the story at his press conference. Stimson did as he was told, but (as he confessed to
his diary) "without doing it so sharply as to discourage or to
make angry the people on the other side of the Atlantic." A
promise to "consult" would imply a commitment to help
maintain the European *status quo*, yet Stimson was critical

[14] Stimson diary, September 15, 1930.

of French efforts to maintain it. As he told Dwight Morrow, France was hindering the disarmament cause by insisting too much on "military" and other "material" means of defense and not enough on "psychological" means. "She would only invite again the jealousy and illwill of other nations, which would result in another war." And when the French opposed an Austro-German customs union, which was intended to save Austria from economic collapse, Stimson agreed with Hoover that the Versailles treaty should be condemned for discouraging the widening of the area of free trade.[15]

The French having defeated the plan for a customs union, the Austrian economy went from bad to worse, until in May of 1931 the great central bank, the Kredit Anstalt, failed. If the drains of money and credit from central Europe should continue, the depression would be aggravated throughout the world. To check this trend, Hoover proposed as an emergency measure a one-year moratorium on the payment of both reparations and war debts. The French proceeded to sabotage the moratorium by taking their bank credits out of Germany. By summer the European crisis, political as well as economic, had reached a new peak of intensity.

That summer, Stimson sailed for Europe to talk face to face with the statesmen of England and Germany, France and Italy. As a gentleman among gentlemen, he hoped to bring Europeans to a better understanding of one another and thus, perhaps, to prepare the way for general disarmament and peace.

While abroad, he got a chance to perform a feat of diplomacy which he afterwards considered "one of the neatest and most successful" of his entire career. It concerned the continuing withdrawals of short-term credits from Germany

15 *New York Times*, November 24, 25, 1930; Stimson diary, November 24, December 8, 10, 11, 12, 1930; January 20, March 2, 30, May 8, 14, 1931.

and Central Europe. In a second effort to stop this dangerous drift, Hoover had suggested to the British government
that a special conference convene in London, and he had
requested Stimson and another traveling Cabinet member,
Secretary of the Treasury Andrew W. Mellon, to attend.

At the London conference, in July, 1931, the French
urged their own scheme for the salvation of Germany: a
half-billion-dollar loan from France, Great Britain, and
the United States. Stimson recommended this to Hoover,
by telephone, but Hoover rejected it because he believed
that the proceeds of the loan would be drained out as fast
as they were put in. He cabled to Stimson and Mellon a
counterproposal of his own. This called for a "standstill
agreement," according to which all banks holding German
and Central European balances would refrain from withdrawing them.

Stimson, when presenting his standstill agreement to the
London conferees, did not do as Hoover had intended.
Instead of disavowing entirely the French scheme for a
loan, he argued, with "the simile of a bathtub with a hole
in the bottom," that "there was no use putting in fresh water
until we had plugged up the hole to stop the withdrawals of
credits." And instead of presenting the new proposal as
Hoover's, he identified it ambiguously as a joint Anglo-
American plan. He reasoned that the French, already antago-
nized by the Hoover moratorium, would turn down the
supplementary agreement if they knew it came from the
same source.

This disguise of the Hoover plan was, in Stimson's belief,
the grand stroke that made success possible. It was the feat
on which he was to pride himself. But Hoover viewed the
affair in quite another light.

Already the President was losing confidence in his Secretary of State. Stimson seemed to reflect the opinion of the
diplomat, French or English, who flattered him last. One

day, from Paris, he telephoned Washington to deplore the American distrust of the French. Next morning, from London, he warned that the French were tricksters and must be watched! At the White House, Hoover remarked to an amused assistant: "Did you ever see such a complete *volte face* in a few hours?"

He wondered whether his Secretary was being taken in. Stimson (and Mellon) had urged him to approve the French loan scheme on the grounds that, otherwise, the United States might be to blame for economic catastrophe in Europe. But Hoover doubted whether the British themselves favored the French plan, and he suspected that they were merely trying to put the burden of opposition upon the United States. His suspicions were confirmed when, through a roundabout inquiry, he learned that the Bank of England opposed the loan.

To keep the American initiative, Hoover determined at the critical point of the London negotiations to give to the press the gist of his standstill proposal. Stimson advised him to wait until the crisis was past, but Hoover went ahead. Meanwhile Stimson was telling reporters in London that the plan was no more American than it was British and that, as a matter of fact, Prime Minister MacDonald had had as much to do with it as anybody! "I may be unfair to him," a State Department official commented at the time, "but I cannot help feeling that he wanted so to be the great man, the great mediator in London, that he failed to take any account of the situation here." [16]

After the London conference had adopted the standstill agreement, Stimson resumed his travels as a kind of mediator

---

[16] *The Memoirs of Herbert Hoover*, Vol. 3: *The Great Depression, 1929–1941* (New York, 1952), 67–68, 73–78; *On Active Service*, 209; Pearson and Brown, *American Diplomatic Game*, 236–40; Stimson diary, July 19, 1931. Hoover's reaction to Stimson's *"volte face"* and the contemporary comment of the unnamed State Department official are from confidential sources.

at large or, in his own words, an "honest broker" for the statesmen of Europe.

In Berlin the Germans cheered his visit as a sign that America was at last awake to their plight. He talked as man to man, or rather as soldier to soldier, with General Von Hindenberg, President of the Weimar Republic. Von Hindenberg "said that he was glad to hear that I was a soldier, that his experience had been that the soldiers on opposite sides did not cherish a bitterness against each other." Stimson "reciprocated," then reminisced about the war, concluding that "we must find a better solution of such questions in the future." The old Prussian "emphatically agreed."

In Rome Stimson received a hearty welcome from Mussolini. He also had a friendly chat with Il Duce's foreign minister, Count Dino Grandi, in which he assured Grandi that it was best for the United States to stay out of the League of Nations, that this country could do Europe more good from the outside. He and Mrs. Stimson went for a speedboat ride with Mussolini, who "showed his attractive side," as Stimson told his diary, "and we both liked him very much."

In London he got down to cases in a confidential talk with MacDonald about France and the treaty of Versailles. Stimson "pointed out that France took her position flatly on a doctrine of cooperation among the Powers for a peace guarantee by military action against an aggressor; that she was also seeking by this to freeze into permanency the extreme oscillation in her favor and against Germany which had resulted from the last war." He asked the Prime Minister point blank "what he proposed to do in the face of the issue presented by France's insistence upon the Versailles Treaty and Germany's rising opinion against the servitude which that treaty imposed." MacDonald frankly replied that he thought the treaty must be amended, sooner or later, but Great Britain would not stand for its amendment by force. How Stimson himself would meet this fundamental issue, he did not record.

Only in Paris did the emissary of good will get a cool reception from the public, though the Premier himself, Pierre Laval, "manifested the utmost friendliness." Laval impressed him as a statesman who was "able," "forceful," "sincere," and "extremely frank." Stimson invited him to Washington to see the President. "I wanted to get Laval talking with him the way he talked with me about European problems."

In Washington, after his return in September, Stimson seemed to expect a great deal from Laval's impending visit. A man who was in a position to observe him closely was asked, in private, "whether the Secretary thought the United States Government could settle these various European questions." This man replied that the Secretary did not think the government could do it but "thought he could personally." If so, the Secretary was due for disillusionment.

The real object of Laval was, of course, the familiar one of Clemenceau and Briand before him: to get from the United States some kind of promise to reinforce the "security" of France. At a meeting with Hoover and Stimson he came promptly to the point with the suggestion of a consultative pact. Hoover told him, coldly, that it was a political impossibility. And Stimson added that "it was perfectly clear politically in this country that America would never agree beforehand to give armed assistance on a contingency in the future." [17]

[17] *On Active Service*, 208–209, 268; *New York Times*, June 5, 1931; U. S. State Department, *Papers Relating to the Foreign Relations of the United States, 1931* (3 vols., Washington, 1946), 1: 545; Stimson diary, July 27, August 8, September 30, October 23, 1931. The contemporary opinion that Stimson "thought he could personally" is from another confidential source.

So ended Stimson's summer adventure in personal, informal diplomacy. It left him in a dilemma, which was of his own making. On the one hand, he clearly recognized (at times) that the Versailles treaty was the heart of the European problem, and he agreed with the President that the treaty ought to be revised. But he ran against the hesitancy of Great Britain and the adamantine refusal of France. On the other hand, he toyed with the idea of a consultative pact which would have had the effect of endorsing the Versailles treaty and freezing even harder the *status quo*. But he ran against the opposition of the President and of American public opinion. He could have avoided his dilemma, though he could not have solved the European problem, if there had been more consistency and less confusion in his own thinking during his first two years as Secretary of State.

And then, as if frustration over Europe were not enough, he suddenly had to deal with an even more urgent crisis in the Far East.

4 Be Gentle with the Japanese

It was a most pleasant interview. Secretary Stimson felicitated his State Department visitor, Ambassador Katsuji Debuchi, on the excellent feeling that prevailed between America and Japan. Ambassador Debuchi returned his smiling congratulations. The two men agreed, with sincere satisfaction, that their countries' relations were better at the moment, in 1931, than for many years.[1]

Later that very same day (September 17, Washington time; September 18, Mukden time) an explosion occurred on a railroad track in faraway Manchuria. It was not much of an explosion, not even enough to delay a single train, but it was enough to start an army going. Japanese soldiers in Manchuria were on the move.

Manchuria was an old battleground for the Chinese, the Russians, and the Japanese. It belonged nominally to China, and the mass of its people were Chinese, but a more or less independent warlord governed and misgoverned it. And on it both Russia and Japan had designs.

As successors of the Russian empire-builders, whom they had defeated in the Manchurian war of 1904–05, the Japanese held treaty rights which gave them some of the powers of a sovereign within the supposedly Chinese province. By treaty right, for example, they kept troops inside a railroad

[1] Stimson diary, January 8, 1932, on microfilm in the Yale University Library; memorandum by Stimson, September 22, 1931, in U. S. State Department, *Papers Relating to the Foreign Relations of the United States: Japan, 1931–1941* (2 vols., Washington, 1943), 1: 5.

zone to guard the Japanese-owned South Manchuria Railway. But they were not content with the *status quo*. They looked to Manchuria as a source of raw materials and as a market for their manufactures, which were being shut out from the rest of the world by various barriers, including the American tariff. They looked to Manchuria also as a buffer against the Soviet Union, which maintained at Vladivostok a huge naval and air base aimed directly at the heart of Japan. For both economic and strategic reasons, the Japanese wanted to bring Manchuria under their control.

The Chinese situation made them all the more anxious to act, and to act in a hurry. After the civil war of 1926–28 China was at least partially unified by the Nationalists under Chiang Kai-Shek. He aspired to extend the unification of the country by incorporating Manchuria unequivocally into it. If he succeeded, the effect would be to frustrate the Japanese program. If he failed, Japanese interest in Manchuria would be left as they were—at the mercy of warlords and bandits or, even worse, at the mercy of Communists, backed by Soviet Russia just beyond the horizon.

The reality of the Communist threat could be seen in the Russian invasion of northern Manchuria in 1929, when Stimson invoked the Kellogg Pact. "The success of the application of the pact of 1928 is problematical," observed the authors of a 1931 American textbook on Far Eastern affairs, fairly representative of contemporary academic opinion in the United States. "The outcome made it additionally clear that Soviet policy is in part similar to that of the Czars, and that Russia is even more determined at present than she was in the nineteenth century to dominate Asia." These authors added: "Contemporaneously Russia is more to be feared by Japan and China than either of these is to be feared by the other." [2]

---

[2] Hosea B. Morse and Harley F. MacNair, *Far Eastern International Relations* (Boston, 1931), 758–69, 777–78. Japan's position in Manchuria was

As of 1931, Stimson himself was not much concerned about Russia as a menace in the Far East. That spring, a couple of his law partners tried to interest him in the subject of the United States's entering into diplomatic relations with the Soviet Union. He said he was "more interested in studying the economic conditions which underlay the question of Russia than to jump to Russia itself first," and he felt sure "that if there was no economic depression nobody would be thinking of Russia." Montagu Norman, governor of the Bank of England, told him that in Europe "Russia was the very greatest of all the dangers," and he noted Norman's remarks without any comment of his own.[3]

Stimson was indeed alarmed, however, about the program of the Chinese Nationalists. They aspired to revise the "unequal treaties" which the powers, including the United States, had imposed upon the old China during the nineteenth century. These treaties granted extraterritorial rights by which foreigners—Americans as well as Japanese, Englishmen, and others—could escape the jurisdiction of Chinese courts. Chiang Kai-Shek seemed determined to put an end to extraterritoriality, by negotiation if he could, by repudiation if he must. The issue was coming to a head early in 1931. American diplomatic and consular representatives in China bombarded the State Department with warnings that lawlessness and banditry prevailed in many parts of the country,

---

legalized by her treaty of 1905 with Russia, ceding to Japan all Russian rights south of Changchun, and her treaties of 1905 and 1915 with China, confirming and extending these rights. See C. W. Young, *Japan's Special Position in Manchuria* (Baltimore, 1931).

[3] Stimson diary, April 1, 8, 1931. With regard to the Soviet Union, Hoover was a very determined advocate of a policy of no credits and nonrecognition, and so was Stimson's State Department adviser on Russian affairs, Robert F. Kelley. "Stimson was in no sense an enthusiast for recognition, but Kelley stoutly resisted any inclination the Secretary may have had in that direction." William A. Williams, *American Russian Relations, 1781–1947* (New York, 1952), 219.

that American lives and property were in constant peril, and that foreign interests must not be left to the jurisdiction of the local authorities.

Giving heed to these reports, Stimson resolved to head off Chiang Kai-Shek. He wondered what to do "in case the Chinese prove finally recalcitrant with regard to the extraterritoriality negotiations." A few years earlier, at the time of the Nanking atrocities in 1927, American and British destroyers on the Yangtze River had lobbed shells into the city to stop the rampaging Nationalist troops. Now, in 1931, Stimson considered the feasibility of another joint demonstration against the Chinese: "the question comes up whether we should use force." The trouble was that "with the new implement of a boycott which the Chinese use, it would be very unlikely that Britain would back us up." [4]

For Stimson, it was a relief in those days to turn from relations with unruly China to those with well-behaved Japan. Not that he or any other informed person supposed the Japanese had given up their old idea of hegemony in Asia, but through the decade 1921–31 they appeared to be pursuing their aim by peaceful and cooperative methods. They worked closely with both Americans and British in dealing with the obstreperous Chinese Nationalists. They collaborated at the London naval conference of 1930. The Japanese leaders—Prime Minister Wakatsuki and Foreign Minister Shidehara—were personal acquaintances of Stimson's. Wakatsuki and Shidehara might have difficulty in carrying on irenic diplomacy, because of the peculiar constitutional structure of Japan, since the civilian heads of state might

---

[4] U. S. State Department, *Papers Relating to the Foreign Relations of the United States, 1931* (3 vols., Washington, 1946), 933–81; Stimson diary, January 21, March 11, April 10, 25, 1931. From 1929 on, taking the advice of his Division of Far Eastern Affairs, Stimson had opposed the abandonment of extraterritorial rights in China by the United States or any other power, but before 1931 he had done so in a patient and conciliatory spirit. Wesley Fishel, *The End of Extraterritoriality in China* (Berkeley and Los Angeles, 1952), 153–63.

pull one way while the army and navy went another. But Stimson was confident that his friends themselves were committed to peace.[5]

As for American interests in Manchuria, these were relatively small in terms of dollars and cents. Despite American tariffs, Japan and the United States continued to be good customers of one another, Japan occupying third place among the nations in the foreign trade of the United States. American trade and investments in Japan were much larger than those in China, and the extension of Japanese control over Manchuria might as likely increase as decrease American economic opportunities in that part of the world.

But there were other considerations for the United States. As has been seen, Americans had treaty rights in China, among them the right to evade Chinese law. And there was a tradition to be maintained or else abandoned, the tradition of the Open Door and the Integrity of China, proclaimed by Secretary of State John Hay in 1899 and 1900. The principles of the Open Door and Integrity had become treaty rights also, since they were embodied in the Nine-Power Pact of the Washington conference in 1922, a pact which Japan as well as the United States and China had signed. The Kellogg Pact could be interpreted as giving the United States additional treaty rights in Manchuria, and Japan had signed this one, too.

Besides economic interests and treaty rights and traditional phrases, there was still another concern for the United States, one that might well have predominated over all the rest. That was the matter of the safety and security of the American nation itself. This strategic interest in Manchuria could have been only indirect at most. It might best be served by supporting Japan against China or Russia, or by

[5] Henry L. Stimson, *The Far Eastern Crisis: Recollections and Observations* (New York, 1936), 34–37.

backing China or Russia against Japan, or perhaps by doing neither.

The extent of American economic, moral, and strategic interests in Manchuria, and the means by which they might appropriately be advanced, were questions for the high policy makers in Washington to decide, subject to the approval of the people of the United States.[6]

In making decisions on the Far East, the two most important officials in the State Department, next to Stimson himself, were William R. Castle, Jr., the Under Secretary of State, and Stanley K. Hornbeck, the chief of the division of Far Eastern affairs. Formerly a history professor in Chinese as well as American colleges, Dr. Hornbeck was scholarly, informed, and tenacious of his well-founded opinions. He was inclined to sympathize with China. Castle, a career diplomat, lately ambassador in Tokyo, was well educated and worldly wise, a person of genial wit and gracious manner. He was inclined to sympathize with Japan.

Castle had been Hoover's choice for the post of Under Secretary, to succeed Stimson's trusted friend, Joseph P. Cotton, who died early in 1931. No one could quite replace Cotton so far as Stimson was concerned, though he accepted Castle's appointment willingly enough.[7] He still had a couple of intimates as advisers upon whom he could call in addition to or instead of Castle and Hornbeck. These were his special assistant, Allen T. Klots, and the Assistant Secretary of State, James Grafton Rogers.

As a personal friend of Hoover's, Castle had ready access to the ear of the President. And the President, though much

---

[6] Eleanor Tupper and George E. McReynolds, *Japan in American Public Opinion* (New York, 1937), 292–93, briefly summarize Japanese-American trade interests and note that the "average American" as of 1931 showed "little curiosity about or concern over events in the Far East."

[7] Stimson diary, March 30, 1931. Stimson later regretted his "administrative blunder" in accepting Hoover's recommendation of Castle. Henry L. Stimson and McGeorge Bundy, *On Active Service in Peace and War* (New York, 1948), 192.

preoccupied with depression problems at home, was not the man to slough off his ultimate responsibility for the conduct of affairs abroad. So long as he remained in office, his was the final say on foreign policy.

The stage was set for a drama of divided counsels.

For the first two or three weeks of the Manchurian crisis, the policy makers in Washington saw eye to eye. Neither President Hoover nor Secretary Stimson believed that American treaty rights would be involved. After the explosion on the railroad track near Mukden, September 18, 1931, Japanese troops had gone out from the railroad zone, occupied the city, and not returned to their rightful place. To the men in Washington it appeared, however, that the army in Manchuria was proceeding without authorization from Tokyo, and therefore the Japanese government could hardly be accused of violating the Kellogg Pact. Day after day Stimson kept looking for signs that the troops were retreating to the railroad zone, were "crawling back into their dens," and he listened eagerly to the assurances and reassurances of Ambassador Debuchi.

Meanwhile the Chinese government and the League of Nations were making futile attempts to enlist the United States in some kind of joint action. China appealed to this country as sponsor of the Kellogg Pact and to the League under the Covenant, requesting the appointment of a commission to investigate the Manchurian affair. The League sent an appeal against war to China and Japan, forwarding copies of its proceedings to Washington, then began to discuss the creation of a neutral commission, which was to include a representative of the United States. The Japanese delegate objected, insisting that Japan and China must settle their differences between themselves, without any interference from the League. But the Chinese delegate refused to hear of direct negotiations so long as Japanese troops remained outside of the railroad zone.

Stimson took the side of Japan. He made it clear that the United States would have nothing to do with the proposed investigation. Privately, he suspected that the League was "trying to pass the buck to us," and he resented the way the League kept "nagging" him. As for himself, he wished to avoid action that might antagonize Japan against the United States, or that might strengthen the military element in Japan, weaken the Wakatsuki-Shidehara ministry, and embarrass it in its effort to recover control over the rampageous army. "My problem," he thought, "is to let the Japanese know we are watching them and at the same time to do it in a way that will help Shidehara, who is on the right side, and not play into the hands of any Nationalist agitators on the other." He cautioned Ambassador Debuchi that, although he was "making every effort to save Japan's face and give them time to settle this by themselves with China," the Japanese must realize that he "thought the situation was very grave" and "they must settle it mighty quick."

To the American minister in Geneva, Hugh Wilson, he laid down three successive lines of action for the United States in relation to the League: First, while opposing the plan for a neutral commission, we should support the League in urging "that Japan and China themselves effect a settlement through direct negotiation." Second, if "outside action" should become necessary, we should "favor China and Japan's submitting to machinery set up in the League of Nations Covenant." Third, "should it develop for any reason that this line is impracticable," we should "consider the machinery of" the 1922 Nine-Power Treaty "or action such as may be practicable under the 1928 Kellogg-Briand Pact." [8]

This program Stimson himself authored, but he did so

[8] Stimson diary, September 19, 21, 22, 23, 24, 28, 1931; Stimson to Hugh Wilson (telegram), September 23, 1931, in *Foreign Relations, 1931*, 3: 49; Sara R. Smith, *The Manchurian Crisis, 1931–1932: A Tragedy in International Relations* (New York, 1948), 28–50.

with the approval of both the President and the top State Department advisers. At the outset Hoover endorsed Stimson's analysis of the problem and, as the days passed, Stimson was reassured to find that Hoover "thoroughly agreed" with him in his "caution."

Under Secretary William R. Castle was pleased to note: "The Secretary was looking at the whole thing very sanely and was not planning to take any such precipitate action as that which he perhaps unfortunately took two years ago when there was danger of a blow up between China and Russia." Castle thought the trouble with Manchuria was that it had no real status: "Ostensibly it is Chinese and because of the Russian and Japanese influences it is never really Chinese." Stanley K. Hornbeck, the head of the division of Far Eastern affairs, shared the views of Castle. "As Stanley says, there will be no real peace until some one of the three nations is able to establish itself firmly in the saddle." Castle suggested that "the best thing which could happen now would be for Japan to get full control and Stanley rather ruefully agreed, although, as he pointed out, the place really belongs to China."

Even the "isolationist" leaders of the Senate could find little fault with the State Department during these weeks of watchful inactivity. True, the irrepressible Hiram Johnson sarcastically inquired: "Where now is the bugle call Mr. Stimson trumpeted so loudly and prematurely but a short time ago, when Russia and China were making faces at each other? Where is the League of Nations? Where is the sacrosanct Kellogg Pact?" But William E. Borah, chairman of the Senate Committee on Foreign Relations, agreed with Stimson "throughout" when Stimson took him aside to explain how he was cooperating with the League while preventing it from "leaving any baby" on his "doorstep."

Stimson learned with satisfaction that Lord Reading, the British Foreign Secretary, was "taking very much the same

policy" he himself was "and not getting excited the way
they did down in Geneva." The *Times* of London, spokesman for the Foreign Office, complimented Stimson on his
"tactful" diplomacy. Tokyo as well as London applauded
him. "The Japanese are very pleased with the consideration
I have shown them in preventing too rough treatment," he
noted in his diary, "and Debuchi has brought in some very
nice messages from Shidehara for me." Words of approval
came from almost everywhere except Geneva—and Nanking.

From Nanking came demands for a stronger stand by the
United States, pleas for action by all the signatories of the
Kellogg Pact, threats of a rapprochement with Russia as
China's only alternative. All this did not swerve Stimson in
the slightest from his adopted course. The League having
adopted a resolution asking "both parties" in Manchuria to
restore "normal relations," he merely advised the Nanking
government that time must be allowed for Japan and China
to carry out the League's request. And at length he reaffirmed his official attitude in a conversation with the Chinese
chargé d'affaires in Washington: "We have not attempted
to go into the question of right and wrong . . . we are not
taking sides . . . we are 'playing no favorites.' " [9]

That was on October 8, 1931. On the same day Stimson's
thinking and American policy reached the first turning
point. The change was precipitated by news that Japanese
planes were bombing the city of Chinchow, in southern
Manchuria, far from the railroad zone. From the "disquiet-

[9] Stimson diary, September 24, 25, October 6, 8, 1931; diary of William
R. Castle, September 29, 1931, typescript in the possession of Mr. Castle,
Washington, D. C.; Drew Pearson and Constantine Brown, *The American
Diplomatic Game* (New York, 1935), 308, quoting Hiram Johnson; Lon-
don *Times*, September 26, 1931, and Tokyo *Jiji*, October 1, 1931, both
quoted in Smith, *Manchurian Crisis*, 44–45, 66–67; *Foreign Relations, 1931*,
3: 104–106, 136–39. Paul H. Clyde, "The Diplomacy of 'Playing No
Favorites': Secretary Stimson and Manchuria, 1931," in the *Mississippi
Valley Historical Review*, 35: 187–202 (June, 1948), summarizes the
material in this *Foreign Relations* volume.

ing telegrams" he read, Stimson had to conclude that, for all Debuchi's promises, the Japanese army was expanding rather than contracting its operations. He told himself: "I am afraid we have got to take a firm ground and aggressive stand toward Japan." So far as he was concerned, the policy of "playing no favorites" was no sooner stated than, by the force of events, it had to be abandoned.

Here his views and those of the President began to diverge a bit. When, the next day, he reported to the Cabinet the new and ominous turn in Manchurian events, he felt that Hoover was not sufficiently impressed. The President did not seem to realize quite what it meant "to have Japan run amok and play havoc with its peace treaties." Instead, he thought we must be careful "not to get ourselves into a humiliating position, in case Japan refused to do anything about what he called our scraps of paper or paper treaties."

Stimson did not like this scraps-of-paper phrase. "The peace treaties of modern Europe made out by the Western nations of the world no more fit the three great races of Russia, Japan, and China, who are meeting in Manchuria, than, as I put it to the Cabinet, a stovepipe hat would fit an African savage," he admitted to his diary. "Nevertheless they are parties to these treaties . . . and if we lie down and treat them like scraps of paper nothing will happen, and in the future the peace movement will receive a blow that it will not recover from for a long time." Admittedly the hat did not fit, but Stimson was beginning to think we should jam it on anyhow!

The time had come, he believed, to take the third step among the alternatives he earlier had outlined—that is, to consider action under the Nine-Power Treaty or the Kellogg Pact. The latter he now put first, thinking that he would "probably push forward the Kellogg Pact" and hold the Nine-Power Treaty "in reserve" to facilitate an eventual peace conference between China and Japan. He decided, however, "not to initiate action" but to wait for the League.

When he discussed his plan with Castle and Hornbeck, he got their concurrence. And when he talked again with the President, he found him more than willing to go along. Hoover "even went so far as to say that we should authorize our man in Switzerland to sit with the Council." This suggestion had come originally from Norman Davis, head of the American delegation to the preparatory disarmament commission in Geneva, and Stimson had dismissed it as one of Davis's "rather wild propositions." He now welcomed the idea.

The United States must be represented officially on the Council of the League! Having arrived independently at the same bold conclusion, Hoover and Stimson together determined to carry it out in the most cautious way possible, so as not to offend public opinion whether American or Japanese. Hence the invitation must appear to come unprompted from the League, and the business of the extraordinary session must be confined strictly to the Kellogg Pact. When the Council began to discuss the invitation Stimson became alarmed at the Japanese opposition. "It lines us up vis-a-vis Japan," he thought, "just the position that I have been trying to avoid." "With the information I have at hand from Manchuria it would be easy to arouse and inflame American sentiment, so that it would stand solidly behind me. But that is just what I don't want to do."

In Cabinet he raised the question whether at the last minute the United States should not decline the Council's invitation. But he discovered that "the President was very strong that we should keep right on. He has been first-rate throughout . . . taking a clear and unequivocal stand."

And so, despite Japan's dissenting vote, the American consul in Geneva, Prentiss Gilbert, sat at the Council table in an open meeting and then in a secret session to discuss the invocation of the Kellogg Pact. The conferees decided, on

October 17, that the Council should call upon all the signatories to remind China and Japan of their obligations under the pact to settle their dispute by pacific means. This decision, with a representative of the United States participating, climaxed the first phase of American policy making with respect to the Manchurian crisis.

The rest was anticlimax. As soon as the decision had been made, Stimson "thought it advisable to terminate the outward appearance at least of Gilbert's connection with the Council." Castle and Hornbeck concurred. But the British and the French protested against the withdrawal of Gilbert: it might look like a gesture disapproving the League's action. Reluctantly Stimson concluded to "let him go on sitting at the damned table" on the condition that he "keep his mouth shut" to show that he was no longer a participant, only an observer. Then, to re-emphasize the League's initiative, Stimson delayed sending his note on the Kellogg Pact to China and Japan until three days after Great Britain, France, and other League members had sent theirs.

And when the Council passed a resolution calling upon Japan to evacuate Chinese territory by November 16, he hesitated to endorse it. Some of its points he thought were "unwise" and might "lead to a deadlock"; his "problem" was to compose for Japan a statement which would "back up the things which we believe in and back their [the League's] position up in general" without committing this country to the "unwise things." He accepted as the basis of his note on the League resolution a draft prepared by Castle, who "had rather cleverly met the difficulties which faced us of putting our statements in an inoffensive form." This note omitted any reference to the November 16 deadline, the nub of the League's resolution, and was not communicated to Japan until two weeks after the League had acted.

So the United States followed the League—at a distance and with qualifications—in making a verbal application of the Kellogg Pact to the Manchurian affair. This was Stimson's policy, and it was also Hoover's. The two men had agreed upon each careful step, but the one was willing to consider going farther, and the other was beginning to fear that they had gone too far already. As Castle observed on November 4, after lunching with the President, "he wants to get completely out of the League connection and thinks it might have been wise, politically, to make Stimson keep out." [10]

The assumption underlying American policy at the start of the Manchurian crisis did not remain tenable for long—the assumption that forbearance by the United States would enable the Japanese moderates to retain power and check the militarists. As early as November 7, 1931, Stimson observed: "It looks now as if the military element in Japan might get control." On November 19, after hearing that Japanese troops had taken Tsitsihar, in far northern Manchuria, he inferred that "the Japanese government which we have been dealing with is no longer in control; the situation is in the hands of virtually mad dogs." On December 11 he imparted to the Cabinet the news that the Wakatsuki-Shidehara ministry had actually fallen, and he pointed out the "imminent danger of a new movement by the Japanese army." On January 2, 1932, he learned that the army had occupied Chinchow and so had brought "the Manchurian matter up to a final climax": the conquest of Manchuria was an accomplished fact.

Meanwhile, as soon as they foresaw this as the probable outcome, he and Hoover had begun to consider "eventualities" and ways to deal with them. The upshot was the announcement of the famous nonrecognition doctrine. That was the work of both the President and the Secretary, the

[10] Stimson diary, October 8, 9, 10, 13, 15, 16, 20, 29, November 3, 1931; Castle diary, October 10, November 4, 1931; *On Active Service*, 232–33; Stimson, *Far Eastern Crisis*, 60; Smith, *Manchurian Crisis*, 92–127; Pearson and Brown, *American Diplomatic Game*, 312–16.

one proposing the general principle and the other developing and applying it, but before concurring in it they debated another possible line of action—cooperation with the League in the exertion of economic pressure upon Japan.

Stimson first broached this subject to Hoover, rather tentatively, on October 17, while the American representative was sitting with the League Council. At that time some of the delegates in Geneva were thinking, unofficially, of the possibility of the League's resorting to economic sanctions. The question arose whether the United States would cooperate, at least passively, by refraining from the use of its Navy to maintain the freedom of the seas against a League blockade. Even before the Manchurian crisis this question had come up repeatedly in a theoretical form, and Hoover always had refused to yield on American neutral rights, while Stimson had inclined to the belief that in an actual test the United States would not employ its Navy to frustrate concerted action against an aggressor.

Now that the issue apparently was becoming a practical one, Stimson faced the problem of making his position acceptable to the President, as well as to the American people, and he thought he had hit upon a brilliantly simple solution when someone suggested to him the relevancy of the Kellogg Pact. Let the pact be the touchstone: the United States could judge other nations by it and refuse to interfere with sanctions against a violator. When Stimson recommended this to the President, it provoked a long argument, but Hoover "promised finally that he would think it over with an open mind."

After thinking it over, the President addressed the entire Cabinet with a statement in which he put strongly his case against the application of sanctions to the Manchurian crisis. First, he said, while the "whole transaction" was "immoral," it was primarily the concern of China and Japan themselves.

The Japanese never could successfully "Japanify" China, and they had some justification for their course in Manchuria, since the disorder there hurt them economically and exposed them to danger from a "Bolshevist Russia to the north and a possible Bolshevist China" on their flank. Second, "Neither our obligation to China nor our interest nor our dignity require us to go to war over these questions." Third, "we have a moral obligation to use every influence short of war to have the treaties upheld or terminated by mutual agreement," and we should "cooperate with the rest of the world" in using "moral pressures" to these ends. "But that is the limit. We will not go along on any of the sanctions, either economic or military, for these are roads to war."

Though not a specific reply to Stimson's proposal, the President's blast seemed to impress the Secretary of State. "I concur with him as to the danger of a blockade leading to war," he told his diary, after Hoover once more had spoken against the use of economic pressure. Again, in answer to Secretary of War Patrick J. Hurley, who insisted in Cabinet that "the Japanese was going to seize Manchuria anyhow," unless stopped by force, Stimson averred that "the policy of imposing sanctions of force" had been "rejected by America in its rejection of the League of Nations." [11]

Then the sudden extension of warfare in Manchuria, culminating in the capture of Tsitsihar on November 17, induced some change of heart in both the President and the Secretary of State. The move of the Japanese army looked like a defiant reply to the League resolution calling for withdrawal from Chinese territory by November 16. The Council now reconvened in Paris, and Stimson prevailed upon

[11] Stimson diary, October 17, November 7, 9, 13, 19, December 11, 1931; January 2, 1932; William S. Myers, *The Foreign Policies of Herbert Hoover, 1929–1933* (New York, 1940), 156–59.

Hoover to send Ambassador Charles G. Dawes there from London to be accessible to its members, though not to join their sittings. Dawes reported to Stimson that the League now would probably consider sanctions and that even Sir John Simon, the new British Foreign Secretary, was "inclined to think" that "the League should go to the limit of its powers."

This was an exaggeration. Actually the air in Paris was quite cynical. Rumors circulated regarding a supposed forthcoming Japanese-American deal—which would be just as well, in the opinion of the Quay d'Orsay. From the French viewpoint China was disorderly, lawless, impossible. Japan was the good gendarme. "If the United States condemns Japan too strongly," one Parisian newspaper suggested, "it realizes that it may interfere with its own actions in Central America, where it has intervened with no more scruples than have the Japanese in Manchuria."

Stimson was inclined to agree, up to a certain point. His own special investigators in Manchuria had reported to him: "The Japanese had long been aggravated by Chinese *intransigeance*. The Chinese would not—wilfully would not, from the Japanese point of view—come to a conclusion with the Japanese in negotiations over problems that affected Japanese economic development in Manchuria." And Stimson informed Dawes: "The situation in Manchuria in some ways resembles a situation that we have had to confront on the borders of Mexico and in Central America. Japan has undoubtedly suffered great aggravation in the past, but in making this attack in September she went far beyond . . . any proper intervention in behalf of lives and property."

On November 19, when some of the League delegates were hinting at economic sanctions and inquiring discreetly about the American attitude, Stimson in Washington had a telephone conversation with Dawes in Paris. In part it went like this:

STIMSON: "We do not ourselves believe in the enforcement of any embargo by our own government, although we would not probably in any way interfere through the fleet with any embargo by anybody else. We believe an embargo is a step to war and if an embargo is decided upon by the League, it would be very likely for that embargo to lead to war."

DAWES: "That is what Sze [Chinese delegate on the League Council] wants to do."

STIMSON: "Yes, Sze would like very much to get all of the nations of the world in war with Japan."

DAWES: "Exactly."

STIMSON: "We have no sympathy with that and we do not intend to get into war with Japan."

Hoover, who impressed Stimson as "quiet but determined," approved the message to Dawes. "The President added," according to Stimson, "that he thought I could tell him [Dawes] again that the sympathy of our people undoubtedly would be with the embargo, and that there might be a private embargo put on here by voluntary action in refusing to trade with Japan."

For the President, this was going pretty far, and yet Stimson soon began to wonder whether it was far enough. On November 27 he proposed to Hoover that they reconsider the question of American participation in an embargo. First, he argued, sanctions against Japan would be brief if all the powers, including the United States, joined in ("She would have to surrender very quickly"). Second, "the militaristic elements in Japan could learn only through suffering and not by the sanctions of public opinion." Third, it would be a tremendous blow to world peace "if Japan really gets away with this." The President, however, refused to reverse himself. He still thought of sanctions as the road to war. His Secretary was beginning to think of sanctions as a way to peace, though he admitted to his diary: "I have not yet made up my own mind on the subject." [12]

While Stimson remained thus undecided on the issue, the League Council was discussing not sanctions but, again, an investigation of the Manchurian affair. This time the Chinese opposed and the Japanese favored a commission of inquiry —similar to the one the Japanese previously had rejected with Stimson's aid. Now, once more with Stimson's backing, the Japanese got what they wanted in Geneva. He approved the investigation plan, committed the United States to participation in it, and urged it upon the reluctant Chinese.

The Chinese continued to hope for sanctions, and so did some Americans. During December Stimson noted that "many people" were "getting impatient and urging drastic steps or words" upon him. Among these people were his closest personal advisers in the State Department: his special assistant, Allen T. Klots, and the Assistant Secretary of State, James Grafton Rogers. Hornbeck inclined at times toward these extremists, but Castle remained the advocate of circumspection.

The four of them, with Stimson presiding, took part in a "vigorous meeting" at Woodley, his Washington residence, on December 6. The question was what "the next step" for the United States should be if the League plans for an investigating commission fell through. Three of the experts, Castle alone dissenting, favored "economic measures." As Stimson noted, however, "We all agreed that if possible action should come from the other nations first." On

---

[12] Stimson diary, November 19, 27, 1931; Dawes to Stimson, November 18, 1931, and memorandum of telephone conversation between Stimson and Dawes, November 19, 1931, in *Foreign Relations, 1931*, 3: 484, 488–98; Paris *Journal des Débats*, quoted in Pearson and Brown, *American Diplomatic Game*, 322–23.

the whole the Secretary himself was noncommittal at the meeting, though he confided to his diary that Hornbeck went "too far against Japan" for him. Castle assumed that the Secretary leaned in Castle's own direction.

After this conference Stimson saw Hoover at the White House and was surprised to find "he was not absolutely and to the last against a boycott." The President felt, however, that we would have to base the action on the Nine Power Treaty and "not go into it behind the League." Accordingly Stimson began hopefully to think of planning a Nine-Power conference, then became discouraged when the President in his special message to Congress on foreign affairs, December 10, omitted a "warning sentence" which Stimson wanted him to include.

The Secretary was in between extremes. Senator Borah decried the current "talk of the use of force or intervention," while the Scripps-Howard newspapers were, as Stimson phrased it, "pounding the government for not being more aggressive towards Japan." He finally invited Roy Howard and his chief editorial writer to lunch and tried to make them "see the folly of taking an aggressive step" at that time.[13]

Casting about for an alternative to economic pressure, the President weeks earlier had begun to make suggestions, and one of these was to lead eventually to the formulation of the nonrecognition policy. On November 7 he proposed to Stimson that the American government recall its ambassador from Japan but at the same time, to make the protest a strictly peaceful one, issue a public statement disclaiming all thought of war. Then he got what he thought was a better idea. "He is beginning to swing against the idea of withdrawing the Ambassador," Stimson recorded as of Novem-

[13] Stimson diary, December 6, 8, 9, 1931; Castle diary, December 7, 1931; *New York Times*, November 22, 1931; William S. Myers, ed., *The State Papers and Other Public Writings of Herbert Hoover* (2 vols., New York, 1934), 2: 76–77.

ber 9, "and thinks his main weapon is to give an announcement that if the treaty [presumably to be made between Japan and China] is made under military pressure we will not recognize it or avow it."

At once Stimson discussed this proposal with his advisers. Castle favored it, especially if the announcement were made "together with the rest of the world," though he cautioned the Secretary that "even then we must be careful" because, "if the resultant treaties should be eminently fair," it might prove embarrassing to refuse to recognize them. Hornbeck opposed the plan, arguing that Secretary of State William Jennings Bryan had tried it in 1915 without results. But Stimson himself thought that, even as used in 1915, by the United States alone, nonrecognition had become "one of the potent forces" that finally brought about a Far Eastern settlement at the Washington conference of 1921–22. Now, if the "disavowal" were "made by all of the countries, it ought to have a very potent effect" in bringing about an "ultimate solution," which would "of course involve elements of compromise."

Stimson delayed acting on the nonrecognition plan, for several reasons. One was that, almost to the last, he had lingering hopes that the Japanese might yet reverse themselves in Manchuria. (As late as November 30, 1931, he said in his diary: ". . . the Japanese Ambassador came in with some more news from Manchuria, which was pretty good this time. I think now the Japanese don't intend to let their army do any more solo work, and I think they will go ahead and make a settlement.") Also, he was waiting to see what the League would do, especially with regard to sanctions. And, finally, some American experts on the Far East, even more cautious than the President, considered the nonrecognition plan too drastic. One of those counseling caution was Stimson's old friend, former law partner, and highly respected mentor in international affairs—Elihu Root.

"Allen Klots brought me back interesting news from Mr. Root," Stimson noted on November 14. "Rather to my surprise Mr. Root is more sympathetic with Japan than with China; and he is very fearful lest we do not recognize her real claims to Manchuria."

Nevertheless the Secretary continued to ponder and to elaborate the nonrecognition idea, associating with it the Nine-Power Treaty and the Kellogg Pact, and planning to reveal, simultaneously with its announcement, some of the documents bearing on the Manchurian affair. As he informed Dawes in Paris, November 19: ". . . the only act we see we could do would be to publish the papers and the correspondence, announce our disapproval of the action of Japan, possibly calling it a violation of these treaties and then announce as we did in 1915 that we would not recognize any treaties that were created under military force." By December 2 he was almost ready to cable Dawes a "final statement" warning Japan about the refusal to recognize. But his assistant Klots, after consulting three State Department experts, reported back to him that they all advised holding up the message for fear "it would make Japan so recalcitrant in any future negotiations over Manchuria that it would simply invite trouble." So he "put aside the cable for the present." [14]

A month later, January 2, 1932, when he got news of the Japanese occupation of Chinchow, which brought "the Manchurian matter up to a final climax," Stimson suddenly decided to act. The next morning, a Sunday, he arose at six with his "mind rather clarified" on what he wanted to do. "I went down to my library and there wrote out in long hand a short note to the Chinese Government and to the Japanese Government, based largely upon the note of 1915. Previously we had been thinking of a longer note. . . ." In

[14] Stimson diary, November 7, 9, 14, 30, December 2, 3, 1931; Castle diary, November 9, 1931; *Foreign Relations, 1931,* 3: 496–97.

the evening he showed his draft to Klots and the foreign policy specialists Hunter Miller, Ransford Miller, and George H. Blakeslee. "They were staggered by it at first because it was so different from what we had been thinking [of], but they gradually came around to it. . . ."

On the following day, January 4, after conferring with Rogers, Klots, and Hornbeck, he took a revised draft of the new and relatively pointed note, together with a copy of the old and more diffuse one, to the White House, where he showed Hoover the short version first. Hoover approved it. Stimson "pointed out the dangers . . . if the Japanese called our position . . . and tried to annex Manchuria," but he found that Hoover was "willing to take that risk."

The President approved, but the Secretary still faced some opposition within the State Department. In a brief final session on the draft of the note, on January 6, Castle was in general enthusiastic and especially liked "bringing the Kellogg Pact in," but he objected to a sentence which made the United States as a signatory of the Nine-Power Treaty appear, incorrectly, to "guarantee" (rather than merely "respect") the integrity of China, and the wording was changed. Hornbeck not only objected to the wording—he thought "do not intend" to recognize was better than "will not"—but, according to Stimson, he also "fought rather tenaciously against a definite statement" at all. "I thought his words were a little too weak," Stimson said in his diary, "although I consented to making the note a little bit softer than it had been originally."

Next day, January 7, 1932, copies of the note went off to China and Japan. The essence of it was that the United States did not intend to recognize as legally valid any situation, treaty, or agreement impairing the treaty rights of the United States in China (the Nine-Power Treaty was not mentioned by name) or brought about by means contrary to the Pact of Paris. This was a unilateral *démarche* by the

United States and not a joint announcement with other powers such as Stimson at first had envisaged. After the sending of the notes, however, and almost as an afterthought, he did carry out Castle's last-minute suggestion of inviting the other signatories of the Nine-Power Treaty (but not those of the Kellogg Pact) to dispatch similar notes.[15]

The British reply was rather abrupt, and it was published in the London *Times* for all the world to see. The Japanese, the British *communiqué* said, recently had made statements to the effect that Japan "was the champion in Manchuria of the principle of equal opportunity and the open door for the economic activities of all nations," and that Japan would "welcome participation and cooperation in Manchurian enterprise." The British government would seek confirmation of these assurances from the Japanese ambassador in London, but meanwhile "in view of these statements" his Majesty's government had "not considered it necessary to address any formal note to the Japanese Government on the lines of the American Government's note." And the *Times* added in an editorial that the British government was right in not going along. "Nor does it seem to be the immediate business of the Foreign Office to defend the 'administrative integrity' of China until that integrity is something more than an ideal."

The Japanese were emboldened. They replied to Stimson's note with what he later referred to as "cool cheek." Agreeing with him about the sanctity of treaties (but having their own treaties with China in mind) they cordially thanked him for his willingness to "support Japan's efforts" to see that treaties were observed!

The reaction in Great Britain did not surprise Stimson,

[15] Stimson diary, January 2, 3, 4, 6, 7, 1932; Castle diary, January 7, 1932; U. S. State Department, *Foreign Relations of the United States: Diplomatic Papers, 1932* (5 vols., Washington, 1948), 3: 8. These sources are supplemented by a communication to the author from a State Department employee of that time who prefers not to be named.

though he would have preferred a more discreet expression of it. He noted in his diary: "it was not at all unexpected so far as I was concerned." True, he had told the British ambassador two days in advance what he was going to do, and had "hoped that his government would take a similar stand." On the night of January 7, however, he learned from the French ambassador that Great Britain was refusing to join in a French protest against Japan's taking Chinchow. "So, therefore, No. 1 is backing out," he inferred, but he did not blame "poor old England," beset as she was by "troubles with India" and "financial troubles at home."

Opinion in the United States was of more concern to Stimson at the moment, and it generally favored his notes. He tactfully explained to Senator Borah that he "had not consulted him beforehand" because he "did not want to dump the responsibility on him," and Borah responded by praising the nonrecognition plan in general and in detail. Then the two men made arrangements for delivering to the Senate certain of the State Department's documents on Manchuria.

Though the publication of this correspondence was intended further to arouse American opinion, Stimson for the time being looked upon nonrecognition as a step toward "the eventual settlement of Manchuria by negotiation" and not as a step toward the use of force. So he could not agree when Senator Claude A. Swanson of the naval affairs committee commented on the unusually "strong" language of the notes, then "suggested that we move the fleet to Hawaii, merely as a demonstration." Stimson remarked to the Senator that *that* would be unusually "strong." And he discouraged Representative Cordell Hull, who was promoting a bill to give the President "discretionary power" to embargo exports to "nations which violate the Pact of Paris." The Secretary said "it would be very dangerous to have it brought up just now, because everybody would discuss Japan." [16]

Within a few days his attitude was to change drastically, as events in the Far East took a new turn.

[16] *The Times*, London, January 11, 1932; Stimson diary, January 7, 9, 14, 21, 1932; *On Active Service*, 238; Tupper and McReynolds, *Japan in American Public Opinion*, 312–18.

5 Get Tough: The Stimson Doctrine

A quiet little dinner party at Woodley, secluded in the midst of Washington. Afterward, when Stimson was dictating his diary entry for the day, he remembered one part of the conversation as "very interesting." James Grafton Rogers, just back from a trip to the Pacific Coast, had been giving his impressions of public opinion in that part of the country. According to him, people there generally felt "that the responsibility of policing the world was now on us, and that we should build a big navy." Stimson reflected: "The Manchurian matter will certainly clinch these opinions." [1]

During the last week of January, 1932, Japanese troops, having completed the conquest of Manchuria, began to move against the Chinese in and around Shanghai. The immediate provocation was a Chinese boycott against Japanese goods, but this was only one manifestation of a more general grievance: the disorder and lawlessness in China proper which, as in Manchuria, rendered Japanese lives and property unsafe.

Just one year earlier Stimson himself had been worried by the bumptiousness and irresponsibility of Chiang Kai-Shek's government, as threatening American interests in China. At that time he had thought that the United States,

[1] Stimson diary, October 10, 1931, on microfilm in the Yale University Library.

if it could gain the cooperation of Great Britain, might resort to force against the Chinese.

Now, in 1932, he reversed his former attitude. Instead of sympathizing with the Japanese, he viewed their action almost as a personal outrage, and he began to think of Anglo-American action against *them*. He was egged on by his Wall Street law partner, Bronson Winthrop, who was "quite het up about the Japanese threat against Shanghai" and wanted "to see the British and American fleets lined up there against any attempt to overawe the Chinese or to prevent a real honest boycott." Under Secretary Castle observed on January 25: "The Secretary is in a high state of excitement about the situation in Shanghai." And again, about a week later: "The Secretary is feeling very belligerent, and nobody can blame him for his fury against the Japanese, but he must be restrained from saying things which we have got to follow up no matter where they lead."

Not only Castle but also Hornbeck, Klots, and others in the State Department were dubious about Stimson's belligerent fury, his eagerness for naval action. The Secretary, as he himself said, "had to put on the pressure" in a conference with them. Castle felt that the Japanese had less justification in Shanghai than in Manchuria. "On the other hand," he wrote, "they have undoubtedly had to stand a lot in connection with the boycott which has been made effective through murder and arson, the Chinese police looking calmly on." And another thing: "What people are inclined to forget in all this Chinese business is that China is not a nation, that there is no Chinese Government which can direct and control."

Even Navy Secretary Charles F. Adams and Admiral Willam V. Pratt, when Stimson approached them, were slow to see things as he did. "They were not alive to the situation," he observed after a conversation with them, "but became so after the talk got on." President Hoover, by con-

trast, was "thoroughly alive" from the start. He quickly endorsed Stimson's "proposition" for Anglo-American cooperation in protesting to Japan and sending naval forces to
Shanghai.

The President promptly dispatched men and ships to join
the British at Shanghai, and he later reinforced the American bases in Hawaii and the Philippines. He was willing
enough to use the Navy, but his purpose was not the same
as Stimson's. He aimed "to protect the lives of Americans,"
as he afterwards said, and "strict orders were issued that
our forces should confine themselves to the task of protecting Americans." Castle believed: "This is, of course, for the
protection of American lives and property, seriously en-
dangered, in all probability more from the Chinese than
from the Japanese."

Stimson, however, had other ends in view. When he
spoke to the British ambassador, Sir Ronald Lindsay, he did
say that "our Consuls up the River were calling for additional war vessels because they anticipated the possibility
that we would have to rescue and remove our nationals." He
also said he "did not intend any threat against Japan; our
Asiatic squadron was not large enough to constitute a
threat." But he added that the presence of American and
British warships would have a "beneficial effect" on Japan,
would "strengthen the hands of Chiang Kai-Shek," and
would help to salvage the Anglo-American policy of the
Open Door.

Despite his disclaimer to Lindsay, Stimson did intend to
threaten Japan. Hoover did not. In Cabinet Stimson quite
frankly said he "realized the importance of having Japan fear
this country," and he was glad it happened that "the fleet
was going to have its battle practice this time off Hawaii."
War Secretary Hurley, opposing further notes and protests
and deprecating nonrecognition, argued that we should put
up or shut up, should either use our fleet (along with the

British) to restrain Japan or else say and do nothing. The President stood in between the two Secretaries. For Hurley's benefit he warned of the "folly of getting into a war with Japan on this subject," and "said he would fight for Con-tinental United States as far as anybody, but would not fight for Asia." Turning to Stimson, he complimented him on his mobilization of public opinion behind the Kellogg Pact in 1929 and his nonrecognition notes of January 7, 1932, but refused to approve a policy of threat.

Stimson afterward recalled to himself how he had suc-cessfully threatened Moncada in Nicaragua, and he mused upon "the great difference and difficulty" he was now hav-ing with Hoover. "He has not got the slightest element of even the fairest kind of bluff." At the next Cabinet meet-ing Stimson requested "that there should be no talk or ac-tion by anyone which should indicate that we were not going to use any weapon that we might have, whether it be the fleet or the boycott." [2]

Instead of heeding this request, Hoover tried to think of conciliatory ways to end the fighting in Shanghai. At the end of January he suggested that he and King George send an open appeal to the Emperor of Japan, but Prime Minister Ramsay MacDonald replied that this would be contrary to

[2] Stimson diary, January 23, 25, 26, 29, 1932; diary of William R. Castle, January 25, February 2, 1932, typescript in Mr. Castle's possession in Wash-ington, D. C.; *The Memoirs of Herbert Hoover*, Vol. 2: *The Cabinet and the Presidency, 1920-1933* (New York, 1952), 374; William S. Myers, *The Foreign Policies of Herbert Hoover, 1929-1933* (New York, 1940), 162; Henry L. Stimson and McGeorge Bundy, *On Active Service in Peace and War* (New York, 1948), 241-45. Stimson further noted in his diary, Janu-ary 26, 1932, regarding his discussion in Cabinet with Hoover and Hurley: "I quoted Roosevelt's saying, 'Speak softly and carry a big stick.'" Also: "In thinking this matter over [that is, the "bluff" against Japan] my mind reverted to my association with Moncada in Nicaragua, when I told him that if he did not lay down his arms, we would have to take them away from him. I was prepared to carry it through, but I knew mighty well that the chances were a thousand to one that I wouldn't have to carry it through; and if I had not been willing to make that threat at that time, I would have been unable to stop a civil war."

royal etiquette. Next morning, February 1, according to
Castle's record, "the President had a new idea which was
to make joint representations to the Chinese and Japanese to
stop fighting and to open direct negotiations with neutral
observers." After Great Britain, France, and Italy had
joined the United States in this mediation offer, the President spoke out to show that it was not intended as a means
of bluffing or coercing Japan. "He came out with one of
his statements that we weren't going to fight," Stimson later
complained, and he thereby "spoiled the impression" which
Stimson had desired to make.

At the moment Stimson was thinking much in terms of
naval power, little in terms of economic pressure. When
China formally appealed to the League for sanctions, the
touchy subject was revived in Geneva. Discussions of an
arms embargo also began "making a good deal of a rumpus,"
as Stimson put it, in the House Committee on Foreign Affairs. Again, as with Congressman Hull a few weeks earlier,
he tried to discourage consideration of such a law. He instructed Rogers to tell Representative Linthicum: "we have
a treaty with Japan which really prevents an embargo, and
to denounce that treaty . . . involves a very serious question because it would terminate all our port arrangements
and everything else with Japan."

And when an emissary came to him with a petition
sponsored by A. Lawrence Lowell, president of Harvard,
and endorsed by Newton D. Baker, former Secretary of
War, "asking us not to block the way for the sanctions of
the League by refusing to refrain from trade with Japan in
case the League leads the way," he replied that the League
members obviously were *not* leading the way: "none of
them were willing to apply sanctions, whatever we did."
He philosophized to himself: "It is very curious now to
have a peace man trying to urge action which normally leads
to war."

For the nonce, he could see no point in trying to co-operate with the League. He was returning to his "old view" that the United States could not "dispense with police force." "And," he thought, "the only police force I have got to depend upon today is the American Navy." [3]

When the Japanese bombed Shanghai from the air, Stimson's sense of righteous indignation increased. More and more he viewed the issue between the United States and Japan as one of right and wrong, white and black. To him, the Japanese attack on Shanghai seemed as evil as the German invasion of Belgium. He recalled "how outraged we were when President Wilson did nothing to show the shame that we felt," and he was "anxious that Mr. Hoover should not be put in the same position." So he wanted to do something "to sum up the situation officially" and "put the situation morally in its right place."

To his relief, he found that Hoover was "very sympathetic" with the idea of a new official statement. But when he spoke his mind to the President about the need for "leadership," the need for avoiding Wilson's timid example, he and the President "had a set-to back and forth."

And he later learned, to his dismay, that Hoover lacked "appreciation of the real nobility of the traditional and standard American doctrine towards China of the 'Open Door.'"

As for himself, Stimson was determined to strike a resounding blow for morality, nobility, and the Open Door policy. The Shanghai incident had given him a chance, and he did not want to let it pass, did not want the fighting to end too soon. So he was sorry to see a "prospect of the cessa-

[3] Castle diary, January 30, February 1, 1932; Stimson diary, February 13, 18, March 29, 1932. By February, 1932, American newspapers were "almost completely hostile to Japan," and there was in the United States a widespread popular demand for an anti-Japanese boycott. Eleanor Tupper and George E. McReynolds, *Japan in American Public Opinion* (New York, 1937), 319–39.

tion of hostilities" in Shanghai. "I am unhappy," he confessed to his diary, "because if they cease they will cease without America having said her word on the morality of this great situation."

He must hurry and have his say, before the shooting stopped. What he had in mind was a restatement of the nonrecognition doctrine. This time he intended to emphasize the Nine-Power (Open Door) Treaty rather than the Kellogg Pact, and he hoped to persuade Great Britain to join with the United States in sending notes to Japan. But Sir John Simon turned him down, saying that Britain preferred to confine herself to cooperation with the League. "Sir John was perturbed," as Hugh Wilson, the American minister to Switzerland, afterwards learned from him. "Mr. Stimson had suggested taking such vigorous action that Sir John felt it might lead to the use of the American and British fleets to enforce it. He added that the British public was in no state of mind to support a war in such a remote region," and "he questioned whether the American public would not also be reluctant to assume such a risk."

Stimson was furious at this rebuff. He felt he had to express his "sentiments on the Open Door," and he did not want to do it in a speech. "The British have pocketed me on the note method of doing it," he fumed. "I do not dare to send a note on the Nine-Power Treaty for fear of the yellow-bellied responses that I will get from some of the countries." On February 21 Rogers suggested that the Secretary "might write a letter to somebody." And after a conference at Woodley that day Castle noted that "it was finally decided that the Secretary should write a letter to Borah, if possible, setting forth the ideas of this Government as to the Open Door, etc. in a fashion which would get public sentiment behind us in this country and at the same time show the League how far we were willing to go."

Stimson's Borah letter, drafted with the aid of Hornbeck,

began with a tedious exposition of the Open Door policy, then came forcefully to the point. It denied the Japanese contention that the Nine-Power Treaty needed to be revised in the light of altered circumstances since 1922. The "recent events" in Manchuria and Shanghai, "far from indicating the advisability of any modification" in either the Nine-Power or the Kellogg pacts, "have tended to bring home the vital importance of their faithful observance." The letter reaffirmed the nonrecognition principle and recommended that "the other governments of the world" adopt it, so as to announce a "caveat" which would "effectively bar the legality of any right or title sought to be obtained by pressure or treaty violations."

The letter also added a new and distinctive element to Stimson's case against Japan. This was his contention that the three Washington conference treaties of 1922—the Nine-Power, Five-Power, and Four-Power Pacts—were "interdependent and interrelated." The United States, he argued, had agreed to limit its battleship construction and to leave its bases at Guam and the Philippines without further fortification in return for Japan's agreeing to respect the Open Door and the integrity of China. He indicated that, if Japan was to persist in violating Chinese integrity, the United States would consider itself released from the limitations on its Navy and its Pacific fortifications.

Castle, "after a hasty reading of the letter," gave it his "wholehearted approval" and said to himself: "That is the kind of thing which the Secretary, a lawyer, can do admirably." But Hoover, when Stimson showed the draft to him, was not so enthusiastic.

Recently Stimson, having changed his mind about sanctions again, had been trying to persuade the President to agree to either an economic or a diplomatic boycott in case the League should act. Hoover consented to withdrawing our ambassador from Japan, if the other powers should withdraw theirs, but that was as far as he would go. Stimson was pleased. "This," he thought, "is a long step toward combativeness for the President."

But Hoover refused to go any farther, and he seemed to suspect that a forward step might be implied in the proposed letter to Borah. So, as Stimson recorded, the President "suggested putting in a sentence which would relate to the public opinion of the world as the sanction behind our note of January 7th and behind the action which the Borah letter proposes." Stimson "persuaded him to cut it out." He argued that the sentence would "be used to indicate that under no possibility would we use any sanction of a boycott." As for himself, he "preferred to leave the Japanese guessing on that point still." [4]

The letter was dated February 23 and published on February 24, 1932. Next day Stimson went to show the President a batch of congratulatory cables he had received. "It was lucky I did," he thought. Hoover "was proposing to tell the people of the United States that under no circumstances would we go to war. He has been rather frightened by the reaction of the big Navy people to my letter . . . without stopping to remember that the reaction of the peace people had been equally favorable." Stimson told Hoover that a no-war announcement "would make people think he did not endorse my letter instead of endorsing it most thoroughly as he had and it would remove the last little lingering doubt in the minds of Japan as to the possibility of our doing something which would be serious against them." And again on the following day Stimson talked Hoover out of making a clarifying, no-war announcement.

The Borah letter, Stimson said in retrospect, was intended for "at least five unnamed addresses" and was designed to

[4] Stimson diary, February 8, 18, 20, 21, 24, 1932; Castle diary, February 12, 15, 16, 19, 21, 23, 1932; Henry L. Stimson, *The Far Eastern Crisis: Recollections and Observations* (New York, 1936), 166–75; *On Active Service*, 246–56.

"encourage China, enlighten the American public, exhort the League, stir up the British, and warn Japan." The immediate reaction was rather mixed. From Tokyo, Ambassador Cameron Forbes reported that the letter had "made the Japanese public feel that the United States" was "their enemy." In London, Sir John's Under Secretary, Anthony Eden, announced: "We should certainly not agree to seeing the terms of the Nine-Power Treaty flouted, but in the face of the assurance given by the Japanese Government, I can see no justification for our assuming that anything of the kind is likely to take place." Stimson, in his own words, felt "slapped in the face." He thought: "This is a singular and rather startling eventuality in view of the attitude which Sir John Simon has been talking to me over the telephone from Geneva."

Then, within a few days, Sir John himself began to champion nonrecognition before the League, and on March 11 the Assembly adopted a resolution incorporating the principle. This was a partial victory for Stimson.

But he had much more in mind than nonrecognition itself when he thought of encouraging China, enlightening the American public, exhorting the League, stirring up the British, and warning Japan. He also looked toward the eventual use of economic sanctions. "If a situation should ultimately arise when the American government felt it necessary to recommend the imposition, in cooperation with the rest of the world, of an embargo upon Japanese goods," he wrote in 1936, "I believed that such a measure would have more chance of being adopted by Congress if it were recommended following the invocation of the Nine Power Treaty than if it had been recommended solely by the League of Nations." And he looked, more immediately, toward the use or at least the threat of American naval power. Though he protested that he "had been very careful not to make any threats" in the Borah letter, his reference to the interdependence of the Washington conference treaties clearly implied the threat of a new naval race, if not actually a war, in the Pacific.[5]

To him, though not to Hoover, the publication of the letter as well as the naval display at Shanghai was a far-seeing move in a game of diplomatic bluff and power politics.

As spring came in 1932, Stimson based his thinking more and more upon the assumption of inevitable war between Japan and the United States. There was "shaping up an issue between the two great theories of civilization," he thought, and it was "almost impossible that there should not be an armed clash between two such different civilizations." Hornbeck, too, predicted that the conquest of Manchuria would lead to the conquest of China and "eventually to war" between the United States and Japan. "And if this might lead to war in the future," queried Castle, "is that any less bad than to take steps with regard to Manchuria which would lead to war now?"

In Cabinet Stimson talked at length on "the challenge which Japan had made to the civilization of the West," and ended with "a warning that the President had better keep his powder dry." The Secretaries of War and the Navy seconded him, but the President was not impressed. He only said something about "phantasmagorias."

War sometime—maybe soon. In view of the "ticklish situation in Shanghai and Tokyo," Stimson feared that "at any moment an accident might occur which would set the whole world on fire." So he consulted Admiral Pratt about the relative states of preparedness of the Japanese and American navies, Chief of Staff Douglas MacArthur about the maintenance of American troops in China, and banker

[5] Stimson diary, February 25, 26, March 3, 1932; Stimson, *Far Eastern Crisis*, 161–62, 175; *On Active Service*, 249, 257. Stimson's Borah letter was highly approved by the great majority of newspapers in the United States. Tupper and McReynolds, *Japan in American Public Opinion*, 339–44.

Thomas W. Lamont about the "financial susceptibility" of Japan in case of war. He became, as he said, "much alarmed about the present situation of the Navy," which appeared to be "more unequal" than he had thought "to meeting Japan." He told Hoover so. "The President said that was all the more reason for not having an offensive Navy," Stimson noted. "I said I wasn't talking about an offensive but a defensive Navy."

His fears mounting, Stimson reached the conclusion that the fleet, after the completion of its battle practice in the Pacific, should continue to be based at Hawaii. With the aid of Admiral Pratt, he persuaded the President. Repeatedly he urged upon Pratt and other admirals "the absolute necessity of keeping the Navy in such a condition in which it would be airtight against any sudden attack by the Japanese." When Senator Swanson expressed concern over a possible diplomatic impasse, Stimson assured him "that we would not go to war unless Japan attacked us, but in that case we would fight like the devil."

Afterwards (in 1936) Stimson wrote that there had been "a real possibility of a Japanese attack being suddenly launched at the possessions of European and American governments" in 1932. "In such a situation the presence of the entire American fleet assembled at a port which placed it on the flank of any such outbreak southward towards Hong-kong, French Indo-China, or the Philippines, undoubtedly exercised a steadying effect. It was a potent reminder of the ultimate military strength of peaceful America which could not be overlooked by anyone, however excited he might be." [6]

The fleet at Hawaii in 1932 provided an unconscious rehearsal for events to come in 1941. The grand maneuvers of

[6] Stimson diary, March 2, 8, 9, 10, 16, April 5, May 16, 18, 19, 20, 1932; Castle diary, April 4, 1932; Stimson, *Far Eastern Crisis*, 137–38; *On Active Service*, 242, 255.

1932 included a test of the joint Army and Navy defenses of Pearl Harbor. At dawn on a Sunday morning "enemy" carriers approaching Oahu from the northeast took the defenders completely by surprise. The attacking planes sank every battleship in the harbor, destroyed all the defending planes before they could get off the ground. So the umpires ruled.[7] This lesson was lost upon Stimson, who supposed that the mere presence of the fleet had a "steadying effect." The lesson was not lost upon the Japanese.

Nonrecognition came to mean different things to the President and to the Secretary of State, and during 1932 a struggle developed between them to name and define the doctrine. As early as February 18, Castle noted:

"The President said a couple of days ago that for the coming election he must have all the support he can get. He wants Stimson—if we get across the Nine Power note making more or less universal the idea that the world will not recognize treaties, etc. which result from the use of force —to make a speech somewhere and proclaim this as the Hoover doctrine. As the President says, it is a tremendous step, a longer step toward eliminating force from international affairs than anything which has been done. He said that he had to wrestle with Stimson for days to get it across, that the Secretary wanted always to go in for withdrawal of diplomats or an economic embargo, either or both of which measures would almost inevitably lead to war. I knew that the Secretary had always played with those ideas, but gathered from him that he had, with great difficulty, put across the idea embodied in his note of January 7. It would hurt his feelings terribly to have this called the Hoover doctrine because he thinks of it as one very important star which history will put to his credit."

Stimson declined to speak out as the President desired him

[7] Edwin Muller, "The Inside Story of Pearl Harbor," *Reader's Digest,* vol. 44, no. 264, pp. 25–27 (April, 1944).

to, on the grounds that it was improper for members of the
State Department to make political speeches. And, weeks
later, he still held back when, as he himself put it, "Secretary Hurley came in to talk to me about the 'Stimson Doctrine' of the Borah letter" and said he was "anxious to have
me say something to indicate that the President had actively
shared in this matter, so that it could be used in the campaign
in his favor. I pointed out that I had already done this in
my letter to Borah, where I pointed out that my note of
January seventh had been sent at the President's instructions."

Stimson having repeatedly refused to champion the
"Hoover doctrine," the President turned to Castle, who
wrote (April 1): "He wants me to talk about the new doctrine . . . of not recognizing . . . which he rightly feels
is his own." [8] And Castle did talk about the new doctrine
—after Stimson had left for Europe.

Stimson's April trip to Europe was prompted by Norman
Davis, chairman of the American delegation to the preparatory disarmament commission in Geneva. Calling at the
State Department (March 29) Davis told Stimson that
Hoover's public disclaimer of any intention to fight, several
weeks earlier, had left a very unfortunate impression on
members of the League. He advised the Secretary to go in
person to Geneva, presumably to correct that bad impression.

According to Stimson's diary, Hoover consented to his
making the trip—to discuss both disarmament and the Far

[8] Castle diary, February 18, April 1, 8, May 2, 1932; Stimson diary,
March 12, 1932. Stimson noted in his diary, March 12, 1932, that in conversation with a couple of newspapermen he had taken occasion to
"emphasize again the President's part in this matter" (the nonrecognition
doctrine). In his book of 1936, however, he did not emphasize the President's part, but wrote of the origin of the nonrecognition idea, without
mentioning Hoover: "I find from my diary that as early as November 9th
I discussed it with my assistants as an ultimate possible weapon to be used,
and thereafter it was constantly cropping up in our discussions." *Far
Eastern Crisis*, 93.

Eastern crisis. According to Hoover's press statement announcing Stimson's departure, the object of the mission was to assist the work of the disarmament conference and nothing else: "This is the sole purpose of the Secretary's visit." And according to Stimson's memoirs "Stimson set himself at Geneva . . . to the purpose of obtaining . . . a world judgment against Japan," so that, if worse should come to worst, "it would lay a firm foundation of principle upon which the Western nations and China could stand in a later reckoning."

While in Geneva, Stimson made a great show of American cooperation with the League. On April 18, 1932, he—the American Secretary of State himself—even took a seat at the Council table, to the gratification of League enthusiasts back home. In all his conversations public and private, however, there was little meeting of minds as between him and the European statesmen. They talked of disarmament. He talked of Manchuria and Shanghai. They were interested in collective security for Europe. He wanted a united front against Japan. One thing he did achieve—an "understanding" with Sir John Simon about "working hand in hand with regard to the Far East."

In his absence Under Secretary Castle took his place in the Cabinet, saying to himself: "I always feel that I am more truly Acting Secretary when he is safely out of the country." And while Stimson was pursuing his own policy, Hoover and Castle laid down a quite different line. Castle, at Hoover's request, made two addresses in which he assured the American people that their government did not contemplate the use of economic pressure or military force.[9] The people had no way of knowing that at the moment the United States, as between the President and the Secretary

[9] Stimson diary, March 29, May 17, 1932; Castle diary, April 8, May 2, 6, 1932; William S. Myers, ed., *The State Papers and Other Public Writings of Herbert Hoover* (2 vols., New York, 1934), 2: 157–58; *On Active Service*, 258.

of State, was engaging in a kind of dual diplomacy almost comparable to that of Japan herself!

Hoover dreaded Stimson's return, and Stimson on his arrival home was indeed wroth on account of Castle's speeches. He waited for an explanation. After a few days, taking full responsibility, Hoover offered one. He said, according to Stimson, that "he had gotten very nervous about the excited feeling in Japan" while Stimson was away. He was "afraid it might lead to some attack on us and thought the best way to prevent it was to come out and say that we were not going to boycott them."

Soon Stimson tried to get Hoover to endorse the principle of cooperation with League sanctions as a corollary of the Kellogg Pact. We should refuse to recognize not only territorial changes made by aggression but also belligerent rights claimed by an aggressor. We should "implement the Kellogg Pact with a declaration as to what we would do in not recognizing a nation which was declared an aggressor by the League of Nations, and who had also broken the Kellogg Pact." So Stimson told Hoover, but Hoover did not agree. Stimson assumed that the President, while "in favor of the proposition," was "afraid to do it during the Presidential campaign."

Hoover looked upon disarmament, rather than economic warfare, as the proper means to implement a pact of peace. The Kellogg Pact, he reasoned, meant that the nations of the world should use their arms only for defense. They should increase the power of defense by "decreases in the power of attack"—by drastic cuts in their land, air, and naval forces. Such was Hoover's idea, but Stimson thought it "just a proposition from Alice in Wonderland," and he objected vehemently to it. "He feels," wrote Castle, "that our fleet, intact, is essential in the Pacific to keep Japan in order." In spite of his opposition the President finally went ahead and, on June 22, announced his comprehensive disarmament

plan: "I propose that the arms of the world should be re-
duced by nearly one-third." [10]

After trying, and failing, to hold Hoover back with regard to disarmament, Stimson set to work on a speech "in
defense of the nonrecognition policy," as he himself interpreted it. He was going to state his own conception of ultimate American aims as distinct from the conception of
Castle and Hoover. "My speech is intended to support the
Kellogg Pact as the fulcrum upon which we will have our
issue with Japan," he said to himself. "The speech is intended
to rally the European countries around the Pact, so that
when the issue with Japan comes up, they will support us intelligently on this central point." When he showed his draft
to Hoover, he ran into trouble. Though he explained that
he was defending the Pact against the assaults of "the in-
telligentsia," he had to cancel part of what he had written
and revise some of the rest.

After arranging for an invitation, he delivered his cen-
sored address on August 8, 1932, before the Council on Foreign Relations in New York. In it he proclaimed a "revolution in human thought" as revealed in the League Covenant
and the Kellogg Pact. War, except for the "right of self-
defense," was now "an illegal thing," and neutrality was
out of place. The nonrecognition policy of the United States
reflected "this new viewpoint and these new covenants."
True, the pact had no "sanctions of force," only those of
"public opinion," but the American notes of January 7,
1932, would lead eventually to a world-wide "moral disap-

[10] Castle diary, May 2, 15, 22, 24, 1932; Stimson diary, May 16, 18, 19, 20,
22, 24, 1932; Stimson, *Far Eastern Crisis*, 137–38; Myers, *State Papers of
Hoover*, 2: 211–13. Castle commented in his diary, June 23, 1932: "The
President's arms statement has been well received in this country and on
the whole well received by Governments abroad. . . . What is unfortunate, I think, is that such a move was not made long ago, and in fact the
President is being criticized just for this. . . . It is very hard to understand
why he allowed himself to be overpersuaded by the Secretary because . . .
he had pled with Stimson at least to send it to Geneva for the Delegation
to discuss."

proval" of aggression and to "consultation between signatories of the Pact." The speech provoked a violently anti-
American reaction in Japan.

If Stimson was a bit cryptic in New York, if he did not
make clear what the objects of "consultation" might be,
the fault was not entirely his own. Years afterward he admitted that, at the time, he "did not himself accept" the
position that public opinion alone was enough. But "he was
bound to . . . acknowledge that the Kellogg Pact would
not have had general support if it had included stronger
sanctions than that of public opinion." He might have added
that the Kellogg Pact, with such a gloss upon it, would not
have had Hoover's support, either. As Castle wrote during
a visit at Hoover's summer camp on the Rapidan: "the President told me . . . he was always afraid Stimson would get
us into real trouble through his earnest and entirely laudable
desire to support the various peace treaties. He said that he
was thankful that he had forced Stimson to omit the last
three pages of his speech on the Kellogg Pact because in
those pages he went the whole limit, expressed our willingness to join in sanctions, etc."

Soon after his defeat for re-election, in November, 1932,
Hoover spoke to Castle about the latter's writing a book on
the foreign policy of the administration. Hoover said Stimson would feel that *he* ought to write it. "But," observed
Castle, "the President does not want Stimson to make himself
the center of the book because, as he said, 'he would have
had us in a war with Japan before this if he had had his
way.' " 11

11 Stimson diary, July 20, 23, 25, 26, 27, August 10, September 16, 1932;
Castle diary, August 20, November 18, 1932; Stimson, "The Pact of Paris:
Three Years of Development," in *Foreign Affairs*, 11: i–ix (special supplement, October, 1932). In a letter from Tokyo, August 13, 1932, Ambassador Joseph C. Grew informed Stimson of the "outburst in Japan
against your speech before the Council on Foreign Relations," and explained that the "violent Japanese press reaction was based . . . on the
Foreign Office's inflammatory interpretation of Debuchi's cabled account."

At the time of Franklin D. Roosevelt's election, Stimson was in the midst of what was to him urgent but unfinished business. Peace had come to Shanghai early in May, the Japanese withdrawing in frustration, which Stimson attributed largely to his own policy of bluff. But in Manchuria they were consolidating their position. On September 15, 1932, while the League's investigators (the Lytton Commission) were preparing their report, the Japanese government announced its recognition of the puppet state of Manchukuo. With this *fait accompli* the Japanese presented a challenge both to the American policy of nonrecognition and to the forthcoming Lytton Report. Stimson grimly accepted the challenge. His object now was to bring the United States and the League of Nations, acting together, to make a final statement of the nonrecognition doctrine—as he interpreted it—and thereby to censure and chastise Japan.

He was not deterred by warnings of Japan's increasing hostility toward the United States nor by rumored threats of a rapprochement between Japan and the Soviet Union. From Tokyo Ambassador Joseph C. Grew cautioned him: "The Japanese regard the United States as their greatest stumbling block, although they expect the report of the Lytton Commission to be unfavorable and the action of the League of Nations to be possibly unfavorable. At present talk of friction with Soviet Russia is comparatively quiescent." And by way of the diplomatic grapevine, information came to the State Department that, as Castle phrased it, "Russia would have no difficulty in recognizing Manchukuo when Japan did," and "this would probably be followed by a nonaggression pact between Japan and the Soviet."

According to Castle, "It makes the Secretary itch to recognize Russia just to prevent this—and why should recognition prevent it?" But the Secretary decided, as he

U. S. State Department, *Papers Relating to the Foreign Relations of the United States: Japan, 1931–1941* (2 vols., Washington, 1943), 1: 99.

announced in another public letter to Senator Borah, that if "we recognized Russia in disregard of her very bad reputation respecting international obligations," the rest of the world would look upon our action as "a maneuver to bring forceful pressure upon Japan." So we would "lose the moral standing we had theretofore had in the controversy" with her. Though Stimson did not shrink from the possibility of an ultimate application of force, he wanted first to make the "moral" issue absolutely clear.

He therefore welcomed the Lytton Report as condemning Japan and justifying his own position. He afterwards said that the report rendered "a decisive judgment against Japan on all major issues" and recommended "the re-establishment of a genuinely Chinese regime in Manchuria." But Castle viewed the report as anything but an indictment— "so judicial in temper, so fair to both countries." [12]

The truth is that the Lytton Commission, while by no means exculpating the Japanese, also placed a heavy share of blame on the Chinese, pointing out that the issues involved in the conflict were not so simple as they were often represented to be. "This is not a case in which one country has declared war on another country without previously exhausting the opportunities for conciliation provided in the Covenant of the League of Nations," ran some of the actual words of the report. "Neither is it a simple case of the violation of the frontier of one country by the armed forces of a neighboring country, because in Manchuria there are many features without an exact parallel in other parts of the world."

As for "the re-establishment of a genuinely Chinese regime," the report did not exactly recommend this. To quote again, "a mere restoration of the *status quo ante* would

[12] Castle diary, September 7, October 5, 1932; Stimson diary, September 26, 1932; *Foreign Relations: Japan, 1931–1941*, 1: 102; U. S. State Department, *Foreign Relations of the United States: Diplomatic Papers, 1933* (5 vols., Washington, 1949–52), 2: 778–79.

be no solution. Since the present conflict arose out of the conditions prevailing there before last September, to restore those conditions would merely be to invite a repetition of the trouble." Instead, the Lytton Commission proposed that the Western powers and Japan cooperate in the "reconstruction" of China.[13]

Disregarding some of the implications of the report, Stimson hailed it as "probably the greatest event that has happened in foreign relations for a long time." To his disgust, however, the President and the Cabinet "did not take any great interest" in it. What was worse, the columnist Walter Lippmann argued that the Lytton Report and the nonrecognition doctrine were incompatible, since the report recommended for Manchuria a set-up different from either the old one under China or the new one under Japan, while the American notes of January 7, 1932, if taken literally, would estop the United States from agreeing to anything except a restoration of the *status quo!*

Indignantly denying this, Stimson went ahead "stiffening up the League on Manchuria" and urging its members to act upon the Lytton Report and nonrecognition together. Some of them, "pretty wishy-washy," hoped to make the report a basis for conciliation between China and Japan, but he insisted that the League must "do its duty as to principles before they start conciliation." [14]

In his self-appointed task of "stiffening up the League," he ran into complications—and also opportunities—as a result of the Presidential election. President Hoover was on the way out. President-elect Roosevelt was on the way in, and the future belonged to him.

[13] League of Nations, *Appeal by the Chinese Government: Report of the Commission of Enquiry* (Geneva, October 1, 1932), 126–28, 131. The commission noted (p. 105) that the Manchukuo government "contains a number of liberal reforms, the application of which would be desirable, not only in Manchuria, but also in the rest of China."

[14] Stimson diary, September 20, 27, October 5, December 12, 15, 1932; Castle diary, October 5, 1932.

The question was whether Roosevelt would continue the policy of nonrecognition. Or, more precisely, whether he would support the Hoover or the Stimson version of it. Nonrecognition itself could be called the Hoover-Stimson Doctrine, since Hoover had suggested and Stimson had formulated it. It could be considered as a final and sufficient measure, a substitute for economic pressure or military force, a policy looking toward conciliation and peace and relying on the moral power of public opinion for its effect. That was the Hoover Doctrine. Or nonrecognition could be viewed not as an alternative but as a preliminary to economic and military sanctions, a way of drawing sharp the issue between the United States (along with the League of Nations) and Japan, a means of laying down the ideological basis for eventual war. That was the Stimson Doctrine.

Where would Roosevelt stand?

6 Selling It to F. D. R.

John Gunther, visiting at the White House one spring day in 1941, overheard a telephone conversation.

For about ten minutes F. D. R. kept saying: "Yes, Harry. . . . No, Harry. . . . Why, I thought that had been done, Harry. But of course it *ought* to have been done, Harry!"

The president looked angry. Nervously he jabbed his pencil at a pad on the desk. "All right, I'll see to it, it's done now, thanks, Harry."

At first Gunther thought this must be Harry Hopkins, the Presidential favorite. Then Roosevelt relaxed a bit, held the telephone closer, and began a long and authoritative exposition of American diplomatic history. Gunther was amazed as he listened. "Well, Harry, as I see it, there have been three cardinal events in the evolution of American foreign policy since 1919. One was . . . . The other was . . . . And the third was your doctrine on Manchuria."

So this was not Harry Hopkins. It was Harry Stimson. And Roosevelt was lecturing *him* on the Stimson Doctrine!

Suddenly Roosevelt put the receiver down, and Gunther noticed a hurt expression on his face. His War Secretary had hung up on him.[1]

"The one problem that comes up in my mind," Stimson had told his diary on election day, 1932, "is the problem of cooperation for the future in order that the nation shall

[1] John Gunther, *Roosevelt in Retrospect: A Profile in History* (New York, 1950), 26.

not lose by the transition." And the next day he wrote: "the great problem is to . . . keep open the chances for capitalizing to the usefulness of the country the experiences I have had." He was even more strongly convinced that the President-elect would need his advice when, about a week later, the journalist Constantine Brown called to tell him about an interview he had had with Roosevelt. "He reported him as not knowing anything about foreign affairs," Stimson noted. "Brown had tried to talk to him about Manchuria, and found that he had no interest in it at all."

What, indeed, would Roosevelt do about the Far East? Many of the Japanese themselves were optimistic. They were speculating that relations with the United States would improve under the new administration. They expected, for one thing, to see a reduction of the American tariff and an increase in trade. The *Japan Advertiser*, of Tokyo, even predicted that Roosevelt would put an end to the Stimsonian policy of "interference in the Manchurian problem."

On the basis of his known record, the Japanese had good grounds for viewing Roosevelt as their friend. At first, as Assistant Secretary of the Navy in President Wilson's Cabinet, he had been a Japanaphobe, but afterwards he had reversed himself. During the Pacific war scare of 1913–14 he sketched a war plan for the Navy to use against the expected foe. Then, with the Washington conference of 1921–22, he began to foresee a new era of Japanese-American amity. He now heartily disapproved those people who were "still thinking in terms of war rather than in terms of trying to remove the causes of war." In 1923 he published in *Asia* magazine an article defending the work of the Washington conference—the limitation of naval armaments, the fixation of Pacific defenses. When Hector C. Bywater, a prophet of war and proponent of sea power in the Pacific, issued a rebuttal, Roosevelt rejoined: "It is exactly that attitude which I have sought to combat." In 1928, writing in *Foreign Af-*

fairs, he not only praised the Washington conference again but also criticized the Coolidge administration for its big-Navy program and declared that naval competition was "today the result of bungling diplomacy." [2]

So, in 1932, Stimson had ample reason to be concerned about the views, or lack of views, of the future President. He said to himself: "I can see countless matters in which it will be important for me to have an interview with him in regard to such matters as Manchuria, the conferences and situations in Europe, about which I personally know so much and he so little, that I think it most important for the United States and her foreign policy during the next four years that we should give this man as fair a chance as possible."

According to a New York *Herald Tribune* writer, Ernest K. Lindley, "Word was conveyed to Mr. Roosevelt almost immediately after his election that Mr. Stimson felt it very important to have the guidance of Mr. Roosevelt's views in his handling of the Far Eastern situation." The go-between was Felix Frankfurter, an old friend of Stimson's and a brain-truster of Roosevelt's. Before Christmas Frankfurter telephoned Stimson to say that Roosevelt would like to see him. But when Stimson spoke to Hoover, the President refused his consent.

Then Frankfurter repeated the invitation, and on January 3 Stimson appealed again to the President. "I told Hoover that I was sufficiently interested in his (Hoover's) policy to want to do anything I could to perpetuate it." Finally Hoover agreed to the meeting on the condition that Roosevelt put the request to him.

---

[2] Stimson diary, November 11, 1932, on microfilm in the Yale University Library; Henry L. Stimson and McGeorge Bundy, *On Active Service in Peace and War* (New York, 1948), 291–92. On Roosevelt's earlier attitude toward Japan, see Frank Freidel, *Franklin D. Roosevelt: The Apprenticeship* (Boston, 1952), 221–26, 232–33; and William L. Neumann, "Franklin D. Roosevelt and Japan, 1913–1933," in the *Pacific Historical Review,* 22: 143–53 (May, 1953).

On January 9, 1933, returning through snow and sleet from Coolidge's funeral at Northampton, Massachusetts, Stimson stopped off at the Roosevelt home in Hyde Park. Here he met F. D. R. for the first time. They had lunch together, then talked all afternoon, just the two of them.

Stimson found his own position much closer to Roosevelt's than to Hoover's on all questions except one—disarmament—and on this point he promptly but politely set his host to rights. When Roosevelt "expressed most warmly his approval" of Hoover's drastic arms reduction idea, Stimson "cautioned him not to be too hasty, pointing out that Japan was not likely to agree to the naval portions of the Hoover plan." He discussed with Roosevelt, much more sympathetically than he could do with Hoover, the question of Philippine independence, the possible imminence of war with Japan, and the naval strategy to be employed when war came. Stimson recorded:

"He told me a story of his own action as Assistant Secretary in getting out the 'orange plan' of the Navy against Japan in respect to the defense of the Philippines and how surprised he had been to find that, under the plan as it then stood, the fleet was to leave the Philippines and the Army in it unprotected and return to the American coast. I told him that that was not the plan now, as I understood it, and I pointed out to him the strategic effect of the Hawaiian position in stabilizing the present situation against any attack either on our coast or on the Philippines."

The gist of the conversation was the Stimson Doctrine. And Roosevelt seemed almost ready to out-Stimson its author. He "fully approved of our policy in the Far East," as his guest described it to him, his "only possible criticism" being that "we did not begin it earlier." He asked whether the American ambassador should not be recalled from Tokyo, as a gesture of disapproval of Japan, and Stimson warned him that it would be fatal for the United States to act alone. Finally Stimson came to the main object of his visit:

"I told him of the present ticklish situation at Geneva and the likelihood that it might be advisable for me to make another statement as to this Government's position. I said to him, 'I do not wish to ask any commitment from you but I certainly do not wish to make any such statement and then have you immediately afterward come out with a contrary position or statement.' He replied, 'You need have no fear of that.' "

After emerging from the Hyde Park conference, Stimson was beset by newsmen requesting a statement. He only grinned and told them he had had a delightful lunch. In New York next day he telephoned Castle to report "that he had had a good talk with Roosevelt, that if you could take at 100% all that he said, the future looked very hopeful as to foreign relations." [3]

With Roosevelt's backing, Stimson could look forward to accomplishing his program before the end of his own and Hoover's term, if he could steer his precarious way between the incoming and the outgoing President. His main object was to align the United States with the League in censuring and punishing Japan. To achieve this, he hoped to do the following: Obtain from Congress legislation permitting this country to cooperate with sanctions by means of an arms embargo. Prevent the passage of a pending bill for Philippine independence, which might look like an American retreat from the Far East. Get from the President-elect a public endorsement of the Stimson Doctrine. Yield to Great

[3] *On Active Service*, 291–92; New York *Herald Tribune*, January 18, 1933; Stimson, "Memorandum of Conversation with Franklin D. Roosevelt, Monday, January 9, at Hyde Park," on microfilm in the Yale University Library; diary of William R. Castle, January 10, 11, 13, 1933, typescript in Mr. Castle's possession in Washington, D. C.

Britain and France on the troublesome war debts question, so as to facilitate the formation of a united front. And, finally, join with the League in adopting the Lytton Report together with the nonrecognition principle as a basis for further action.

Stimson during the winter of 1932–33 "felt rather conscience stricken that we had not legislation enabling the President to forbid the traffic in arms last winter when the Manchurian trouble was at its height and Congress was apparently anxious to do it." There was already a law which empowered the President to prevent the export of munitions to revolutionaries in this hemisphere (as was done at the time of the Brazilian revolution of 1930). Now that Bolivia and Paraguay were warring over the Chaco region, a State Department man suggested to Stimson that he "get the President to send a message to Congress asking for an extension of the power to prevent the sale of arms to two countries in the situation in which Paraguay and Bolivia" were. Of course, such an extension of the law could be made to apply to the Manchurian affair as well as the Chaco dispute. But Stimson presented it to Hoover as a South American matter, and the President "readily consented" to sending the desired message.

Days passed, and no message was sent. Then Hoover asked Stimson to draw up the message himself, and Stimson did so, but still it was not delivered to Congress. Stimson kept urging Hoover to act, and Hoover kept refusing. "Stories have cropped out in the press, rather fantastic," Stimson noted in his diary, "about a fight between the President and me over the arms embargo bill."

Finally, on January 11, 1933, two days after Stimson's Hyde Park meeting with Roosevelt, Hoover submitted to Congress the Stimson memorandum with a brief and perfunctory covering note of his own. Roosevelt spoke out to endorse it much more enthusiastically than Hoover did. But the embargo bill was to bog down in Congress.[4]

The Philippine question had been a sore point between Stimson and Hoover for much longer than the embargo. It was the very first matter that Stimson, upon his return from Manila in 1929, had taken up with the President. He then importuned the President not to let the islands go. "How long must we keep them in order to do our duty to them?" Hoover dryly asked, but Stimson, after arguing his case, concluded: "I think I converted him to the importance of the question." The independence agitation continued, however, and Hoover repeatedly showed that he was no convert to Stimson's cause.

One day (in February, 1932) Stimson asked him whether "he really believed that the United States was not enough of a governmental power and did not have enough of constitutional freedom to evolve [a] relationship to another country like the Philippines similar to the relationship of England to the British Commonwealth of Nations."

Hoover did not deny that the United States had the power. He only said: "Well, that's the white man's burden."

Stimson replied: "Yes, that's what it comes down to and I believe in assuming it. I believe it would be better for the world and better for us."

The crises over Manchuria and then Shanghai made Stimson all the more determined to keep the Philippines. When, at the height of the trouble in Shanghai, the House of Representatives passed the Hare bill for independence, he saw it as "a terriffic blow to our position in the Far East."

To him the danger seemed greatest of all early in 1933, both houses of Congress finally having passed the Hare-Hawes-Cutting bill. Insisting that Hoover veto it, he argued

[4] Stimson diary, December 14, 23, 1932; January 12, 1933; William S. Myers, ed., *The State Papers and Other Public Writings of Herbert Hoover* (2 vols., New York, 1934), 2: 565–66; Raymond Moley, *After Seven Years* (New York, 1939), 93–95.

that this was the worst of all possible times for withdrawing from the Philippines, that the prospect of such withdrawal had brought on the aggressive expansion of Japan in the first place. Yet he did not like the veto message that Hoover prepared. Hoover assumed that independence was the ultimate goal—a complete and absolute separation—though he thought it should be delayed until the economic stability of the islands was assured. Stimson accused him of making a "misstatement of Philippine history" by confusing independence with "self-government"—a very different thing. "But I could not get him to see it," Stimson complained to his diary, "because he said he differed with me radically on our views of the Philippines and that discouraged me a good deal after my association with him for four years."

Hoover did veto the bill, on January 13. Both the House and the Senate promptly overrode him—"I feel very badly about it," Stimson said—and the bill became law on January 17.[5]

On the day of the veto Stimson called up Roosevelt to say he was going to inform the British that he did "not expect the American policy towards the Japanese to be changed." Roosevelt "at once responded that that was all right" and would have his support. A few days later he hinted to reporters that his administration would hew to the line that Stimson had laid down. Then, on January 17, he issued a public statement in which he said: "American foreign policy

[5] Stimson, "Memorandum of Events Since Becoming Secretary of State, Dictated August 28, 1930," on microfilm in the Yale University Library; Stimson diary, February 14, April 6, 1932; January 12, 13, 1933; *The Memoirs of Herbert Hoover*, Vol. 2: *The Cabinet and the Presidency, 1920–1933* (New York, 1952), 359–61; Garel A. Grunder and William E. Livezey, *The Philippines and the United States* (Norman, Oklahoma, 1951), 208–209. The grant of independence in the Hare-Hawes-Cutting Act was conditional upon Filipino approval, which was not forthcoming, because of the tariff provisions of the act. In 1934, however, the Tydings-McDuffie Act containing slight modifications was accepted. It provided for a "commonwealth" government until 1946 and then independence. *On Active Service*, 149–50.

must uphold the sanctity of international treaties." To the man in the street this may have sounded like a meaningless platitude, but not to the man in the State Department. "It was a very good and timely statement and made me feel better than I have for a long time," he told his diary.

It did not make Roosevelt's brain-trusters, Raymond Moley and Rexford Tugwell, feel so good. It was no platitude to them, either. They supposed it to be a "wholehearted acquiescence in the Hoover-Stimson rejection of the traditional American concept of neutrality, of disinterestedness, impartiality, and nonparticipation in foreign quarrels." They thought it "endorsed a policy that invited a major war in the Far East." On January 18 they spent hours with Roosevelt at his New York City home trying to convince him he was making a tragic mistake. He suddenly put an end to their pleas by looking up and recalling, quite irrelevantly, that his Delano ancestors used to engage in the China trade. "I have always had the deepest respect for the Chinese," he said. "How could you expect me not to go along with Stimson on Japan?"

On that same January 18 the New York *Herald Tribune* printed a critical letter from a writer who signed himself Scramasax. "Mr. Stimson has flourished the Kellogg Pact under Japan's nose as a business contract," Scramasax declared. "It is taking mean advantage of her subscription to a few paragraphs of pleasant persiflage." Calling attention to Scramasax's letter, an editorial went on to say: "This country is drifting into a quarrel with Japan to no clear end. The question naturally arises whether an understanding with Japan based upon our own rights and interests would not be possible of arrangement and whether, if it were arranged, the net result might not work more powerfully toward peace and sanity in the world as a whole than does the present situation, as dangerous as it is ineffective."

Stimson deplored such journalism as that. The *Herald*

Tribune, he complained, "had chosen just the time when everybody else was so satisfied with my policy and the fact that Roosevelt had backed it up to make an attack on it, or rather a query about it."

The newspaper had referred to Roosevelt's "putting himself behind what is alternately called the Hoover doctrine or the Stimson doctrine." Like Moley and Tugwell, everyone outside the administration supposed that there was but one doctrine, whatever its name. And yet, at this very time, Hoover was drawing for history a distinction between his own and Stimson's policies. He requested and received written statements from two of his Cabinet members, Secretary of War Hurley and Secretary of the Interior Ray Lyman Wilbur, testifying that he himself had proposed nonrecognition, insisted upon it as against sanctions or other "aggressive action," and started the "discussions and decisions" out of which "came the Hoover doctrine." [6]

Meanwhile Stimson and Roosevelt were drawing closer and closer together. On January 19 they held a second tête-à-tête, this one in a Washington hotel. In the course of it Roosevelt remarked: "We are getting so that we do pretty good teamwork, don't we?" Stimson laughed and said "Yes."

But relations between Stimson and Hoover became increasingly strained, especially after Roosevelt visited the White House, on January 20, to discuss the question of war debts. Stimson, unlike Hoover, wanted to see the debts canceled, the moratorium of 1931 made permanent. He hoped to produce a joint Hoover-Roosevelt statement which would lump the debts together with other international economic problems, such as currency stabilization, and provide for immediate Anglo-American conversations to lay the

[6] Stimson diary, January 17, 18, 1933; Castle diary, January 17, 1933; Moley, *After Seven Years,* 94; New York *Herald Tribune,* January 17, 18, 1933; William S. Myers, *The Foreign Policies of Herbert Hoover, 1929–1933* (New York, 1940), 163–68, 229 n.

ground for an economic conference to meet in London during the summer. "This was a ticklish task," he admitted in
his memoirs, "for Mr. Hoover was preoccupied with the
task of defending and reinforcing his own record on debts,
and the defense of one policy was not easy to reconcile with
the beginning of a somewhat different one." He ran into
trouble both with Hoover and with Roosevelt's aide, Moley.
He tried, and failed, to bulldoze Moley into accepting his
own draft of a note to the British. And, when Hoover instructed him to send a note demanding debt payments from
the French, he stalled—until Hoover jogged him with a
sharp memorandum. "I told him," Hoover noted, "that it
should be sent at once and that I was irritated at the delay."

And then, at his press conference on January 23, Stimson
remarked (though not for publication): "I am Roosevelt's
acting Secretary of State."

Castle observed: "The President is in a very embarrassing
position since his own defense of American rights is ignored
in the press accounts and Roosevelt and Stimson are played
up as the heroes." The Secretary's incautious remark at his
press conference, it seemed to Castle, was almost the last
straw. "Poor Hoover feels that Stimson comes very close to
disloyalty and poor Stimson feels that his loyalty is a terrible
strain on his conscience." And Stimson himself told Hoover
that "the only thing that upset" him was the thought that
Hoover "felt that he was being humiliated" by what Stimson
"had done with regard to Roosevelt." [7]

Despite the "terrible strain on his conscience," Stimson
was pressing onward toward his main object. After being
reassured of Roosevelt's support, on January 13, he telephoned London to say that "as a lawyer" he did not see

---

[7] *On Active Service*, 293; Moley, *After Seven Years*, 96–104; Myers,
Foreign Policies of Hoover, 238–39; Stimson diary, January 24, 1933;
Castle diary, January 24, 1933.

how the British and the other League powers "could get away without approving of the Lytton Report, which amounted to findings of fact, and then making a decision of the League on these findings, which should include an application of the non-recognition policy directly to Manchoukuo." At the end of January, however, he heard from Geneva that the British did not want to commit themselves to nonrecognition "for an indefinite time and under any conditions." And he was told that Sir John Simon desired, in return for a British commitment, a guarantee of close American cooperation with the League.

It was hard for Stimson to satisfy the British because of Hoover's continuing restraint. On February 14 Hoover returned with corrections and additions a review of the administration's foreign policies which Stimson had prepared. "I feel the memorandum gives the impression of too strong an alliance with the League," Hoover said. "I have insisted upon the aloofness of the United States from the League of Nations in that the sanctions of the League are those of force either economic or military, whereas the United States could not and would not enter into force sanctions."

Nevertheless, Stimson did commit the United States in a confidential message to Sir Eric Drummond, the Secretary General of the League. Drummond had inquired through Hugh Wilson, the American Minister to Switzerland, whether Stimson could approve a certain communication from the League to the signatories of the Nine-Power Treaty and the Kellogg Pact. This letter was to announce "the Assembly's hope that they will associate themselves with the views expressed in the [Lytton] report and that they will if necessary concert their action and their attitude with the members of the League." Stimson cabled to Wilson: "You may in your discretion tell Drummond in confidence that I am assuming that upon being informed of your receipt of such a letter and after examination by me of the text, I shall be able to reply promptly and favorably and make his letter and my reply public."

On the day of Stimson's promise to Drummond, February 24, events in Geneva reached their fateful denouement. The Assembly adopted the Lytton Report with essentially the recommendations Stimson had desired—recommendations which did "not provide for a mere return to the *status quo*" but did "exclude the maintenance and recognition of the existing regime in Manchuria." In Washington the British ambassador, congratulating the Secretary of State, said that at last the nations of the world had done a good job. "And he added," according to Stimson, "that he thought I had hot-housed them a little into 'more prompt action than they would have taken.' " [8]

Stimson's triumph was, however, to be qualified. On that same February 24 he and the President had a final show-down about the meaning of nonrecognition.

Stimson had passed on to Hoover a cable from Ambassador Grew in Tokyo about Japan's probable reaction to the League resolution. "There is no bluff in her attitude," Grew warned. "The military themselves, and the public through military propaganda are fully prepared to fight rather than to surrender to moral or other pressure from the West." This ominous message raised in Hoover's mind "a most serious question," and he at once sent word to Stimson that "some occasion should be taken to make it clear" that non-recognition presupposed absolutely no sanctions other than those of public opinion. Furthermore: "The whole doctrine of non-recognition is not alone a method of invoking world

[8] Stimson diary, January 13, 16, 1933; U. S. Department of State, *Foreign Relations of the United States: Diplomatic Papers, 1933* (5 vols., Washington, 1949–52), 3: 137–39, 186–87, 197, 204; U. S. Department of State, *Papers Relating to the Foreign Relations of the United States: Japan, 1931–1941* (2 vols., Washington, 1943), 1: 114; Myers, *Foreign Policies of Hoover*, 251–54; League of Nations, *Official Journal*, Special Supplement No. 112 (Geneva, 1933), 75.

opinion but it is equally important in the phase that it avoids precipitant action and allows time to work out proper solutions." Stimson promptly talked Hoover out of making any such public declaration.

But the next day Stimson's official response to the Assembly's resolution fell far short of the reply he had so recently promised Sir Eric Drummond. Minister Wilson seemed a little surprised. "As I read your reply to Drummond," he cabled to Stimson, "we have neither 'associated the Government of the United States' with the views expressed in the Assembly's report although we declare ourselves to be in substantial accord therewith nor have we stated that we would 'concert our action and attitude if necessary.' "

And Stimson had to keep on explaining, in answer to Chinese, British, and other inquiries, that the United States, because of the failure of Congress to act, did not and could not contemplate an arms embargo for the time being. Making the best of the situation, he reminded his questioners that "forty-two nations in the Assembly had delivered a moral judgment on the situation in the Far East, the most dramatic and formal which had been delivered in human history." His own "hunch," he said, was that "the moral judgment might lose force if we attempted to couple it with ineffective material action."

Japan's recourse was to resign from the League. But some of the Japanese still hoped to come to an understanding with the United States once Roosevelt was in the White House. Stimson, to the last, did all he could to frustrate them. A rumor ran that the head of the Japanese delegation in Geneva intended to go to Washington with the notion of "discussing the political situation with the incoming President." On March 1 Stimson instructed Ambassador Grew in Tokyo: "If you are approached on the subject of such a visit to the United States, the Department suggests that you discreetly and as on your own responsibility encourage the impression that it would be desirable if that delegate did not seek to visit this country for the purpose of conferring with high officials here." [9]

After March 4, 1933, Hoover no longer stood in the way. Roosevelt was in power, and Stimson set himself to the task of keeping the new President up to his own high mark. At first the outlook, as he saw it, was extremely bright, and then it suddenly grew dark.

At the inauguration Roosevelt declared: "In the field of world politics I would dedicate this nation to the policy of the good neighbor . . . who . . . respects the sanctity of his agreements in and with a world of neighbors." Which sounded like another fine platitude, except to those who, like Stimson, believed that the sanctity of agreements justified the coercion of Japan.

At the very first business meeting of his Cabinet, according to James Farley's story, Roosevelt presented his strategy for a war in the Pacific, the Navy to be based on Hawaii and to strike out from there. From Tokyo, Ambassador Grew forwarded a hint from a "reliable Soviet source" that the Soviet Union had troops in eastern Siberia which would be very handy "in case of an American-Russian-Chinese war against Japan."

The new administration seemed willing to cooperate closely with Great Britain and the League, if not also with Soviet Russia. Amid dozens of New Deal proposals, Roosevelt also sent to Congress an urgent request for authority to impose arms embargoes where and when he might see fit. Congress, however, amended the administration measure so as to require the President to be impartial, to embargo arms for all belligerents—or none. Roosevelt ceased to care much about the resolution thus amended, and nothing came of it. So the British government, which in anticipation of Ameri-

[9] *Foreign Relations, 1933,* 3: 195, 197-98, 204-205, 209-11, 214; *Foreign Relations: Japan, 1931-1941,* 1: 114-16.

can action had imposed a temporary embargo on both China and Japan, soon lifted it, explaining that there was no prospect for an international agreement on the subject in the near future.

The punishment of Japan had to be postponed, but Stimson was determined that Roosevelt must not weaken or forget the cause. After leaving the State Department he had resumed his law practice in New York, but he continued to spend a good deal of his time at Woodley, and during 1933 and 1934 he frequently visited the White House.

In May, 1933, he called to head off the veteran Japanese diplomat Viscount Ishii, who had a date with Roosevelt and who was expected to use his wiles to secure the recognition of Manchukuo. Stimson went in with a worried frown on his face and came out with a beaming smile. On a later visit, when Roosevelt was moving toward an American-Russian alignment by recognizing the Soviet government, Stimson applauded—though only recently he himself had hesitated to go so far, lest he weaken the morality of his case against Japan! He approved again, of course, when Roosevelt began to build up a big Navy. And he rejoiced to discover that Roosevelt agreed with him about the absolute necessity of keeping a hand on the Philippines.

Neither man publicized these cozy chats, but on one issue the former Secretary came openly to the support of the President. The subject was the reciprocal trade agreements bill of 1934, which was to give the executive a part of Congress's tariff-making power, enabling him to lower duties as much as 50 per cent. Only two years before, Stimson had been an outspoken high-tariff man, defending the Hawley-Smoot tariff, the highest in American history, in the campaign of 1932. Unembarrassed by that, he now reversed the field and, in a radio speech on April 29, came out for the administration bill.

At a White House luncheon a few weeks later Stimson

heard from the President "an extraordinary but impressive tale of the long-term ambitions of the Japanese as they had been explained to young Franklin Roosevelt by a Japanese friend at Harvard in 1902." In his diary Stimson recounted the remarkable story at length.

His White House visits came to a sudden end on October 30, 1934. At that time the Japanese troublemakers were demanding naval equality while they were also setting up an oil monopoly in Manchukuo. The *New York Times* guessed that the President, anticipating a new Far Eastern crisis, had called upon his old counselor for more advice. "He and President Roosevelt, long close friends, think alike on these issues." But they did not think alike this time. As Stimson revealed long afterward, the talk "produced a misunderstanding" which "clouded Stimson's confidence in the President." [10]

Though they corresponded occasionally after that, they did not meet again until 1940. Their estrangement was increased by the fact that, as Stimson later put it, "after 1934, bowing to the overwhelming opinion of his countrymen, Mr. Roosevelt for some years pursued a policy in foreign affairs which seemed to Stimson not sufficiently positive or active." Their estrangement was increased also by the fact that Roosevelt pursued policies in domestic affairs which seemed to Stimson entirely *too* positive and active.

On the New Deal, Stimson kept quiet as long as he could, though his law firm early declared unconstitutional the Wheeler-Rayburn holding-company law, only to be reversed by the United States Supreme Court. When Roosevelt pressed his ill-starred proposal for reorganizing the federal courts, however, Stimson spoke out to denounce it in

[10] James A. Farley, *Jim Farley's Story: The Roosevelt Years* (New York, 1948), 39; *Foreign Relations, 1933*, 3: 229; Drew Pearson and Constantine Brown, *The American Diplomatic Game* (New York, 1935), 369-77, 384-88; *On Active Service*, 286, 297-98, 301-302; *New York Times*, May 1, 18, October 31, 1934.

indignant tones. To him the New Deal as a whole meant a
dangerous trend toward national control of business enterprise, Presidential dictation to Congress and the courts, and
a swollen and inflationary public debt. That his own kind
of foreign policy might hasten these very evils—such a
thought apparently never occurred to him.

While estranged from the President, Stimson remained on
the best of terms with the new Secretary of State, Cordell
Hull. These two had begun their cooperation while Stimson
was still in office, and from the first they had agreed on Far
Eastern policy. During Hull's long tenure in the State Department they "worked together as would double cousins,"
as Hull said in his memoirs. Once or twice a week Hull and
his cronies went out for a game of croquet on the Woodley
lawn. "To some, croquet may seem namby-pamby," Hull
thought, "but it is really a very scientific game." Stimson
did not play croquet, but he came out on the lawn now and
then, to have a little talk with the Secretary of State.[11]

From 1933 to 1940 Stimson cast himself in the role of
elder statesman. As such, though he ceased to enjoy direct
access to the President, he occupied an Olympian height.
From it he continually lectured the American people
through books, articles, and letters to the *New York Times*.
In time the Italians invaded Ethiopia, Franco's legions invaded Spain, the Japanese invaded China, the Germans invaded Poland, and the Russians invaded Finland. At every
turn the Elder Statesman called upon his country to do its
part by imposing on them all a Stimsonian peace.

In an article in *Foreign Affairs* in 1933 he assumed, as already the fact, what he was really trying to create—a revolu-

[11] *New York Times*, July 31, 1935; February 7, 1937; *On Active Service*,
302-305; *The Memoirs of Cordell Hull* (2 vols., New York, 1948), 1: 159-
60, 179, 208. Moley warned F. D. R., November 30, 1935: "I found in the
State Department under Stimson . . . an atmosphere foreign . . . to the
vital spirit which characterized the campaign of 1932. That atmosphere has
not changed since Stimson's departure." *After Seven Years*, 323.

tion of public opinion in favor of maintaining peace by collective action. This article elaborated upon the theme of his 1932 speech on the Kellogg Pact. That pact, he again declared, signified a complete change in "world opinion toward former customs and doctrines." Then, to contradict himself, he said the pact would be "irresistible" if only the people of the world would "desire to make it effective"! The "critics who scoff at it," he added, "have not accurately appraised the evolution of world opinion since the World War."

Critics did indeed scoff. Foremost among them was the dean of American international lawyers, John Bassett Moore, who replied in the next issue of *Foreign Affairs*. "Mr. Stimson, just as might have been expected, has not changed front on the Kellogg Pact," Judge Moore wrote. "He still says that its efficacy must depend on public opinion and not on force. It is only when the sanctions of the Covenant and the alleged 'decisions of the League' are invoked that he welcomes, as agencies of peace, the menaces and measures of war which the Covenant prescribes. I have no quarrel with Mr. Stimson. He is present in my reflections only as the spokesman, and as a sincere spokesman, of a group identified with a certain type of mind and thought, and a belief in methods and measures which I, who modestly pray for peace in my own time, profoundly distrust not only because they have no visible moorings on earth or in the sky, but also because they have infected many of my countrymen with confused notions of law and conduct which, while they endanger our most vital interests, hold out hopes of partisan intervention that encourage European governments to defer the readjustments which only they can make and which are essential to peace and tranquillity in that quarter."

Judge Moore denied Stimson's allegation that international law, with its rules of neutrality, had ever "legalized" war. He argued that it was, rather, the new gospel as preached by Stimson which would make war "legal." The "legal" processes of sanctions economic and military were "merely the legitimate offspring of the new and consoling theory that peoples may with force of arms peacefully exterminate one another, provided they do not call it war." Again: "In the days of the old psychology, before the crafty throat of war began to coo of peace, neutrality was chiefly offensive to war-mongers and war profiteers. Today, however, and very naturally, it is even more detested by the devotees of the war-gospel of peace through force."

Judge Moore refused to cringe at the cry of "isolationist." That, he explained, was the label which believers in the new dispensation applied to "those who do not believe in war as the prime, or as the natural and appropriate, creator of peace." As for himself, he was glad to be dissociated from the "moralists now proposing to regenerate the world by violence, without regard to the consequences to their own country or to any other." He knew that "wars have often been fomented by agitations recklessly conducted by persons who professed a special abhorrence of war." [12]

Undeterred by such criticisms, Stimson called for the application of his special brand of unneutrality when Mussolini adventured into Abyssinia in 1935. Congress passed a law which seemed to satisfy the President—the first of the neutrality acts—but it did not satisfy Stimson, because it did not give the President enough discretion in discriminating against the aggressor. The neutrality law was not unneutral enough! In the *New York Times* he accused the American government of handicapping the League in the imposition of sanctions. After the quick success of Italian arms he demanded, in another letter to the *Times*, that his nonrecogni-

[12] Henry L. Stimson, "Bases of American Policy During the Past Four Years," in *Foreign Affairs*, 11: 383–96 (April, 1933); John Bassett Moore, "An Appeal to Reason," in the same magazine, 11: 547–88 (July, 1933).

tion doctrine be applied. A few years later Roosevelt told James Farley how he had "inherited" the Stimson policy. "If I recognize Italy's conquest of Ethiopia," he said, "I would have a Japanese problem on my doorstep." [13]

Meanwhile, in 1936, Stimson restated his case against Japan in his book *The Far Eastern Crisis*, a defense of his policy as Secretary of State.[14] And when, in the Chicago speech of October 5, 1937, the President boldly, if vaguely, recommended a "quarantine" of aggressors, Stimson tried to bring him up to his word. To "quarantine" means literally to compel to remain at a distance, without intercourse. Lo, the President, whether he knew it or not, was asking for an embargo against Japan! In another communication to the *Times* Stimson commended Roosevelt and proposed an immediate suspension of war-material exports. Roosevelt, heeding the public outcry against the quarantine, seemed to forget all about the idea.

But he had already awakened the war fears of many congressmen, and they began to discuss the Ludlow Amendment, which would have forbidden a war declaration without a popular referendum first, except in case of an attack upon American soil. Stimson came forth as a leading critic of the Ludlow proposal. He denounced it as a come-on to aggressors, and argued that it would make war more likely, not less. In this he probably was right. The real danger was that, in preparing to wage war, or to wage peace in Stimson's terms, a President would be tempted to whip up the

[13] *New York Times,* October 11, 1935; April 30, 1936; *Jim Farley's Story,* 198. After the first Stimson letter on the Ethiopian crisis, "government officials" were reported to have "expressed pleasure over its nonpartisan tone" but they "confessed mystification" at its hint of criticism and were "at a loss as to what more Mr. Stimson would have them do." A couple of weeks later Stimson discussed the neutrality issue with Secretary Hull. *New York Times,* October 12, 26, 1935.

[14] This book provoked discussion in the House of Commons because of Stimson's implication that, in 1932, the hesitancy of the British government had handicapped him in his efforts to bring Japan to terms. *New York Times,* November 6, 1936.

public for the referendum by means of contrived war scares
and even actual attacks.

As the Japanese war against China progressed, without a
declaration of war by Japan or the finding of a state of war
by Roosevelt, who refrained from applying the neutrality
law, Stimson made himself the outstanding American
champion of the Chinese cause. To him the advocates of
getting tough with Japan inevitably turned when, in the
summer of 1938, they organized the American Committee
for Non-Participation in Japanese Aggression. Its leaders—
Roger S. Greene, Harry B. Price, and other old China hands
—invited him to serve as its honorary chairman, and he
agreed to do so. Strengthened by the prestige of his name,
the committee agitated both for a voluntary boycott and
for government embargoes against Japan.

During the winter after the Munich deal of 1938, when
the administration asked for changes in the neutrality law
to give the President a freer hand, Stimson again made himself heard, not only writing to the *New York Times* but
also testifying before a Senate committee. He insisted on
what he called affirmative action for peace, which meant enabling the President to discriminate against those he considered aggressors, and which implied more than that, even
a direct military understanding among Great Britain,
France, and the United States for use in the event of war.

At last ex-President Hoover spoke out to disagree. "I
regret to differ so widely from my friend," Hoover said,
carefully avoiding personalities, in a newspaper interview.
"I am convinced that taking sides in European conflicts by
any program of economic support to one side or economic
defense against the other will stop no wars and heads the
United States straight toward being involved in war. It
leads there because no war can be won by economic methods, and once we are in the controversy we have to win, and
only military force will win wars."

When Great Britain and France declared war on Germany in 1939, Stimson was pleased to see action being taken against an aggressor at last. "The coming of war in 1939," said his memoirs, "not for the first or last time in Stimson's life, was a relief."

He kept hammering away at the Japanese. Few Americans, he said, approved of abetting the evildoers in the Far East with oil and scrap iron from the United States, but many of them feared that war would follow if anything were done to stop it. He advised them to put aside their fear. "Experienced observers have promptly recognized and publicly stated that such a fear was without credible foundation; that the very last thing which the Japanese Government desires is a war with the United States." An embargo, he contended, would deprive Japan of the means of carrying on war and so would bring peace to the Pacific.

He told the Yale graduating class of 1940 that compulsory military training was the way to peace, the democratic way. In a radio broadcast the next day, June 18, as France was on the point of surrender, he topped the grand crescendo of his long campaign. He demanded that the United States repeal the neutrality law, open ports to British and French vessels for supply and repair, stop the shipment of oil and scrap to Japan, and carry planes and munitions to the allies in American ships and convoys.

Next day he got a telephone call from the White House.[15]

As summer came in 1940 President Roosevelt had two resolves, in politics and foreign affairs. One was to run for

[15] *On Active Service*, 311–20; *New York Times*, October 7, 8, December 22; 1937; February 13, August 23, 1938; January 19, April 6, 8, 1939; January 11, 1940. Theodore D. Wolsey, in a reply to one of Stimson's letters, said that his attempts to play upon the public's emotions were unworthy of a man of his stature. *Times*, October 12, 1937. In Congress, Republicans attacked and Democrats defended Stimson. *Times*, March 10, 1939. For information on the American Committee for Non-Participation in Japanese Aggression, I am indebted to Professor Fred H. Harrington, of the University of Wisconsin, who has had access to the papers of its organizer, Roger S. Greene.

a third term, and the other was to give aid and comfort to the enemies of Germany and Japan. He had a couple of Cabinet vacancies to fill—War and Navy. The War Department had not been warlike enough to suit him, but at last he was getting rid of the noninterventionist Secretary, Harry Woodring.

On the eve of the Republican national convention Roosevelt schemed to strengthen his policies and confound his critics by creating a "coalition" government, a "Cabinet of national unity." His plan was to appoint as his War and Navy Secretaries the titular leaders of the Republican party, its candidates of 1936, Alfred M. Landon and Frank Knox. For the Navy, Knox was available and eligible. "He is just our type," Theodore Roosevelt had written long before in introducing him to the young Henry L. Stimson. For the War office, however, Landon disqualified himself by persisting in his public criticisms of F. D. R.

The "Talleyrand of the times," Justice Felix Frankfurter, then took a hand. Preoccupied as much with patronage and power as with his work on the Supreme Court, Frankfurter operated a kind of informal but wide-reaching employment agency for Roosevelt. Frankfurter recommended his old friend Stimson; the financier and adviser of Presidents Bernard Baruch seconded the nomination, and Roosevelt readily accepted it. There is a story—rather hard to believe —that Roosevelt explained to a disappointed aspirant for the job (Louis Johnson): "Felix has assured Bernie that if I make Stimson Secretary of War the Republicans will call off their Philadelphia Convention." [16]

Stimson was willing, as always, to serve. When Roosevelt

[16] Eliot Janeway, *The Struggle for Survival: A Chronicle of Economic Mobilization in World War II* (New Haven, 1951), 125–45. After a review in which Henry Steele Commager denounced the story about the Republicans' calling off their convention, Janeway protested that his "source was an eyewitness," and Commager replied "categorically" that the story was "wholly without foundation." New York *Herald Tribune Book Review*, February 3, 1952.

called him he agreed to take the position if he could have his own way with departmental reorganization and with key appointments. "Stimson never knew whether the President had originally intended that he should stay indefinitely as Secretary of War," his memoirs said. In other words, he never knew whether his appointment was originally intended to last beyond the second Tuesday in November, never knew whether it was at first only an electioneering trick. Nor, apparently, did he care.

To be named by the President was one thing; to be confirmed by the Senate was another. Senator Arthur H. Vandenberg, the ranking Republican on the Foreign Relations Committee, said on his way to the Philadelphia convention that he would vote against confirmation if Stimson repeated before the committee his recent statement about convoying materials to the allies. Vandenberg thought convoying would be an act of war, and so did most other Republicans.

At the Senate hearing on his appointment Stimson did not speak quite so frankly as before. When Vandenberg asked him if his policies would not amount to acts of war, he answered that he preferred to call them acts of self-defense. (Afterwards he sent a letter to Vandenberg in which he insisted that aid to the allies would be legal under international law, for neutrality in the face of aggression, he said, was inconsistent with the Kellogg Pact.) When confronted with quotations intended to show his long record of bellicosity, he said with a smile: "If you go on reading from my past statements, you'll make me feel like Winston Churchill for having been right so often."

He took the position, however, that this whole line of questioning was beside the point. He protested that the Secretary of War runs the Army but does not make foreign policy. The only relevant questions, he said, were those touching upon his ability to direct the military establishment. Senator Robert A. Taft, directly contradicting him, insisted that his views on foreign policy did bear upon his functions as a member of the Cabinet. Taft compelled him to back down. In the end both Taft and Vandenberg voted to confirm his appointment, and it was confirmed.

His friends on the American Committee for Non-Participation in Japanese Aggression rejoiced at the news. They took it for granted that, as Secretary of War, he would help make foreign policy and not confine himself to administering the War Department. They had lobbied to speed his confirmation because, as one of them said, "he will be interested in getting the embargo applied." Now, along with Navy Secretary Knox, he was expected to "get a backbone into the President" and keep him from compromising or temporizing with Japan.[17]

[17] *New York Times*, June 24, July 9, 10, 1940; Edward T. Folliard and William Costello, "Secretary of War Stimson," i t the *American Mercury*, 59: 272 (September, 1944); *On Active Service*, 327–29; Roger S. Greene to Mrs. Greene, June 21 and July 27, 1940, from the Greene papers, by the courtesy of Professor Fred H. Harrington.

7 *How We Should Maneuver Them*

At noon, November 25, 1941, five men met in the White House to talk secretly with the President. One of them was the Secretary of War, Henry L. Stimson. He was expecting to take part in a discussion of the government's strategic plan for war in Europe (nicknamed Victory Parade) and so he was surprised at the turn the conversation actually took. As he said in his diary:

"There the President, instead of bringing up the Victory Parade, brought up entirely the relations with the Japanese. He brought up the event that we were likely to be attacked perhaps (as soon as) next Monday, for the Japanese are notorious for making an attack without warning, and the question was how we should maneuver them into the position of firing the first shot without allowing too much danger to ourselves. It was a difficult proposition." [1]

Stimson had joined the Roosevelt administration at a most critical moment in the history of the republic and of the world. France had just fallen, and England was about to meet, alone, the German onslaught. Behind Germany stood the Russia of Stalin in enigmatic partnership with Hitler. The Nazi and the Communist, between them, seemed on the point of dominating all Europe. And in the Far East the militarists of Japan, though still fighting in unconquered

[1] U. S. Congress, *Hearings before the Joint Committee on the Investigation of the Pearl Harbor Attack* (Washington, 1946), pt. 11, p. 5433. Stimson apparently added the parenthetical phrase ("as soon as") at the time he submitted portions of his diary to the committee.

China, nourished ambitions of creating a vast Pacific empire and realizing at last their age-old dream of Asian hegemony.

Such was the outlook in the summer of 1940, but it changed considerably in the course of the following year, as some of the cracks in the supposed solidarity of the conquerors began to show. Repulsed from Britain, Hitler turned on his quondam partner and launched his invasion of Russia. The Japanese had joined the Rome-Berlin Axis and had signed a nonaggression pact with the Soviet Union, though they distrusted the one and feared the other.

In 1941 some of the Japanese leaders wanted to temporize with the United States. One question for American policy makers was whether to temporize with Japan. They might try to detach her from the Axis, so as to avoid having to fight on both the Pacific and the Atlantic fronts at the same time, if not to aviod war entirely. If Russia should withstand the Nazi assault, an American-Japanese conflict might seem less feasible for Japan, less desirable for the United States. During the first week in December the Russians threw back the invader in front of Moscow and started a great counteroffensive. It was too late for peace in the Pacific. By that time the temporizers, both Japanese and American, had lost out.

Once installed in the War Department, Stimson by no means confined himself to the administration of the Army. Though at the Senate hearing on his appointment he had tried to tell his questioners that his views on foreign affairs were irrelevant, he immediately afterward began to take a hand in the determination of foreign policy. One of the first things he did was to propose to Secretary of State Hull and Secretary of the Navy Knox that the three of them hold regular meetings to discuss and agree upon policy recommendations for the President. Adopting his suggestion, they met every Tuesday morning at nine-thirty (and oftener in the fall of 1941) in Hull's office. Significantly, they called themselves the "War Council."

They also met less regularly in what was referred to as the "War Cabinet." This group—including the Army Chief of Staff, General George C. Marshall, and the Chief of Naval Operations, Admiral Harold R. Stark—frequently got together in the White House at the call of the President. The Secretaries attended ordinary Cabinet meetings, too, though these were few and relatively unimportant, and they often conferred individually with one another and with the President. So Stimson kept himself well acquainted with foreign affairs. When asked later about his knowledge of the diplomacy of 1940–41 he answered: "I think I knew it as fully as anybody in the Government."

He did not know military plans quite so fully, for Roosevelt, who conceived of himself as a master strategist, kept secrets from his own War Secretary. "Stimson is obviously unhappy because he is not consulted about the strategy of the war" (that is, the war to come). So said the presidential intimate Harry Hopkins after visiting the War office one autumn afternoon in 1941.[2]

Though Stimson contributed little to war planning, he contributed much to Army preparation. He, more than any other one man, was responsible for the passage in 1940 of the nation's first peacetime draft law.

The impetus for this had come not from the Army or the President but from a civilian group outside the government, the Military Training Camps Association, led by Stimson's friend and fellow Wall Street lawyer, Grenville Clark. In the spring of 1940 Clark urged General Marshall to recommend a draft, but Marshall refused to do so. The general realized that President Roosevelt was unwilling to champion

---

[2] *Hearings . . . Pearl Harbor Attack*, pt. 3, p. 1215, and pt. 29, pp. 2065–68; Robert E. Sherwood, *Roosevelt and Hopkins: An Intimate History* (New York, 1948), 397.

such a measure at that time, with a presidential campaign in the offing. Besides, the general did not want to disrupt his trained units, which he needed for hemisphere defense, in order to provide instruction for a mass of draftees, nor did he want to raise a controversial issue which might endanger the impending bill for an increased Army appropriation. He contented himself with advocating a strong program for voluntary enlistments. Without the backing of the Army or the President, administration senators and congressmen were reluctant to sponsor a conscription bill, and so the Training Camps Association turned to Senator Edward R. Burke of Nebraska, an anti-Roosevelt Democrat, and Representative James W. Wadsworth of New York, a Republican. The latter introduced his measure in the House on June 20—the day that Stimson was nominated as Secretary of War.

Stimson got right to work, before his confirmation, to clear the way for the Burke-Wadsworth bill. Spurred on by Clark, he dissuaded the President from approving the volunteer plan that Marshall favored. Then, conferring with Marshall at Woodley on July 8, Stimson and Clark induced him to withhold a War Department study of peacetime conscription, which they feared might jeopardize the passage of the Burke-Wadsworth bill, and to support the principle of that bill, instead. In a few days Marshall, with Roosevelt's blessing, testified before the Senate Military Affairs Committee in favor of the proposed draft law. It finally passed, though not until September.[3]

When the selective service lottery was begun, Stimson quite fittingly was the man who, blindfolded, drew out the capsule containing the first unlucky number. Some twelve months later, the terms of the earliest conscripts were about

[3] Mark S. Watson, *United States Army in World War II, The War Department, Chief of Staff: Prewar Plans and Preparations* (Washington, 1950), 189-96. Watson says (p. 189 n): "This account of the initiation of the 1940 draft legislation is based largely upon detailed manuscript memoirs of Grenville Clark."

to run out, and the mood of the men and of the country was such that, in an election year, Roosevelt hesitated to ask Congress for an extension of their service. Stimson prevailed upon him to take the chance. It was a narrow squeak, as the House agreed to the extension by a majority of only one vote.

A war for the draftees to fight was almost sure to come if the government should stick to the principles and implications of the Stimson Doctrine. As Stimson's memoirs proudly said: "A careful reading of the diplomatic negotiations that preceded Pearl Harbor can lead to no conclusion but that it was American support of China—American refusal to repudiate the principles of Hay, Hughes, Stimson, and Hull—which proved the final cause of the breakdown of negotiations and the beginning of war." [4]

Cut off all trade with Japan. This will stop the Japanese armies in their tracks. It is the way to peace in the Far East. So Stimson had reasoned during the later phases of the Manchurian crisis in 1932 and 1933. So he had argued continually after the beginning of the Japanese invasion of China in 1937. So he continued to say to his colleagues and the President after joining the Roosevelt administration in 1940. He found eager agreement on the part of Secretary of the Interior Harold L. Ickes and Secretary of the Treasury Henry Morgenthau, Jr. But he ran against the skepticism of Secretary of State Hull, Under Secretary Sumner Welles, Ambassador Grew, General Marshall, and Admiral Stark.

During the first couple of years of Japan's so-called "China incident," from 1937 to 1939, the Roosevelt administration had not contented itself with Hull's verbose reassertions of the Open Door policy and the Stimson Doctrine. It had also aided the Chinese by purchasing their silver, lending

[4] Sherwood, *Roosevelt and Hopkins*, 366–67; Henry L. Stimson and McGeorge Bundy, *On Active Service in Peace and War* (New York, 1948), 256, 345–48.

from the Export-Import Bank, and refraining from an application of the neutrality law, which would have prohibited sales of war materials to China (as well as Japan). Then, in 1939, the administration began to apply "moral" embargoes by requesting citizens not to sell aviation supplies to the Japanese, though this violated the commercial treaty of 1911 which guaranteed Japan exactly the same trading privileges as other countries. The United States finally denounced the treaty, and it came to an end early in 1940. By the time Stimson became Secretary of War, the administration was free to proceed without that embarrassment, and Congress soon authorized further restrictive measures.

After the fall of France the Japanese threatened to move into Indo-China, and they soon did so, occupying the northern part of that French colony. On July 18, 1940, as reports came to Washington that the Japanese were beginning this movement, Stimson, Knox, and Morgenthau dined with the British ambassador and the Australian minister. Stimson was afraid the British might consent to appease Japan with French Indo-China. In the dinner conversation he "brought out that we now had an opportunity under the new legislation of stopping the supplies of oil to Japan." The British ambassador, Lord Lothian, responded that his country might cooperate by destroying the oil wells in the Dutch East Indies.

Stimson noted that this suggestion seemed deeply to impress Morgenthau. And so it did. Next morning Morgenthau urged it on Roosevelt, and promptly the President called Stimson, Knox, and Wells to the White House to talk it over. Welles objected that the Japanese, if deprived of oil in this way, would probably make war on Great Britain. Stimson pooh-poohed Welles's prediction.

Out of this disagreement emerged two separate embargo plans. The State Department proposed to stop the export to Japan of aviation fuel and lubricants, plus the finest grades of scrap iron and steel, but nothing more. Stimson, Knox, and Morgenthau got together and shared their complaints about State Department timidity. Then the Treasury Department prepared a more drastic project which would have prevented the sale to Japan of all kinds of petroleum and all kinds of scrap metal. Morgenthau took a suitable proclamation to Roosevelt, and Roosevelt signed and published it. Then, yielding to State Department protests, he withdrew the Morgenthau proclamation and put forth a new one which mentioned only the highest grades of petroleum products and iron and steel scrap.

Stimson continued to demand a more extensive embargo, and Hull continued to demur. Stimson scored another point when, immediately after news of Japan's joining the Axis in September, 1940, Roosevelt ordered controls on all grades of scrap iron and steel, though he said nothing about oil. Now Stimson concentrated on getting a complete petroleum embargo too.

Throughout the fall and winter the President's advisers kept on debating the oil embargo issue. Summing up his opinions, Stimson asserted (in a memorandum of October 2): Japan has "historically shown that when the United States indicates by clear language and bold actions that she intends to carry out a clear and affirmative policy in the Far East, Japan will yield to that policy even though it conflicts with her own Asiatic policy and conceived interests." But Ambassador Grew warned from Tokyo that increased economic pressure by the United States "would tend to push the Japanese people onward in a forlorn hope of making themselves economically self-sufficient." The danger was that a complete embargo on American oil might start the Japanese on an expedition to take the Dutch and British East Indies and get what they wanted, by force.

Stimson himself did not worry about this danger, of which his more cautious colleagues and advisers made so much.

He tried to tell the President that the thing to do, if the Japanese threatened the East Indies, was to send American warships there to scare them off! Both the Chief of Naval Operations and the Commander in Chief of the United States Fleet opposed Stimson's idea. His friend and former adviser, Herbert Feis, a State Department economics expert, questioned it. As Feis afterwards wrote: "The tactics of Theodore Roosevelt—who sent the fleet around the world in 1908 to impress Japan—were out of date." Even F. D. R. seemed taken aback by Stimson's suggestion, and he passed it off by saying he would study the maps.

It was all very well for Stimson, now head of war and not diplomacy, to assure the officials of the State Department that his "clear and affirmative policy" of economic pressure and naval threat contained no dangerous implications for the United States. "But to the officials who had the decision to make, various points seemed suffused with doubt," as Feis, one of those officials, later said. "If the Japanese Army, for whatever reason, got into greater trouble in China, would it become discredited? Or would it, by placing all blame on us, be able to win more tenacious loyalty? And if, as a result of our action, Japan should really be faced with defeat in China, would it give in or would it make a desperate attempt to save itself by war? Mr. Stimson's opinions on these points seemed to them dubious, and his dismissal of the chance that Japan might dare to fight the United States too confident."

Heeding the warnings of Ambassador Grew, the doubts of his State Department experts, and the cautions of Navy leaders, Secretary Hull during that winter of 1940-41 stood adamant against provoking the Japanese any further until both Great Britain and the United States were ready for a Pacific war.

And then, in the summer of 1941, the debate was ended by a new move of the Japanese, who proceeded to occupy strategic points throughout all of French Indo-China. In reply the President issued an order, July 26, freezing Japanese assets in the United States and in American territories. The British and the Dutch did the same with respect to their possessions. This freeze meant that the Japanese could get no more currency with which to buy American, British, or Dutch supplies.[5]

The embargo was now complete, so far as the United States could make it so. The Stimson Doctrine was at last in full effect.

In his recommendations to the President regarding the Far East, Stimson talked of pacifiying the Japanese by economic action and threats of force. In his recommendations for Europe he did not hesitate to use the language of war itself, though not in public. He backed all of Roosevelt's steps "short of war" in 1940–41, but these were not enough for him. The President seemed to be waiting for war to come to the United States. Stimson preferred to see the United States go right out and join the affray.

In the matter of transferring American destroyers to Great Britain, in September, 1940, he was at the President's elbow with counsels of boldness. When he along with Hull and Knox met with Roosevelt to discuss the plan, Hull was at first dubious about its legality, in view of an existing American statute and the old rules of international law. But Stimson brushed both statute and neutrality aside. He also rejected the suggestion that the administration might first consult the representatives of the people. The destroyer deal, he argued, was simply "an exercise of the traditional power of the Executive in foreign affairs."

In his opinion the President lawfully could do much more than exchange ships for bases, and he must do more, at once.

<hr/>

[5] *New York Times*, November 13, 1940; *On Active Service*, 384–87; Herbert Feis, *The Road to Pearl Harbor: The Coming of the War between the United States and Japan* (Princeton, 1950), 49–50, 89–93, 97, 103, 106, 123–24, 126, 136, 239.

A way must be found, he thought, to provide American goods for Great Britain and get them safely across the Atlantic. As early as December 19, 1940, Stimson told the Cabinet that the Navy must soon begin to convoy ships. Later he ran across a statute of 1892 which authorized the Secretary of War to lease Army property "when in his discretion it will be for the public good." This, he believed, would authorize him to transfer materiel to the British without bothering to go to Congress for a new law.

When, early in 1941, Roosevelt nevertheless went to Congress for fresh and broad legislation, Stimson chimed in with all the friends and members of the administration who clamored for lend-lease. At the hearings he was asked whether lend-lease aid to a belligerent would not be unneutral, and he replied that it would not, that the Kellogg Pact had changed international law so as to free nonbelligerents from any obligation to withhold aid as against an aggressor. When asked whether lend-lease would not be a step toward actual war, he replied: "I do not see that it would be from anything now before me at all a consequence that would necessarily follow from that." But would we not have to convoy the goods? And would not convoying lead to war? "As Secretary of War, I became a subordinate of the President and was directed to follow out his policies," Stimson responded, "and those policies, as I understand them, have always been, as shown by many, many occasions, a desire, if possible—if possible—to effect the safety of this country without becoming involved in any warlike or forcible or military measures." [6]

[6] *The Memoirs of Cordell Hull* (2 vols., New York, 1948), 1: 838; Sherwood, *Roosevelt and Hopkins*, 228; Feis, *Road to Pearl Harbor*, 141–42. Stimson's testimony on lend-lease is quoted at length in Charles A. Beard, *President Roosevelt and the Coming of the War, 1941: A Study in Appearances and Realities* (New Haven, 1948), 31, 34–37, 40–41. Henry Morgenthau, Jr., "The Morgenthau Diaries: IV—The Story behind Lend Lease," in *Collier's*, October 18, 1947, p. 74, implies that Stimson wanted to by-pass the Senate foreign relations committee. Stimson was "just

In private he could express himself somewhat more straightforwardly. Lend-lease, he admitted to his diary, was "a declaration of economic war." Already he had told the Cabinet that "we ought to forcibly stop the German submarines by our intervention." Soon he was counseling Roosevelt to ask Congress for explicit authorization to convoy. The President, however, preferred to evade Congress, use what he called "patrols," and emphasize their "defensive" character. Stimson reminded him that he was going to have American vessels report the locations of German submarines to the British authorities, and assured him that this was a "clearly hostile act to the Germans." He wanted him to recognize the fact and not try to "hide it into the character of a purely reconaissance action."

In a radio speech on May 6 Stimson declared publicly that lend-lease by itself was not enough. Though speaking less frankly than in his private conversations, he strongly implied that the government must resort to a systematic use of convoys—which would require repeal of most of what was left of the neutrality act. The President's secretary, Stephen Early, indicated that Roosevelt had approved the Stimson broadcast. At the next Cabinet meeting, however, Hull spoke out against the speech (and a similar one by Knox) as making unnecessary trouble for the administration. And Roosevelt agreed with Hull that the time had not yet come to talk about eliminating the neutrality law.

When, on June 22, the German armies invaded Russia, many Americans thought it was time to relax a bit, while the two great totalitarian powers preoccupied themselves with one another. Stimson was afraid that Roosevelt might share this widespread sentiment. So he promptly sent him a letter of advice. "For the past thirty hours," he said, "I have done little but reflect upon the German-Russian war

shocked" at the thought of "damn fools" like Hiram Johnson and Gerald Nye discussing the bill at length and delaying its passage.

and its effect upon our immediate policy. To clarify my own views I have spent today in conference with the Chief of Staff and the men in the War Plans Division of the General Staff." The result of all this reflecting and conferring was, first, an estimate of the "controlling facts" and, second, a recommendation of policy. Most important of the "facts" was that Germany would be "thoroughly occupied in beating Russia for a minimum of one month and a possible maximum of three months." The recommended program was that "this precious and unforeseen period of respite should be used to push with the utmost vigor our movements in the Atlantic theater of operations."

On July 3 Stimson sent another note to the President, this one urging him immediately to ask Congress for a declaration of war. He enclosed his own draft for the war message, in which the President was to explain that he had done all he could for the cause of peace, but events at last had proved too strong for him. Again the President was too timid for the War Secretary. Roosevelt did send a message to Congress but it did not even hint at a war declaration, though it announced a warlike act, the moving of American forces into Iceland.

The Iceland occupation was intended to further Roosevelt's scheme of "patrolling" the Atlantic. And that scheme eventually brought forth its incidents of war, when German submarines, pursued by American destroyers, began to fire back. After the first of these incidents, involving the destroyer *Greer*, Stimson was all for a fighting speech by the President, but Hull cautioned against it. So, on September 11, Roosevelt broadcast: "The aggression is not ours. Ours is solely defense. But let this warning be clear. From now on, if German or Italian vessels of war enter the waters, the protection of which is necessary for American defense, they do so at their own peril." In this "shoot on sight" address Roosevelt was, perhaps, asking for war, but Stimson did not want to ask for it: he wanted to declare it.

The more cautious Hull requested the Chief of Naval Operations to present his views, and the forthcoming memorandum was such as to give Roosevelt pause. "A declaration of war by the United States against Germany, unless Germany had previously declared war against the United States, might bring Japan into the war as an active belligerent." So Admiral Stark warned, and he added a reminder that it would be a tremendous disadvantage for the United States to have to wage hostilities on two fronts.

And so, on October 9, the President did not ask Congress for out-and-out war but only for an amendment to the neutrality law. He desired permission to arm merchant ships and send them into war zones. Stimson appeared at the congressional hearings to add the weight of his authority to this proposal. But he was not satisfied with it. As Harry Hopkins noted at the end of the month: "Both Stimson and Marshall feel that we can't win without getting into the war but they have no idea how that is going to be accomplished." [7]

That October the Japanese, already entrenched in Indo-China, stood poised for new and wider adventures in the southwestern Pacific. Not that they seemed to menace directly the United States or its territories, but they did appear ready to strike out against the colonies of Great Britain or the Netherlands.

Stimson, preoccupied with his old proconsular domain, the Philippines, was preparing a "strategy of national defense" with which to forestall the Japanese. He was thinking now in terms of air rather than sea power. His idea was to make the Philippines a base for B-17 bombers which could attack any Japanese expedition daring to move southward past the islands. He wanted to put in the Philippines at least

[7] *New York Times*, May 7, 1941; *On Active Service*, 360–62, 367–74, 383, 386–87; Feis, *Road to Pearl Harbor*, 197, 219–20, 279; Hull, *Memoirs*, 2: 943, 1047; Sherwood, *Roosevelt and Hopkins*, 303–304, 379–80, 397.

a hundred of the Flying Fortresses, and he calculated on October 6 that he could provide that many in about three months. On October 21, when only a few had arrived, he reported to the President: "even this imperfect threat, if not promptly called by the Japanese, bids fair to stop Japan's march to the South and secure the safety of Singapore."

To gain time for assembling his air armada in the Philippines, he was willing to see Roosevelt and Hull keep up their month-old conversations with Ambassador Nomura, but he did not want them to concede anything but talk. When, in September, Premier Konoye proposed to meet Roosevelt in the Pacific, Stimson favored "stringing out negotiations" but opposed an actual conference or even a preliminary discussion of concrete terms. And when, early in November, the "troubleshooter" Saburo Kurusu headed for Washington to join Nomura, Stimson commented to himself: "Japan is sending somebody to us who, I think, will bring us a proposal impossible of acceptance."

He was not quite so much concerned about the need for gaining time, however, as were General Marshall and Admiral Stark. On November 5 they sent the President a joint Army-Navy memorandum advising that "no ultimatum be delivered to Japan." Apparently impressed by this memorandum, Roosevelt the next day told Stimson he thought he might propose to Kurusu a six months' truce during which neither Japan nor the United States would make any military advance or increase of armaments in the Far East.

Stimson did not like this truce plan. It would check his own scheme of building up an overpowering air force in the Philippines, and the Chinese would object to it, as he told Roosevelt. "I reminded him that it has always been our historic policy since the Washington conference not to leave the Chinese and Japanese alone together, because the Japanese were always able to overslaugh the Chinese and the Chinese knew it." (Here Stimson was a bit forgetful.

Just ten years before, in the fall of 1931, he himself had insisted on leaving the Chinese and the Japanese alone together, in spite of strong objections from China and the League.)

After listening to Stimson, the President turned from talk of truce to talk of war. On the following day (November 7) he polled his Cabinet on the question of the southwestern Pacific—"whether the people would back us up in case we struck at Japan down there and what the tactics should be." Should we strike first? What should the tactics be? Would the people back us up? One by one the Secretaries—Hull, Stimson, and the rest—expressed their opinion that the public would support the government, and Roosevelt agreed. Stimson was pleased. This, he rejoiced in his diary, was much the best Cabinet meeting yet. His colleagues seemed to be coming around to his idea of an offensive-defensive move from the Philippines. "The thing would have been much stronger if the Cabinet had known—and they did not know except in the case of Hull and the President—what the Army is doing with the big bombers and how ready we are to pitch in."

For Stimson, the next step was to send poison gas to the Philippines, for ultimate use against the Japanese, who, he told the President, had already used it against the Chinese. "And yet we have been afraid to send it for fear it would leak out and be misconstrued during these negotiations." Having convinced Roosevelt that we should prepare at once for gas warfare, he started things going in the War Department to "get ready for the possible shipments with the idea that it should be done so that it would not come out in the press."

Meanwhile Secretary Hull's seemingly endless talks with Nomura and Kurusu were coming to a head. On November 20 the two envoys presented Hull a note which demanded, as the price of peace, that the United States withdraw its

material and moral support from China and relax its re-
strictions on trade with Japan. Five days later Stimson met
with Knox and Hull in the latter's office for their usual
Tuesday morning get-together. Hull explained that he was
thinking of countering the Japanese demand with a proposal for a truce of three months. Stimson did not oppose it,
as he earlier had opposed Roosevelt's idea for a truce of
six months. He explained to his diary about the Hull plan:
"It adequately safeguarded all our interests, I thought as we
read it, but I don't think there is any chance of the Japanese
accepting it, because it was so drastic." Hull's terms: the
Japanese were to evacuate their recent conquests and cease
from carrying on or preparing new aggressions, and in return the United States was to supply them with a modicum
of oil, enough for their civilian uses only.

At noon that same day, November 25, Stimson went to
the "War Cabinet" meeting in the White House at which
the President "brought up the event that we were likely to
be attacked perhaps (as soon as) next Monday, for the Japanese are notorious for making an attack without warning,
and the question was how we should maneuver them into
the position of firing the first shot without allowing too much
danger to ourselves." As Stimson said, "It was a difficult
proposition." [8]

"*We* were likely to be attacked"! The pronoun, as Stimson here used it, was broad and inclusive. It included the
British and the Dutch, who in his own and his colleagues'
thinking were already our Pacific allies in effect. Earlier
in the year American, British, and Dutch staff officers in
the Far East had agreed that "joint military counteraction"
should be undertaken if Japan attacked or directly threatened the territory of either the United States or Great

[8] Stimson's statement to the joint committee, March, 1946; Stimson to
Roosevelt, October 21, 1941; Stimson diary, November 5, 6, 7, 10, 21, 25,
1941, all in *Hearings . . . Pearl Harbor Attack*, pt. 11, pp. 5419–21, 5432–
33; pt. 20, 4442–44. See also Hull, *Memoirs*, 1077.

Britain or the Netherlands—or, for that matter, if Japan should "move forces into Thailand west of 100 degrees or south of 10 degrees North" or into Portuguese Timor, New Caledonia, or the Loyalty Islands. Stimson repeatedly had tried to get Roosevelt to approve war plans based on this A. B. D. agreement, and Roosevelt had refused to commit himself. Nevertheless, the British and the Dutch in the Pacific were, in the language of the administration, identified with *us*.

On that November 25 the White House conferees were expecting Japan to strike soon at British or Dutch but not American soil. They were confident that the Japanese would not dare to start hostilities against the United States. That is precisely the reason why the question "how we should maneuver them into the position of firing the first shot" was, as Stimson put it, such a "difficult proposition." Since, as he and his associates supposed, the Japanese would not actually fire the "first shot" as against the United States, the problem was how to maneuver them into the position of *seeming* to do so when they moved upon Dutch or British possessions in the Pacific.[9] To this problem the men in the White House proceeded to seek solutions. As Stimson recorded:

"Hull laid out his general broad propositions on which the thing should be rested—the freedom of the seas and the fact that Japan was in alliance with Hitler and was carrying out his policy of world aggression. The others brought out the fact that any such expedition to the South as the Japanese were likely to take would be an encirclement of our interests in the Philippines and cutting into our vital supplies of rubber from Malaysia. I pointed out to the President that he had already taken the first steps towards an ultimatum in notifying Japan way back last summer that if she crossed

---

[9] See Richard N. Current, "How Stimson Meant to 'Maneuver' the Japanese," in the *Mississippi Valley Historical Review*, 40: 67–74 (June, 1953).

the border into Thailand she was violating our safety and
that therefore he had only to point out (to Japan) that to
follow any such expedition was a violation of a warning we
had already given. So Hull is to go to work on preparing
that."

That is to say, Secretary Hull at first proposed putting the
matter to the American people this way: the Japanese have
fired the first shot at us by infringing our freedom of the
seas and by allying themselves with the Germans in a program of aggression against the world, of which we are a
part. Others added these arguments: the Japanese have fired
the first shot at us by threatening an encirclement of our
interests in the Philippines and by threatening to cut off our
rubber supply from Malaya. Then Stimson, recalling Roosevelt's secret warning to Japan of August 17, put it this
way: the Japanese have fired the first shot at us by disregarding that near-ultimatum.

No sooner had Stimson left the White House and got back
to his own office than he learned from G-2 reports that the
long-awaited Japanese expedition was under way. "Five divi-
sions have come down from Shantung and Shansi to
Shanghai and there they had embarked on ships—30, 40, or
50 ships—and have been sighted south of Formosa." Immediately Stimson prepared a paper on the subject for the
President. At last the time had come for the United States
to act!

The next morning Stimson heard from Hull over the
phone that the latter had "about made up his mind" not to go
through with his plan for a three months' truce but, instead,
to "kick the whole thing over" and tell the Japanese that he
had "no other proposition at all." (That day, November 26,
Hull replied to the Japanese note of November 20 by adding
the complete evacuation of China to his conditions for a
settlement.) A few minutes later Stimson talked to Roosevelt on the telephone. Had the President received Stimson's

paper about the new Japanese move? "He fairly blew up—jumped up into the air, so to speak, and said he hadn't seen it and that changed the whole situation because it was an evidence of bad faith on the part of the Japanese that while they were negotiating for an entire truce—and entire withdrawal (from China)—they should be sending that expedition down there to Indochina."

"A very tense, long day," as Stimson recorded in his diary, followed on November 27.

The first thing in the morning, as soon as he got to his office, he called up Hull to find out what had become of the truce idea. Had Hull broken "the whole matter" off, as he had been thinking of doing? Yes, he answered. "As he put it, 'I have washed my hands of it and it is now in the hands of you and Knox—the Army and the Navy.'" (Afterwards Hull denied using these exact words, but he did not disclaim the general idea, except for the possible implication that the State Department was abandoning its responsibilities.) Then Stimson phoned Roosevelt and learned that the conversations with the Japanese had "ended up," all right, but with "a magnificent statement prepared by Hull." Which was reassuring to the Secretary of War.

Later in the morning he met with Secretary Knox, Admiral Stark, and General Leonard T. Gerow, Chief of the War Plans Division. Stark and Marshall had drawn up another memorandum for the President, in which they cautioned him: "Precipitance of military action on our part should be avoided so long as consistent with national policy." They recommended that the United States should go to war only if one of the contingencies specified in the A. B. D. staff agreement should arise. This did not suit Stimson. "I said that I was glad to have time but I didn't want it at any cost of humility on the part of the United States or of reopening the thing which would show a weakness on our part." Or in the words of Gerow: "The Secretary of War wanted to be sure that the memorandum would not be construed as a recommendation to the President that he request Japan to reopen the conversation."

Having made sure that the Marshall-Stark memorandum could not possibly be mistaken for a counsel of peace, Stimson at once tried to get the President to adopt its recommendations. But Roosevelt still held back, declined to make any outright promise to go to war, or issue an ultimatum leading to war, if British or Dutch territory alone was threatened. So it remained uncertain whether he would send American forces into action unless American territory itself were attacked.

Stimson did not let up. Early Friday morning, November 28, he received from G-2 a summary of the developing movement of the Japanese expeditionary force. He decided to take the news to the President before Roosevelt got up, so he might be better prepared for the "War Cabinet" session to meet at noon. Sitting on his bed, Roosevelt told Stimson he could see only three alternatives: "first, to do nothing; second, to make something in the nature of an ultimatum again, stating a point beyond which we would fight; third, to fight at once." Here was an opening for Stimson. Quickly he said he himself could see only two courses, since he doubted if anyone would consider doing nothing. Roosevelt agreed. Then "I said of the other two my choice was the latter one." That is, fight at once.

As Stimson afterward explained, "I was inclined to feel that the warning given in August by the President against further moves by the Japanese toward Thailand justified an attack without further warning, particularly as their movement southward indicated that they were about to violate that warning. On the other hand, I realized that the situation could be made more clean cut from the point of view of public opinion if a further warning were given."

At the noon meeting of the "War Cabinet" (November

28) its members agreed that "if the Japanese got into the Isthmus of Kra, the British would fight," and that "if the British fought, we would have to fight." But the consensus was that, "rather than strike at the Force as it went by without any warning"—which Stimson wanted to do—the American government should first warn Japan that if her expedition "reached a certain place, or a certain line, or a certain point, we should have to fight." He and the others then considered a warning to Japan and a message to Congress "reporting the danger, reporting what we would have to do if the danger happened."

The warning to Japan was to be a diplomatic maneuver, and the message to Congress a political maneuver. Both were to be phrased in such a way that, if the Japanese proceeded with their southward movement, even though they did not touch any American territory, they would nevertheless appear to be deliberately assailing our vital interests and, in that sense, attacking *us*.

Congress was to meet on the following Monday, December 1. In the interim Roosevelt left for Warm Springs, Georgia, after telling reporters that the crisis with Japan might bring him back at any minute. Stimson refused to let the President relax while away from Washington. Preparing several war-message drafts, he sped them to Warm Springs by plane. Then he and Knox and Hornbeck busied themselves with revising the warning intended for the Japanese Emperor. "This," as Stimson described it in his diary, "was in the shape of a virtual ultimatum to Japan that we cannot permit her to take any further steps of aggression against any of the countries of the Southwest Pacific, including China." It would certainly be strong and inclusive enough to justify a declaration of war.

Monday, December 1, came and went. The President, though back in Washington, sent no message to either the Emperor or the Congress. Stimson worried. He was reas-

sured by Harry Hopkins that the President had not weakened. Next morning Dr. Alfred Sze and Dr. T. V. Soong
called at the War office to see if they could get a guarantee
of strong American policy for the impatient Chiang Kai-
shek. "I said," Stimson recorded, "I can only say that
there is no change in the American policy from what I said
to Dr. Soong some time ago, and he can report that to the
Generalissimo and tell him that I also counsel him to have
just a little more patience and then I think all things will be
well." And that afternoon, at another White House conference of the "War Cabinet," as Stimson noted, "The President went step by step over the situation and I think has
made up his mind to go ahead." [10]

At last the way out of Stimson's and the administration's
dilemma seemed clear. The President would warn the Emperor: thus far and no farther. The President would inform
and alert Congress and the American people. By his words,
he would maneuver the Japanese into the position of *seeming* to fire the first shot—at *us*—if they crossed such-and-
such a line. Soon, now, they would cross that line. The
British would fight. We would have to fight—if Roosevelt
stuck to the program and did his part.

During that first week in December, 1941, the American
people knew from the newspapers only that all was not
well in the relations between the United States and Japan.
Members of the administration—Roosevelt, Hull, Knox,
Welles, and Stimson—did hint at all-out hostilities. But, as
Stimson's memoirs phrased it, "even Stimson did not publicly preach to the American people the necessity of fighting," and "Stimson never allowed himself to say that the
final result of President Roosevelt's policy would be war."

[10] Testimony of General Marshall before the joint committee; Stimson
diary, November 26, 27, 28, December 2, 1941; Hull's written replies to
the joint committee, May 16, 1946, all in *Hearings . . . Pearl Harbor
Attack*, pt. 3, p. 1294; pt. 11, pp. 5383–85, 5392, 5433–36; Stimson diary,
December 1, 1941, in Feis, *Road to Pearl Harbor*, 336.

His own knowledge of events to come was remarkable, or at least it should have been, because of the success of Army and Navy intelligence in cracking Japan's most secret codes. As a result of this "Magic," as it was called, he could peruse the confidential communications sent from Tokyo to Japanese representatives all over the world.

In combing through the decoded intercepts, he (like Hull and Knox and the rest) did not look for items indicating a Japanese move against Hawaii or even the Philippines. He looked for evidence that the Japanese were going to cross that line in the southwestern Pacific which the "War Cabinet" had agreed should mark the final division between peace and war for the American people.

On Sunday morning, December 7, Stimson met with Knox and Hull for a special "War Council" session in Hull's office. A Japanese reply to Hull's note of November 26 was expected. "Today is the day that the Japanese are going to bring their answer to Hull," Stimson dictated for his diary, "and everything in MAGIC indicated that they had been keeping the time back until now in order to accomplish something hanging in the air." This was the reason for the special Sunday meeting, and the atmosphere was tense, the faces of the conferees grim. "Hull is very certain that the Japs are planning some deviltry and we are all wondering where the blow will strike." No one mentioned Pearl Harbor.

That afternoon, about two, Stimson was just sitting down to lunch at Woodley when the President called him on the telephone and asked in a rather excited voice, "Have you heard the news?" Stimson said, "Well, I have heard the telegrams which have been coming in about the Japanese advances in the Gulf of Siam." Roosevelt said, "Oh, no. I don't mean that. They have attacked Hawaii. They are now bombing Hawaii."

"Well," thought Stimson to himself after he had left the

phone, "that was an excitement indeed." During the morning the reports of Japanese movements in the Gulf of Siam
had been excitement enough for him. He was already keyed
up by the uncertainty, by the approach of the hour demanding an active solution for his problem—how to make a
Japanese movement on the other side of the world look to
the American people like a shot fired at the United States.
"But now the Japs have solved the whole thing by attacking us directly in Hawaii."

To Stimson these were, on the whole, glad tidings. "When
the news first came that Japan had attacked us, my first
feeling was of relief that the indecision was over and that
a crisis had come in a way which would unite all our people," he told his diary. "This continued to be my dominant
feeling in spite of the news of catastrophes which quickly
developed." [11]

[11] *On Active Service*, 365-66; Hull, *Memoirs*, 1093-95; Marshall's testimony and Hull's and Stimson's written replies to the joint committee;
Stimson diary, December 7, 1941, all in *Hearings . . . Pearl Harbor Attack*, pt. 3, p. 1506; pt. 11, pp. 5393, 5437-38, 5461.

8 The Old Army Game

A couple of *Washington Post* men, writing in a popular magazine in the midst of the war, described the Secretary of War for the American public. He was, according to the authors, "probably the hardest worker in his department and the most thorough." A case in point:

One day an Army officer laid a report on the Secretary's desk, then stood around while Stimson riffled through the papers.

Stimson looked up. "Is there anything else?" he asked.

"I thought perhaps you'd like to initial it," the officer explained, "so I can move it along."

"Do you mean you expect me to sign this without having read it?" Stimson demanded, sternly.

And the officer, according to his own account of the incident, "got the hell out of there—fast." [1]

For months before December 7, 1941, Stimson had expected eventual war with Japan. It seems—in retrospect —that he should have foreseen the Pearl Harbor attack. After all, the Japanese had a reputation for striking without warning, a reputation dating at least from 1904, when they launched the Russo-Japanese war with a surprise blow at Port Arthur. The Navy in its Hawaiian maneuvers of 1932 staged a successful raid on Pearl Harbor with carrier-borne aircraft, and thereafter American war planners repeatedly

[1] Edward T. Folliard and William Costello, "Secretary of War Stimson," in the *American Mercury*, 59: 270–71 (September, 1944).

calculated on the probability of the enemy's beginning hostilities in that way. In January, 1941, Ambassador Grew in Tokyo warned Washington of rumors that Japan might begin war without declaring it, and begin it with an assault upon Hawaii from the air. The "Magic" intercepts of Japanese communications in the fall of 1941, if the pieces of the puzzle had been properly put together, would have spelled out the very time as well as the place of the attack.

The fact is that Stimson did see the danger early in the year. On January 24 the Secretary of the Navy, writing to the Secretary of War about the Hawaiian situation, reported that the "dangers envisaged in the order of importance and probability" were these: first, an "air bombing attack"; second, an "air torpedo plane attack"; and third, "sabotage." Stimson wrote back: "In replying to your letter of January 24, regarding the possibility of surprise attacks upon the Fleet or the Naval Base at Pearl Harbor, I wish to express complete concurrence as to the importance of this matter and the urgency of our making every possible preparation to meet such a hostile effort."

Stimson considered Hawaii "the best equipped of all our overseas departments," though he conceded that it was lacking in pursuit and patrol planes, anti-aircraft guns, barrage balloons, and "aircraft warning service." To overcome this last deficiency, he worked hard to provide radar equipment, though he failed to check up to see how much of it, or how little, was actually ready and in use. Various investigations by war planners showed that only a continuous, long-range, wide-arc reconnaissance by air could give adequate warning of an enemy approach. Yet Stimson did little or nothing to make additional patrol planes available for Hawaii.[2]

[2] Knox to Stimson, January 24, 1941, and Stimson's reply; examination of General Marshall before the joint committee; Stimson's written statement to the committee, March, 1946; Stimson diary, November 24, 1941; Marshall's testimony before the Army Pearl Harbor Board, August 7, 1944, all in U. S. Congress, *Hearings before the Joint Committee on the*

Instead, as the crisis with Japan developed, he concentrated more and more upon sending bombers to the Philippines. On the Philippines, not Hawaii—on offense, not defense—he focused the greater part of his attention. His Philippine preoccupation shines through his handling of what he considered the War Department's final alert to the Army outpost commanders.

This so-called "war warning" was dispatched from Washington on November 27. Three facts about it should be noted. First, Stimson and not Roosevelt or Marshall took the initiative in making the decision to send the message (in a telephone conversation with the President that morning, as Stimson recorded, "I suggested and he approved the idea that we should send the final alert"). Second, he was thinking primarily, and at first exclusively, of the Philippines ("The main question has been over the message that we shall send to MacArthur"). Third, the wording of the alert, in the form or forms it ultimately took, was complex.

At Stimson's instance, General Gerow and Colonel Bundy composed a draft of the message, then presented it to a conference of Stimson, Knox, and Stark (Marshall being absent from Washington that day). The draft began by saying simply that negotiations with Japan had terminated. After calling up Hull, the War Secretary corrected the first sentence to read: "Negotiations with Japan *appear* to be terminated *to all practical purposes* with only the barest *possibilities that the Japanese Government might come back and offer to continue.*" As if to offset the ambiguities he thus introduced, Stimson added to the second sentence these words: "hostile action possible at any moment." The rest of the message he examined carefully and approved without change.

Investigation of the Pearl Harbor Attack (Washington, 1946), pt. 3, pp. 1058, 1115–16; pt. 11, pp. 5419, 5421, 5432–33, 5454; pt. 27, p. 14.

All along he had been thinking of MacArthur in the
Philippines, but he finally decided to send warnings to the
rest of the outpost commanders also. The Army commander
at Pearl Harbor was General Walter C. Short. To the message intended for him was added a caution against alarming
the civilian population of Oahu. Here is the complete dispatch as sent to General Short:

"Negotiations with Japan appear to be terminated to all
practical purposes with only the barest possibilities that the
Japanese Government might come back and offer to continue period Japanese future action unpredictable but hostile
action possible at any moment period If hostilities cannot
comma repeat cannot comma be avoided the United States
desires that Japan commit the first overt act period This
policy should not comma repeat not comma be construed as
restricting you to a course of action that might jeopardize
your defense period Prior to hostile Japanese action you are
directed to take such reconnaissance measures as you deem
necessary but these measures should be carried out so as not
comma repeat not comma to alarm civil population or disclose intent period Report measures taken period Should
hostilities occur you will carry out the tasks assigned in
Rainbow Five so far as they pertain to Japan period Limit
dissemination of this highly secret information to minimum
essential officers."

To General Short, this message was not very informative.
It told him, on the one hand, that hostile action was possible
and, on the other hand, that negotiations might be resumed.
It told him to let the Japanese commit the first overt act,
but not to let this consideration jeopardize his defense. He
was to take such reconnaissance measures *as he deemed necessary*, and yet he was not to carry them out in such a way as
to alarm the civil population or disclose his intent. He was
left with the inference that, if and when hostilities came, his

job would not be to drive attackers off from his own base. Instead, he was told, "you will carry out the tasks assigned in Rainbow Five." So far as it applied to Japan, this war plan called for defending the Philippines, raiding Japanese installations and communications, and cooperating with the Dutch and the British in the southwestern Pacific.[3]

To General Short, then, the wording of this "war warning," taken by itself, was ambiguous and misleading enough. But he did not and could not take that message by itself. It was only one of several that he received, and the others confounded his confusion. From G-2 and from General Arnold he got instructions to be on the lookout for sabotage.

His superiors might have expected something other than sabotage if they had interpreted aright the Japanese "bomb plot" message of September 24 which had been intercepted and decoded. In this communication the Japanese government asked its consul general in Hawaii for detailed information about the precise berthing of the ships in Pearl Harbor. This information, one might have reasoned, was not intended for saboteurs, as they would get their data by local observations of their own. General Short did not have access to this or other "Magic" intercepts, and he was estopped by a recent Supreme Court decision from tapping Japanese communications, himself.

Having been asked to "report measures taken," he immediately replied to the War Department: "Report [Hawaiian] department alerted to prevent sabotage period Liaison

[3] On the composition and nature of the "war warning," see the testimony of Marshall, Stimson, and Gerow, and the text of the message in *Hearings . . . Pearl Harbor Attack,* pt. 3, pp. 1096, 1262–63; pt. 11, pp. 5423–26; pt. 23, p. 1106; pt. 29, pp. 2073, 2082–83, 2162 ff., 2173 ff. On "Rainbow Five," see Mark S. Watson, *United States Army in World War ll, The War Department, Chief of Staff: Prewar Plans and Preparations* (Washington, 1950), 103–104, 445–46. Rainbow 1 and 4 provided primarily for the defense of the continental United States and the western hemisphere. Rainbow 5 included the objectives of 1 and 4 but was itself a plan for action outside this hemisphere against the Axis powers.

with Navy re URAD [your radio message] four seven two twenty seventh." This reply General Marshall brought to Stimson's desk for the Secretary's eye. After all, it was a response to what was actually Stimson's own "war warning," sent out over Marshall's name during Marshall's absence. With the message from Short was one from MacArthur, and apparently the two were clipped together, Short's underneath. Stimson paid close attention to the one on top, that is, MacArthur's. His mind, as usual, was on the Philippines. If he as much as looked at Short's, he never gave it a second thought. Afterwards he could not remember ever having seen it, though he must have, for his initials, in his own hand, were on it.[4]

Stimson and Short misunderstood each other completely, because Stimson was concerned with only his own "war warning," while Short was responding to a whole group of warnings he had received. Stimson never inquired into the sabotage warnings that the War Department had sent. He never questioned (till after December 7) the sufficiency of Short's reply. He never ordered any answer to it. He left the Hawaiian commander to take it for granted that the War Department was satisfied with his antisabotage measures—which included bunching his planes on the ground in such a way as to make them useless for defense and vulnerable as targets in case of an air attack.

The Pearl Harbor disaster, costly though it was in men and material, came in some respects as a godsend to the Roosevelt administration. It seemed to place war guilt squarely upon the Japanese. It seemed to justify the administration's foreign policy in the Pacific. No wonder that Stimson, as his first reaction, felt a sense of profound relief.

[4] *Hearings . . . Pearl Harbor Attack*, pt. 3, pp. 1097, 1100–1101; pt. 11, p. 5443; U. S. Congress, *Report of the Joint Committee on the Investigation of the Pearl Harbor Attack* (Washington, 1946), 576–80.

Relief was followed by concern, concern over the difficulty of waging hostilities in the Pacific with a broken fleet, concern also over the possible public response to the sudden loss of ships and lives. Suppose people should say that the leaders in Washington were themselves at least in part to blame? Something must be done to forestall such criticism.

And Stimson began, at once, to do something. As soon as Knox got back from Pearl Harbor, whither he had flown for a hasty inspection of the disaster scene, the two Secretaries put their heads together. Of all the men in Washington, they had the most at stake, since they were directly responsible for the administration of the Army and the Navy. On December 16, 1941, after conferring with Knox, Stimson took a couple of steps toward clearing his own name in particular and the names of his administration colleagues in general. To Roosevelt he recommended Supreme Court Justice Owen J. Roberts as chairman of a Presidential commission to find who or what was to blame for the Pearl Harbor defeat. He also advised a thorough "housecleaning" of both the Army and the Navy, and without waiting for the findings of the Roberts Commission he immediately began to clean house by recalling General Short from Hawaii.

He did not need to wait for the commission's report, for he could be sure from the outset that it would contain pretty much what he wanted to hear. And Justice Roberts, as Stimson had told Roosevelt, would "command the confidence of the whole country."

On the morning of December 17, Roberts and the four members of his commission met, at Stimson's invitation, for an informal chat at the War office. "Secretary Knox was there," as Roberts afterwards related, "and Mr. Stimson very characteristically said that the Army and Navy wanted to cooperate fully with us and he added that he felt really that it was not a question of Army versus the Navy or Navy versus the Army and he turned to Knox and said, 'How about that, Frank?' and Secretary Knox said, 'That is absolutely right.'"

Thereafter, except for the most casual conversations with Stimson and Knox and Marshall and Stark, the investigators turned their attention away from Washington and toward Hawaii. They did not have access to the intercepted "Magic" messages but would have considered them not worth looking into anyhow. Or so Justice Roberts afterwards said.

As finally drawn up, the Roberts Report commended Secretary Stimson and his colleagues in Washington and censured the Hawaiian commanders, Admiral Kimmel and General Short. "The Secretary of War and the Secretary of the Navy," the report concluded, "fulfilled their obligations by conferring frequently with the Secretary of State and with each other and by keeping the Chief of Staff and the Chief of Naval Operations informed of the course of the negotiations with Japan and the significant implications thereof." The War and Navy departments, according to the report, adequately warned the Hawaiian outpost against an air attack, and yet, warned though they were, the local commanders "persisted up to December 7, 1941," in thinking that "Japan had no intention of making any such raid." So the attack came as a "surprise to all of the superior officers stationed in the Hawaiian area."

Not a hint that Stimson, too, had been surprised. Not a word about the fact that Stimson, for all his conferring with Hull and Knox and the rest, did not even know what warnings had been sent to Short.

Before submitting the report to the President, Roberts showed it to Stimson and Knox for their approval. (Needless to say, he did not show it to Short and Kimmel.) Stimson later dashed off a note of appreciation to Roberts—"just a hasty line to tell you what an admirable job I think that you and your colleagues have done . . . a masterpiece of candid and accurate statement based upon most careful study and analysis." [5]

On January 25, 1942, the Roberts Report was published. Newspaper readers, now that they had what were represented as the facts, could draw their own conclusions.

And now—in the newspapers—General Short himself had a chance to learn the findings of the board. He was unprepared for what he read. True, he had been relieved from command of the Hawaiian Department, but he had been directed to proceed to Oklahoma City "on temporary duty" and then, "on further notice," to report in Washington for "further temporary duty." He was expecting nothing more than some new assignment.

When he discovered that he, along with Kimmel, was receiving all the obloquy for Pearl Harbor, he telephoned General Marshall and asked whether he should retire. Marshall advised him to "stand pat" but told him he would consider this conversation as "authority" for his retirement if it should become necessary. The next day, January 26, Marshall recommended to Stimson that Short's application for retirement be accepted "today" and "quietly without any publicity at the moment." But Stimson did not accept Short's application that day. He waited a whole month.

There was a reason for Stimson's delay. He was facing another dilemma. If he let Short go without court-martialling him, he would invite public criticism for allowing a guilty man—*vide* the Roberts Report—to escape. If, on the other hand, he ordered a court-martial first, he would leave himself open to evidence and argument which might tar him along with Short as guilty of at least contributory negligence. The Judge Advocate General, Myron C. Cramer,

[5] Stimson to Roosevelt, December 16, 1941; Stimson to Roberts, January 27, 1942; Roberts to Stimson, January 31, 1942; testimony of Roberts before the joint committee, all in *Hearings . . . Pearl Harbor Attack*, pt. 7, pp. 3260–63, 3273, 3279, 3283, 3297.

was cautioning Stimson that it would be very hard to make the charges against Short stick. Cramer suggested a way out of the dilemma: retire Short now—but leave the threat of a future court-martial hanging over his head! That was simple enough, but there remained the complication of devising a verbal formula by which Short's retirement could be accepted without embarrassing the administration.

Day after day the administration leaders fretted over this problem of wording. President Roosevelt himself suggested that Short and Kimmel be required to agree that their retirement would be "no bar" to "subsequent court-martial proceedings." But Attorney-General Biddle in a memo to Stimson objected to mentioning a court-martial at all, lest Kimmel and Short, after their retirement, demand an early trial. And the Judge Advocate General in a memo to Marshall warned that at their trial, if they were granted one, "the defense would certainly attempt to pass part of the blame to the War Department."

Stimson himself, in a letter to Knox, January 14, 1942, proposed the essence of the "saving clause," as he termed it, part of which was finally used: "without condonation of any offense or prejudice to any action on behalf of the Government." He added: "Any reasons we want to give for our action can be said to the press." Two weeks later the administration published a statement incorporating the Stimson formula, and in a supplementary announcement he and Knox gave the reasons they wanted to give. The statement said that the retirement applications of the two commanders had been accepted "without condonation of any offense or prejudice to any future disciplinary action." The supplementary announcement informed the people that court-martial preparations had been ordered on the basis of the Roberts Report "alleging" derelictions of duty, but that no trial would be held until "such time as the public interest and safety would permit."

Stimson and Knox were never to find conditions suitable for holding the court-martial. Short and Kimmel themselves could not demand a hearing, for the Secretaries had required them to waive their rights to a prompt trial. And when the two-year statutory period for instituting court-martial proceedings was about to expire, the Secretaries requested them also to waive the statute of limitations, which they did.[6]

Not all the people or their congressmen were satisfied with the disposition that the government had made of the cases of Kimmel and Short. So, in June, 1944, Congress directed the Secretaries of War and the Navy to undertake further investigations of their own. Accordingly Stimson appointed an Army Board and Knox a Naval Court of Inquiry to hold hearings and draw up reports. But neither Knox nor Stimson gave his investigators an entirely free hand. At the outset both denied them access to the Japanese communications intercepted by "Magic."

The members of the Army Board centered their questioning upon the adequacy of the War Department's information to General Short. In particular, they concentrated upon Stimson's "war warning" of November 27, Short's reply to it, and the failure of the War Department to respond to that reply. "I could draw only one conclusion," Short himself testified, "—that as far as the War Department was concerned they approved of my action, because they had ten days after telling me to report to tell me that they did not approve it."

Short had appeared before the Board in the role of a defendant. Stimson, who deigned to make a personal appearance, played a much more complex part. "I am somewhat in

---

[6] *Report . . . Pearl Harbor Attack*, 266-P-S. Charles A. Beard, *President Roosevelt and the Coming of the War, 1941: A Study in Appearances and Realities* (New Haven, 1948), 393–99, gives a more extended account of the disposition of the cases of Kimmel and Short. "The procedure in General Short's case was handled by the Secretary of War," according to General Marshall's testimony, in *Hearings . . . Pearl Harbor Attack*, pt. 3, pp. 1528–29.

the position," he explained to the Board, ". . . of a district attorney in his relations with the grand jury. And by becoming a witness, I have to 'watch my step' very carefully that I do not get into a position of advocacy or bias towards any person who may afterwards be proceeded against or concerned with the action which your report may recommend." At first, he said, he had doubted the propriety of his testifying at all. "But I made up my mind that you were entitled to all the facts that I could give you." Facts he now promised to supply, but no inferences from the facts. He would have to withhold his judgments till the Board had reported—"so that I will be in a position which is not open to criticism."

The grand jury proceeded to quiz the combined prosecutor and witness about the wording of that crucial message to Hawaii of November 27. General Russell asked what Stimson thought Hull meant by the statement, incorporated into the warning, that the Japanese negotiators might come back and offer to continue. This, said Stimson, was a matter of inference and so he would rather not say. The colloquy went on, with General Grunert, the president of the Board, chiming in later.

RUSSELL: "Well, to be perfectly frank about the line of questioning that I am doing at the moment, it appears from the record that the Japanese people did come back on the 1st, 2nd, and 5th of December, following November 27, and did continue to discuss possible adjustments of the situation in the Pacific; and the thinking that I have been doing personally is whether or not the return of the Japanese, the continuation of the negotiations, and the publicity which was given to those continued negotiations had the effect of weakening the message of November 27th which went out to the four commanders."

STIMSON: "No message went out relating to those further coming-backs, if they occurred, that I know of."

GRUNERT: "It was mentioned in the press, though."

STIMSON: "Well, we weren't running the war on the press."

General Russell then tried to point out another ambiguity in the war warning. What had the Secretary told Short to do? "Make a reconnaissance," said Stimson. Was that the actual wording? Stimson read from a copy of the message: "such reconnaissance and other measures as you deem necessary." Did the Secretary regard *that* as a direct order to carry out reconnaissance? "Well," said Stimson, beginning to show irritation, "I am not going into that. The message speaks for itself. That is what I regarded it."

General Frank joined with Russell in raising the question whether the message was not, in several respects, confusing and self-contradictory. Asked General Frank: "Did it ever occur to you, when the message went out, that the part of the message following the first two sentences might have had some effect in minimizing its critical nature to the recipient of that message?" And Stimson replied: "No. I don't remember now having that occur to me. Of course, it is awfully easy to speculate with the knowledge of 'hindsight,' but you must remember this, that we in Washington faced a whole horizon of danger, a good many different outposts." But, the questioners persisted, Short had been told "not to alarm the civil population or disclose intent"; they wondered whether that phrase in any way "curtailed the action that the Commanding General might take, or in any way weakened the directive to take action." Stimson said he didn't think so: radar reconnaissance could be done inconspicuously. "Then you had in mind more a reconnaissance, as you call it, by radar, rather than a reconnaissance by air?" "I had no limitation." "Do you know what state the [Hawaiian] department was in, as far as the so-called 'long-distance reconnaissance' was concerned?" "Well, I only knew by hearsay. . . ."

More questions. Had the Secretary known of the other War Department warnings to Short, those advising him to guard against sabotage and particularly the sabotage of airplanes? Had the Secretary kept himself informed about the Navy Department messages? No, he could recall seeing no warning messages at all, except that one of November 27.

What about Short's reply? The warning to Short had called upon him to "report measures taken." Had the Secretary followed through on this? He had not. "You didn't take the same interest in the reply as you did in the preparation of the original message?" "It wasn't my matter, any more than the other message was. It was my duty to get through the President's directive in regard to that first one in accurate form, and in General Marshall's absence I was the messenger, so to speak, from the President."

But the questioning generals, apparently convinced that Stimson's role had been far more than the passive one of a mere messenger (as in fact it had been), kept pressing the Secretary. "Then, it was not out of the ordinary for this message of Short's and the message of MacArthur to have been sent in to you by the Chief of Staff?" "Well, he sends to me at quite frequent intervals messages which are deemed by him to be important in keeping me up and abreast of the times."

Stimson could not remember actually having seen this particular message from Short. He supposed he had, since his initials were on it.

Under all this pressure Stimson retained his composure pretty well, but he became a bit flustered under another line of questioning. Again, General Russell began it and General Grunert joined in.

RUSSELL: "Then you were not surprised at the air attack on the 7th of December?"

STIMSON: "Well, I was not surprised, in one sense, in any attack that would be made; but I was watching with considerable more care, because I knew more about it, the attack that was framing up in the southwestern Pacific. And I knew also that there was a concentration in the mandated islands—I know now, because the fact is that General Arnold showed me a proposed message for a photographic reconnaissance, so that there was an additional threat, and that might fall on either Hawaii or Panama."

GRUNERT: "Do you know whether or not this message about the task force assumed to be assembling in the mandated islands was transmitted, or whether that information was transmitted, to the outposts, especially Hawaii?"

STIMSON: "Oh, I am sure it was; but don't the papers show it? I really do not know."

GRUNERT: "Do you consider that that information or that such information was necessary to an outpost?"

STIMSON: "Frankly, I don't know what happened in all those details. I didn't meddle with what were military staff matters, barring when I was conveying a message from the President, and barring when I was taking up a new weapon, like radar."

A little later Stimson tried to strike out part of this testimony, and the Board accepted all his emendations except one. In this instance he wanted to edit out the whole of his answer to the question whether news of the Japanese task force assembling in the mandated islands had been sent to Short ("Oh, I am sure it was; but don't the papers show it? I really do not know"). As the generals put it: "The Board did not believe it was justified in making that change."

All in all, the generals had given the Secretary a rather rough time. He was not satisfied with the way their inquiry was going. And when they finally drew up their conclusions, in the fall of 1944, he was still less satisfied. The main points of their report, briefly summarized, were these: The Pearl Harbor attack was a surprise to all concerned—to the public at large, to the Hawaiian command, and to the War Depart-

ment. The extent of the disaster was due to failures both
on the scene and in Washington. General Short failed adequately to alert his command for war. The War Department, knowing the type of alert he had taken, failed to direct
him to take a more suitable one and also failed to keep him
fully enough informed about American-Japanese relations
that he might have corrected his own error.[7]

Stimson refused to let the Army Board's findings stand
unchallenged. He assigned the assistant recorder of the
Board, Lieutenant-Colonel Henry C. Clausen, to a one-man
mission of re-investigation. Except for the last week of the
Board's hearings, testimony regarding the "Magic" intercepts had been excluded. The later witnesses having referred
to phases of that subject, Clausen was supposed to complete
the evidence by gathering information on it from some of
the earlier witnesses, since scattered all over the world. The
tendency of Clausen's re-examination was to strengthen the
case against General Short by showing that the general knew
more than had previously appeared, and the Secretary of
War less, about the precise warlike intentions of the Japanese in 1941. When confronted by Clausen, many of the
witnesses changed the testimony they earlier had sworn to,
or added to it, or professed to have forgotten certain things.
Clausen did not give General Short another chance to speak.

Nor did Clausen call upon Stimson to appear again as a
witness, nor did he look into the Stimson diary. "Why not?"
he was later asked. "Well," said Clausen, "you mean I should
investigate the investigator?"

Stimson knew that, in a less one-sided proceeding than
this, his acts of omission in the fall of 1941 might look as
bad as Short's. The Judge Advocate General, Myron C.
Cramer, had told him as much. In a memorandum of November 25, 1944, Cramer again cautioned Stimson about

7 *Hearings . . . Pearl Harbor Attack*, pt. 27, p. 158; pt. 29, pp. 2063-86;
pt. 35, pp. 131-40, 151, 178-79.

the dangers of an actual trial. "As I have already indicated," said Cramer, "upon any charge of neglect of duty, or of his various duties, General Short would have the formidable defense that he responded to the request to report measures he had taken with a message, incomplete and ambiguous it may be, but which should have prompted doubt as to the sufficiency of the action taken." The court probably would not convict, Cramer added, or if it did, probably would impose no sentence harsher than a reprimand.

So Cramer advised Stimson not to "permit the case to linger on as a recurrent public irritation" but, instead, to make "some disposition of the matter other than by a trial." Specifically, the J. A. G. suggested "that a public statement be made by you giving a brief review of the Board's proceedings and pointing out that General Short was guilty of errors of judgment for which he was properly removed from command, and that this constitutes a sufficient disposition of the matter at this time." Stimson made such a public statement on December 1, 1944.

After the end of the war, on August 29, 1945, President Truman released to the press the Army Board report, as well as the report of the Navy Court of Inquiry. Withheld from the Board's report were certain "top secret" sections dealing with "Magic," and added to it was a Stimson memorandum taking exception to some of its conclusions.

Stimson in this memorandum stressed what he called "the clear and explicit warning of the War Department of a possible attack from without." He insisted that "General Short had been fully advised by the War Department that war with Japan was imminent and might commence at any time." True, he conceded, Short's fundamental error—his assumption that the Japanese would not attack Pearl Harbor —"was shared by almost everyone concerned, including his superior officers in the War Department." True, also, the War Department warnings regarding sabotage, and the War

Department's silence in regard to his report of November 27, may have "confirmed him in his conviction that he had chosen the correct form of alert." True enough. "But these matters, although they make his action more understandable, do not serve to exonerate him." [8]

Like most congressional investigators, those who looked into the Pearl Harbor defeat had other motives than a unanimous and passionate desire to find the plain truth. Four members of the joint committee were Republicans, and six were Democrats. Naturally the majority were interested in protecting the reputations of their former chief and his advisers. And most of the minority, with their own partisan ends to serve, wanted to cast as much discredit as they could upon the administration. Hence, though the committee held hearings for more than six months—from December, 1945, to May, 1946—it did not devote itself continuously and wholeheartedly to the real issues.

Some of the Republican members spent much of their time in trying to prove the unprovable, namely, that Roosevelt and Stimson and the rest had desired the Japanese to attack Pearl Harbor, had known before the event just where and when the attack would fall, and had waited for this "first shot" which they had deliberately provoked. The majority, in turning aside to refute such charges as these, could the more easily evade a head-on approach to the actualities of misguided policy and bungled execution. And yet, in spite of themselves, the congressional investigators did produce a mass of evidence bearing upon the responsibility and irresponsibility of the men at the top as well as those on down the line.

Before the committee, General Short had another chance to be heard, though not of course a chance to be tried and

[8] *Report . . . Pearl Harbor Attack*, 266-P-S; *Hearings . . . Pearl Harbor Attack*, pt. 3, p. 1519; pt. 9, pp. 4413, 4426–28, 4447, 4451; pt. 35, pp. 13–19, 151–79; *New York Times*, August 30, 1945.

either condemned or cleared. He protested that the War Department had used him as a scapegoat—that not only himself but also Generals Marshall, Gerow, and Niles and Secretary Stimson had been to blame. The Army Board, he reminded the committee, had come to that conclusion in its original report. Instead of accepting the report, he went on, Stimson and Marshall had decided to send "a selected individual" around to make a new investigation. "They apparently didn't think they could get what they wanted out of the board," he said.

Stimson himself, pleading ill health, declined to appear before the congressional committee. He did consent to submit copies of parts of his diary for the fall of 1941, and he also sent in a long written statement. In it he undertook, among other things, a refutation of the charge that the administration had been practicing diplomacy so secret that neither the public nor the outpost commanders knew what was going on.

"From some of the comments quoted in the public press," he now wrote (March, 1946), "one would get the impression that the imminent threat of war in October and November 1941 was a deep secret, known only to the authorities in Washington who kept it mysteriously to themselves. Nothing could be further from the truth. At least one of our destroyers had been attacked by German war vessels. Aside from the war warnings which were sent to our military and naval commanders in the various theaters of danger, the imminence of war with Japan was a matter of public knowledge and the people were being warned time and again of the danger which was approaching. One need only read the headlines of the newspapers during this period." Here Stimson listed a number of minatory announcements by the government and speeches by public men. "In Honolulu itself the papers were carrying equally sensational headlines. For example, on November 30 appeared the headline 'Japanese May Strike over Weekend.'"

Thus Stimson now was saying that Short should have been forewarned in the fall of 1941 by reading the Honolulu newspapers. Previously he had implied that Short should have ignored what the papers were saying. He had told the Army Board that news of continuing conversations with the Japanese did not justify Short in assuming there had been no final break. We were, he then said, "not running the war on the press."

The fact is, of course, that the papers during those days before Pearl Harbor were full of all kinds of contradictory information. As late as December 5, 1941, Stimson himself had informed the public that the negotiations were still in progress, and until the very day of the attack other official and unofficial commentators gave hints from which any newspaper reader justifiably could draw the conclusion that the crisis might yet pass. In his statement of 1946 Stimson, with the advantage of hindsight, culled the news of 1941 so as to present only those items that had seemed to indicate an early war.

After denying that American policy had been secret, Stimson proceeded to enlarge upon his previous report assessing blame. He led up to this with some observations on two different kinds of military responsibility. "The outpost commander is like a sentinel on duty in the face of the enemy," he said. "He must assume that the enemy will attack at his particular post; and that the enemy will attack at the time and in the way in which it will be most difficult to defeat him. It is not the duty of the outpost commander to speculate or rely on the possibilities of the enemy attacking at some other outpost instead of his own." Quite different is the position of the Commander in Chief and his advisers. Their duties are more difficult and complex, for they must "constantly watch, study, and estimate where the principal or most dangerous attack is most likely to come."

Now, Stimson went on, the outpost commander in Hawaii had been told "without equivocation" in the message of November 27 that war with Japan was threatening and that hostile action by Japan was possible at any moment. And yet he had clustered his planes on the ground so that they could not readily take to the air (no mention of the War Department's alert against sabotage) and he had used his radar reconnaissance only part of the time (no hint of expert Army opinion that at best radar was no substitute for long-range air reconnaissance).

That was not all. "He then sent a reply to Washington which gave no adequate notice of what he had failed to do and which was susceptible of being taken, and was taken, as a general compliance with the main warning from Washington." That is to say, Short was the one who had sent an ambiguous communication. *He* was to blame for misleading the War Department with his report that he was taking antisabotage measures! "My initials show that this message crossed my desk," Stimson said, "and in spite of my keen interest in the situation it certainly gave me no intimation that the alert order against an enemy attack was not being carried out."

Stimson admitted that some of Short's superiors might also be deemed guilty of neglect, but only in the light of "hindsight." "With the aid of 'hindsight' I believe now," said the statement of 1946, "that to a staff officer whose specific duty was to make dead sure that the warning order was being intelligently and thoroughly put into effect, the lack of detail in the reply should have suggested the importance of a follow-up inquiry." Seemingly it was no part of the duty of the War Secretary himself, even though he had given the impetus to the drafting of the "war warning" and personally had revised it. He conceded that the men in the

War Department might have done some things better than they did, but he insisted to the last: "None of these things in my opinion alter in any material degree the responsibility of General Short." [9]

Eventually, on the basis of such evidence as had been made available to it, the joint committee investigating the Pearl Harbor attack produced a total of three reports: that of the majority, signed by the six Democrats and one of the Republicans; that of the minority, signed by two of the Republicans; and a separate dissenting view, signed by the fourth Republican.

In assessing responsibility, the majority first laid down certain rules, among them the following:

"Any doubt as to whether outposts should be given information should always be resolved in favor of supplying the information." "The delegation of authority or the issuance of orders entails the duty of inspection to determine that the official mandate is properly exercised." "Communications must be characterized by clarity, forthrightness, and appropriateness." "No considerations should be permitted as excuse for failure to perform a fundamental task."

Then the majority gave its general conclusions, including these:

"Perhaps the most signal shortcoming of administration, both at Washington and in Hawaii, was the failure to follow up orders and instructions to insure that they were carried out." "It would seem that War and Navy Department officials both in Washington and Hawaii were so obsessed by an executive complex that they could not besmirch their dignities by 'stooping' to determine what was going on, or more especially what was not going on, in their organizations." "The record tends to indicate that appraisal of likely enemy movements was divided into *probabilities* and *pos-*

[9] *Hearings . . . Pearl Harbor Attack*, pt. 11, pp. 5416–18, 5429–31; *New York Times*, December 6, 1941; January 27, 1946.

sibilities. Everyone has admitted that the attack on Pearl Harbor was regarded as at least a possibility. It was felt, however, that a Japanese movement toward the south was a probability. The over-all result was to look for the probable move and to take little or no effective precautions to guard against the possible action."

From the preliminary observations and the general conclusions of the majority, it would seem that the Secretary of War should have been listed among the specific individuals in some degree responsible for what had happened. But he was not.

Quite different were the conclusions of the Republican minority. Whatever errors of judgment the commanders at Hawaii may have committed—ran the minority report—those men were links in a chain of command which dangled down from Washington. The men in Washington had appointed the men in Hawaii and should have had a care for their competence.

But that was not all, according to the minority report. "The defense of Hawaii rested upon two sets of interdependent responsibilities: (*1*) The responsibility in Washington in respect of its intimate knowledge of diplomatic negotiations, widespread intelligence information, direction of affairs, and constitutional duty to plan the defense of the United States; (*2*) the responsibility cast upon the commanders in the field . . . to do those things appropriate to the defense of the fleet and the outpost. Washington authorities failed in (*1*); and the commanding officers at Hawaii failed in (*2*)." Those responsible in the first category were Roosevelt, Stimson, Knox, Marshall, Stark, and Gerow; in the second category, Short and Kimmel; and in a special third category, since he was outside of the command chain, Hull.

In passing, the minority took note of Stimson's plea of "hindsight." "For every failure to exercise prudence and foresight with reference to knowledge in his possession he must bear a corresponding burden of responsibility for the consequences that flow from that failure," the minority declared. "By virtue of his office he is presumed to have special competence and knowledge; to act upon his special knowledge, and to be informed and alert in the discharge of his duties in the situation before him. The introduction of hindsight in extenuation of responsibility is, therefore, irrelevant to the determination of responsibility for the catastrophe at Pearl Harbor."

The dissenting Republican expressed "additional views" which were closer to the minority than to the majority report. "What was done in Washington as well as what was done in Hawaii was admittedly done in the light of the universal military belief that Hawaii was not in danger from an initial attack by Japan," he pointed out. So "the mistake lies on the Washington doorstep just as much as it does on that of Hawaii."

The majority report Stimson viewed as "both fair and intelligent." And why not? It commended him, along with the President and other high officials, for having done his duty with "distinction, ability," and of all things "foresight." The minority report, which blamed him along with Short, he resented as a concoction of "twisted and malicious views." [10]

To an impartial observer—if such there be—it might perhaps seem that Stimson's gross miscalculation of the danger to the United States before Pearl Harbor was excusable enough. He had been concentrating on his own "first shot" —the aerial blow he was going to launch from the Philippines against the southward moving Japanese ships. He had been impressed by the recent demonstration of air against

[10] *Report . . . Pearl Harbor Attack*, vii–viii, 251 ff., 266 ff., 457 ff., 505, 524, 540, 557–58, 571–73; Henry L. Stimson and McGeorge Bundy, *On Active Service in Peace and War* (New York, 1948), 393.

naval power given by the British against the Italians at Taranto. He overlooked the possibility that the Japanese might also have taken a lesson from Taranto—a lesson to be applied at Pearl Harbor. He was like a chess player who becomes so preoccupied with his own next move that he overlooks what his opponent may be up to. His error was grave, but understandable.

What was hard to understand, or to reconcile with his reputation for honor and integrity, was his refusal to own up to a share of responsibility, his insistence on passing the buck to a subordinate in the field.

9 *Military Necessity*

Afterwards, Henry L. Stimson was well satisfied with his handling of Army affairs during the war. Though he had aroused some criticism, he could and did dismiss it as merely the ranting of the misguided and misinformed. His critics in Congress, he believed, had "looked at every wartime act through the distorted lens of rancorous mistrust." His critics within the administration had been "self-righteous ideologists"— "New Deal cherubs"—who simply "would not understand that the natural enemy was in Germany and Japan, not in Wall Street or among the brass hats."

As for himself, he had been completely dedicated to "the proposition that the only way to fight a war is to fight it with your whole and undiluted strength." He had proceeded with "a complete lack of apprehension lest war destroy any of the lasting values of American democracy." The "militarism," about which a few Americans had professed concern, was to him nothing but a "bogy." [1]

It was, ostensibly, a great crusade. It was a war for freedom and human rights, a war to overthrow the tyrants in other lands who damned a man because of race or creed and threw him into a concentration camp. And one of the war measures was the forcible uprooting and "relocation" (within stockades) of thousands of American citizens who were guiltless of any crime—unless it was the crime of having Japanese ancestors.

[1] Henry L. Stimson and McGeorge Bundy, *On Active Service in Peace and War* (New York, 1948), 470–73.

True, this was a response to cries of imminent danger on the West Coast, but the "yellow peril" in that part of the country had been invented long before 1941. It had been preached by self-interested groups in California, Oregon, and Washington for more than a generation. To truck farmers who faced a frugal and efficient competitor, anti-Japanese agitation was good economics. To hereditary patriots who despised the Japanese as an inferior and unassimilable race, it was good Americanism. To office-seekers who needed a sure-fire popular issue, it was good politics.

The agitation led to a series of discriminatory measures against the alien and the native-born Japanese in California and the other Pacific states. It embarrassed the Federal Government in respect to relations with Japan and culminated in the Japanese Exclusion Act of 1924. And that act, by strengthening the anti-American element in Japan, contributed to the creation of the diplomatic impasse out of which ultimately came the Pearl Harbor attack.

Then Pearl Harbor suddenly gave the anti-Japanese groups an opportunity to achieve an aim they had cherished all along. At last they could, perhaps, get rid of the Japanese-Americans entirely! They seized their chance.

Various agricultural, labor, and business organizations chimed in with the American Legion and the Native Sons and Daughters of the Golden West to demand a mass evacuation from the Pacific Coast. They argued that the Japanese had sabotaged the defenses of Hawaii and were plotting to do the same in California. The wily "Japs"—according to this propaganda—deliberately had settled close to strategic points so as to be ready for a concerted and effective uprising. It was admitted that none of these people, so far, had sabotaged anything. In the reasoning of the evacuationists, however, this lack of sabotage only proved the existence of the nefarious plot: the "Japs" were all lying low and awaiting a secret signal to rise and strike at the moment when their blood brothers from Japan would attempt to land.

Little distinction was made between American-born citizens and Japanese-born aliens, or between residents as a whole and the forces of the enemy. They were all viewed as members of the same treacherous and barbarous race, and no matter how cagily some of them might pretend to be Americanized, the taint was in their blood. Besides, the Japanese Americans were a nuisance to good, white Americans engaging in the vegetable and fruit business. As the secretary of the Grower-Shipper Vegetable Association frankly admitted, members of this organization had "selfish reasons" for wanting to see all Japanese removed, permanently, from California.

In the beginning, the anti-Japanese propagandists ran against the opposition of churchmen, social workers, and educators who insisted upon fair treatment for the despised and denounced minority. But these advocates of human rights faced several disadvantages. They could not match the influence of politicians, patrioteers, and big businessmen. They found it hard to meet the argument that the public safety must not be trifled with. So they had to qualify their stand against mass evacuation. They could only say that this must not be done—unless it was "required by the military."

The military held the key. What they said, went. The military man on the scene, the commanding officer of the Fourth Army and the Western Defense Command, was Lieutenant-General John L. De Witt, and he had not the slightest doubt as to the merits of the debate. The advocates of quick and stern action, finding a receptive listener in De Witt, focused much of their pressure upon him. And he responded by urging the War Department to get tough.

But the War Department, in the beginning, did not have

a completely free hand. The Justice Department was responsible for precautions against alien enemies and suspicious persons in general. For more than a year before December 7, 1941, a special defense unit under the Attorney General had been carrying on undercover work in preparation for just such a problem as that which suddenly arose on the West Coast, and when war came, the Justice Department was ready. Its policy was to deal with every case individually and to distinguish between alien enemies and citizens—the former if dangerous to be arrested, the latter if dangerous to be closely watched. Right after Pearl Harbor the F. B. I. did nab a number of Japanese aliens, but Attorney-General Francis Biddle announced: "The great majority of our alien population will continue to be loyal to our democratic principles if we . . . permit them to be."

General De Witt was not satisfied with what the F. B. I. was doing. From the outset he wanted to go much farther, and as time passed he increased his demands. Descend on "Jap" homes in "mass raids" to look for spies and contraband. Lay out extensive "restricted areas" and keep the "Japs" away from them. Make the entire West Coast a restricted zone, and ship the "Japs" out of it. Such were the recommendations that De Witt sent, one after another, to the War Department.[2]

The decision was up to the Secretary of War: he could modify or veto De Witt's proposals, or he could endorse them and urge the President and the Congress to put them into effect.

The responsibility of Secretary Stimson was of a different order from that of General De Witt. It was the duty of the military commander to provide, at whatever cost, for the security of the area under his immediate command. He had to

[2] Morton Grodzins, *Americans Betrayed: Politics and the Japanese Evacuation* (Chicago, 1949), 1–91, 231–36, and *passim*.

focus his attention there, listen to rumors, and assume the worst. Otherwise, he ran the risk of sharing the fate of General Short, who was being publicly censured for alleged dereliction of duty at Pearl Harbor. (The public excitement in California increased markedly after the publication of the Roberts Report on January 25, 1942.) But the Secretary of War was in a position to take a more comprehensive and more critical view than the general in the field. In the light of his presumed knowledge of the military and political scene as a whole, Stimson might have been expected to behave somewhat more judiciously than De Witt in relating the Japanese-American question to the facts of war and politics.

Stimson, however, did nothing during that winter of 1941–42 to allay the growing panic on the West Coast—to lessen the fears of an attack from without and sabotage from within.

During the weeks after Pearl Harbor military intelligence as well as civilian gossip gave rise to such stories as the sighting of a Japanese force off San Francisco, then its heading for Los Angeles, and the construction of secret airfields in Lower California. "The wild, farcical and fantastic stuff that G-2 Fourth Army pushes out!" exclaimed Vinegar Joe Stilwell in Los Angeles on December 19.

Stimson seemed to share Stilwell's skepticism when, on February 8, he called the vinegary general into his office to ask him about the "Jap situation on the coast," as Stilwell put it. Stilwell told about the wild rumors in Los Angeles. According to him, "Henry let it drop that the Fourth Army was always exaggerating things." But Stimson dropped no such hint to the California public.

Nor did he evince any doubts when, a few weeks later, antiaircraft batteries fired nearly fifteen hundred rounds at a phantom air force during a Los Angeles air-raid alarm. In Washington Secretary Knox dismissed the alarm as false.

But not Secretary Stimson. He told reporters that unidentified airplanes had appeared over Los Angeles, and he read a telegram which said that these planes might have been "some from commercial sources operated by enemy agents for the purpose of spreading alarm, disclosing positions of antiaircraft positions or effectiveness of blackouts." A couple of weeks after that, however, he had to confess to newsmen that there was nothing to this story.

Whatever the possible danger from Japan, by air or by sea, the supposed danger from resident Japanese-Americans, as potential saboteurs, was an entirely different matter. The widespread fear of concerted sabotage was based upon the popular belief that the same thing had already happened in Hawaii. Secretary Knox reinforced this belief on his return from inspecting the disaster scene, when he indicated to newspaper reporters that a Japanese fifth column had been active there. *The fact was that there had been no sabotage at Pearl Harbor.*

Stimson knew there had been none. He eventually admitted (March 19, 1942) to the Tolan committee investigating the Japanese-American situation: "The War Department has received no information of sabotage committed by Japanese during the attack on Pearl Harbor." In the meantime the Tolan hearings in California had been giving wide publicity to false reports of such sabotage. But neither Knox nor Stimson had raised a finger to correct these reports and thereby temper public opinion on the Coast. "Why had the Secretaries done nothing to silence these rumors before?" one student of the subject (Bradford Smith) questioned afterward. "Were they willing to let the Japanese take the heat off them for what had happened in Hawaii?" [3]

[3] Theodore H. White, ed., *The Stilwell Papers* (New York, 1948), 3–10, 35; *New York Times*, February 26, March 6, 1942; Robert E. Sherwood, *Roosevelt and Hopkins: An Intimate History* (New York, 1948), 504–505; U. S. Congress, *Fourth Interim Report of the Select Committee Investigating National Defense Migration* [Tolan Committee] (Washington,

While doing nothing to correct the misinformation or calm the fears of the California public, Stimson accepted and approved the increasingly drastic proposals of General De Witt which were inspired by the mixture of racialism, false rumor, and panic. Stimson urged these plans upon the Justice Department. Up to February 9, 1942, Attorney-General Biddle gave in at every point and saw that the program was carried out.

Then Biddle drew the line. Stimson was asking for the removal of Japanese-Americans from zones including most of the western half of Oregon and Washington and the whole Los Angeles vicinity. "The Department of Justice is not physically equipped to carry out any mass evacuations," Biddle protested to Stimson. "It would mean that only the War Department has the equipment and personnel to manage the task." Anyhow, Biddle said, De Witt had not shown any need for such an extreme measure: "No reasons were given for this mass evacuation." So Biddle refused to act, and the War and Justice Departments clashed head on.

While the two Departments remained at loggerheads, anti-Japanese groups in California concentrated the greatest pressure of their whole campaign on General De Witt. And the general broadened his program again. On February 14 he recommended to the War Department that the Secretary get from the President authority "to designate military areas in the combat zone of the Western Theater of Operations (if necessary to include the entire combat zone), from which, in his discretion, he may exclude all Japanese, all alien enemies, and all other persons suspected." Stimson adopted this recommendation and prepared for a showdown with Biddle.

But Biddle yielded without a fight. He was tiring of the

1942), 48; Bradford Smith, *Americans from Japan* (Philadelphia, 1948), 265, 268; Carey McWilliams, *Prejudice: Japanese-Americans: Symbol of Racial Intolerance* (Boston, 1944), 107-10.

abuse which rabid columnists—including Henry Mc-Lemore, Westbrook Pegler, and even Walter Lippmann—were heaping on him. He was disinclined to hold out against the Army on an issue which the Army defined as one of national defense. And so, though not himself convinced that mass evacuation was necessary, he met with Stimson in the latter's office on February 18, 1942, and surrendered Justice to War. The two men put the finishing touches on a Presidential proclamation, directing the Secretary of War to prescribe areas and exclude persons therefrom, and both of them signed it.

Ostensibly the decision to relocate the Japanese-Americans was a "military" one, because it had been recommended by a military officer. But General De Witt later demonstrated, in his final report on the subject, that he had not based his reasoning on any special military knowledge or insight. Indeed, his brief for mass evacuation followed point by point the argument of the various civilian pressure groups. And his basic assumption was the same: a "Jap" was a "Jap," whether he happened to be an American citizen or not, and his racial characteristics made him peculiarly dangerous. "The Japanese race is an enemy race," De Witt averred, "and while many second and third generation Japanese born on United States soil, possessed of United States citizenship, have become 'Americanized,' the racial strains are undiluted."

Stimson did not question this racialist view. It seemed to convince him that mass evacuation was a matter of "military necessity," and he sent his proclamation to the President, and the President issued it, on those grounds. Then, fearing for the constitutionality of the President's order, Stimson submitted to Congress the draft of a bill to legalize the evacuation and provide criminal penalties to enforce it. With the bill he included a letter emphasizing his contention that military requirements made it absolutely necessary for Congress to act, and to act without delay.

Up to this time Congress as a whole had shown little interest in the excitement on the West Coast. Senators and representatives from the Pacific states, of course, had said a good deal about the "Jap" menace, but they had aroused almost no response except among a few Southerners, such as Senator Tom Stewart of Tennessee and Representatives Martin Dies of Texas and John E. Rankin of Mississippi. Rankin coupled the Japanese with the Negroes as an inferior race and outspokenly demanded "concentration camps" for Japanese-Americans. He denounced his critics as persons who would "mongrelize America and drag her people down to the level of the Japanese." For all that Rankin could say or do, however, the question remained a regional one, resounding in the Far West and echoing rather lightly in the South.

Stimson turned it into a national issue with his appeal to Congress. And he made it an issue of military mystery such as few civilians either in or out of Congress felt competent to discuss. In sponsoring the War Department's bill, the chairmen of the House and Senate Military Affairs Committees presented only one argument in favor of it: the military authorities desired it and considered it essential. No congressman or senator so much as suggested looking into the background and the reasonableness of the War Department's request. There would hardly have been time for that: Stimson himself had said that Congress should act with the utmost speed. Only one member of either house spoke out in direct opposition to the bill. "I think this is probably the 'sloppiest' criminal law I have ever read or seen anywhere," said Senator Robert A. Taft. "I certainly think the Senate should not pass it." But the Senate did pass it, and so did the House.

Having secured the approval of Congress, the Army proceeded to herd to "relocation centers" in the interior all the people of Japanese birth or ancestry on the West Coast— old and young, able and infirm, male and female, alien and citizen.

The majority were citizens, Americans. They were being deprived of their liberty, though not because even one of them had been convicted of any crime. The American Civil Liberties Union called their case "the worst single wholesale violation of civil liberties of American citizens in our history." It set a precedent for "a policy of mass incarceration under military auspices," declared the most thorough student of the subject, Morton Grodzins. "This is the most important result of the process by which the evacuation decision was made. That process betrayed all Americans." [4]

In the process by which the decision was made, Stimson as Secretary of War played a crucial part. The demand for evacuation had arisen in the first place from the long-standing desire of certain regional pressure groups to get rid of a minority for reasons of economic competition and racial prejudice. The demand was increased because of falsely grounded fears of sabotage at a time of anticipated enemy attack. Then, by the magic words "military necessity," Stimson transmuted the local agitation into a transcendent national cause. A wholesale violation of civil liberties was made acceptable to most of the American people, to the President, to Congress, and to that ultimate guardian of constitutional rights, the Supreme Court.

Fred Korematsu, born in California, had never been outside of the United States. He had never acknowledged allegiance to any country except his own. When war came he was eager to serve against Japan or any other enemy, and he

[4] Grodzins, *Americans Betrayed*, 129–79, 240–302, 325–48, 368–74. The present treatment of the "relocation" relies very heavily on Grodzins' excellent study. Grodzins is not concerned with pointing up the specific responsibility of Stimson, but that responsibility is implicit in the book, especially in its discussion (as on pp. 206–207) of "military necessity."

said so. Having recently come of voting age, he was a registered voter. In short, he was a good American, undistinguishable from millions of other young men except for the cast of his features.

Among his neighbors in San Leandro he was accepted as one of them. He had many friends not of Japanese ancestry —one girl in particular. He did not want to leave her, and when the general exodus began, he stayed home. He was arrested.

As an American schoolboy, Fred had heard of the Constitution with its bill of rights. One item, the Fifth Amendment, provided that no person should be "deprived of life, liberty, or property, without due process of law." And the Thirteenth Amendment declared: "Neither slavery nor involuntary servitude, except as punishment for crime whereof the party shall have been duly convicted, shall exist within the United States, or any place subject to their jurisdiction."

Fred sued for his freedom. His attorneys argued that he was being deprived of rights guaranteed him by the American Constitution. His loyalty to the United States, which no one denied, was not an issue. Eventually his case reached the Supreme Court, and the high judges gave their decision a week before Christmas, 1944.

The majority of the Court held that, under the circumstances, the forced migration and confinement of thousands of American citizens, without trial, was constitutional enough. Said Chief Justice Stone: "Where . . . conditions call for the exercise of judgment and discretion for the choice of means by those branches of the Government on which the Constitution has placed the responsibility of war-making, it is not for any court to sit in review of the wisdom of their action or substitute its judgment for theirs." And Justice Douglas agreed: "We cannot sit in judgment on the military requirements of that hour."

Three of the judges dissented: Roberts, Jackson, and

Murphy. Justice Jackson observed that the Court might "as well say that any military order will be Constitutional and have done with it." Justice Murphy said a good deal more.

"There was no adequate proof that the Federal Bureau of Investigation and the military and naval intelligence services did not have the espionage and sabotage situation well in hand," Murphy pointed out. "Nor is there any denial of the fact that not one person of Japanese ancestry was accused or convicted of espionage or sabotage after Pearl Harbor while they were still free, a fact which is some evidence of the loyalty of the vast majority of these individuals and of the effectiveness of the established methods of combatting these evils. It seems incredible that under these circumstances it would have been impossible to hold loyalty hearings for the mere 112,000 persons involved—or at least for the 70,000 American citizens—especially when a large part of this number represented children and elderly men and women."

Justification for exclusion was sought, Murphy said further, "mainly upon questionable racial and sociological grounds not ordinarily within the realm of expert military judgment, supplemented by certain semi-military conclusions drawn from . . . use of circumstantial evidence."

The whole procedure, Murphy concluded, fell into "the ugly abyss of racism" and bore a "melancholy resemblance" to the Nazi treatment of the Jews in Germany.[5]

The contest between the War and Justice Departments on the relocation issue was one of several battles that Stimson fought, and won, against civilian agencies on the home front. He also won the battle for control of news about the war. The question was this: should the military themselves de-

[5] New York Times, December 19, 1944; Nanette Dembitz, "Racial Discrimination and the Military Judgment," in the Columbia Law Review, March, 1945, pp. 175–239; Grodzins, Americans Betrayed, 351–58.

cide what the people might be told, or should a separate and strictly civilian agency make the decisions? President Roosevelt seemed to favor such a civilian authority when, on June 12, 1942, he set up the Office of War Information and put Elmer Davis, a thoroughly seasoned and levelheaded newspaperman, at the head of it. Washington reporters assumed, at the start, that the President had given Davis and the O. W. I. full power over the information services of the Army and the Navy. But the Secretary of War assumed no such thing.

A few days after Davis's appointment, Stimson held a press conference. The reporters, aware that Davis had recently seen Stimson, wanted to know whether the O. W. I. was going to handle the Army's news releases. Stimson looked a little shocked. "Is Mr. Davis an educated military officer?" he asked, heavily. Of course, Mr. Davis was not, but in the opinion of some of the newsmen present, that was beside the point. One of them, Bruce Catton, later observed that, "however great Davis's ignorance of military matters might be," it could not compare with the "arrogant ignorance of civilian emotions, morale, and ideals which sat entrenched under the brass hats" in the Pentagon. "Someone with at least a faint understanding of such matters should have had something to say about the way in which the people were told about the fighting."

A showdown between the O. W. I. and the War Department came with the trial of the eight Nazi saboteurs who had been captured after landing on the Atlantic coast in the spring of 1942. Davis sent a man to cover the trial, but the Army officers would not let the man in. The most that General McCoy would concede to the O. W. I. was the privilege of publishing the Army's daily communiques, which told practically nothing except that there was a trial going on. When Davis went directly to the White House, Roosevelt sustained the Army at every point. Stimson was thereafter to have his own way with military censorship.

This outcome was, in Bruce Catton's belief, only one of several signs that, "in place of the all-out people's war we thought we were fighting," it was in fact to be "a purely military war." Neither Davis nor anyone else "could keep the War Department from throwing its weight around and making far-reaching decisions in purely non-military fields, because that was inherent in the kind of war we were fighting." The kind of war we were fighting—as Stimson had defined it.[6]

The Army had to have supplies. Stimson therefore assumed that he and his Assistant Secretary, Robert P. Patterson, in charge of procurement, ought to decide what war materials should be produced, and how much. But if they had the final say about production for war, they would also have the last word about production for civilian needs. So, to arbitrate between military and civilian demands, President Roosevelt in 1942 set up the War Production Board (successor of earlier "defense" mobilization agencies) and put at the head of it an executive of Sears, Roebuck and Company—Donald M. Nelson.

Nelson did not propose to allow the continued manufacture of luxury goods, such as radios, phonographs, and the like. He did not even intend to allow the production of essential civilian goods to proceed at full blast. He was willing to cut down on such items, at least temporarily, so as to make certain that the output of munitions would be adequate. But he disagreed with Stimson about what was adequate for the Army and what was essential for civilian life.

Stimson tried to stop the manufacture of such things as farm and coal-mining machinery and repair parts, railroad equipment, and synthetic rubber for civilian use. He also

[6] Bruce Catton, The War Lords of Washington (New York, 1948), 186, 190–91.

tried to prevent what he considered the waste of newsprint in the comic sections of Sunday newspapers.

Nelson, however, believed that the Army's demands, if heeded, might not only damage the war production effort itself but also "have a serious effect on our democratic institutions." He could not understand, for example "how we could hope to turn out a maximum volume of munitions unless we obtained enough coal to power the munitions-making plants," and he did not see how we could get the coal unless we had machinery for the mines. He feared that if the Army could abolish the funny papers, it would be well on the way toward controlling the press. "If it can stop the printing of comic strips it can—and inevitably *will*—forbid the publication of cartoons and other material, perhaps, ultimately, of certain classes of editorial matter which, in its opinion, represents a waste of newsprint."

So Nelson soon found himself in the position, not of arbiter between military and civilian demands, as originally intended, but of champion of the civilian economy. He was no match for his antagonists in the War Department. For him—and the civilian economy—it was a losing struggle from the start.

"Officials in high places," according to Nelson, gave out stories that "the production program was in a mess." Hints and rumors spread to the effect that the war on the battle-fronts might be lost—all because of the obstructionism of W. P. B. After a few months of this sort of thing, the President superimposed a new agency (which was to become the Office of War Mobilization, headed by James F. Byrnes) upon the Nelson board, thus drastically reducing his authority.

Not satisfied with that, Stimson determined to have him fired, in February, 1943, but Nelson outmaneuvered him and hung on to his job, such as it was. The internecine conflict went on, more bitterly than ever.

It reached a climax in the summer of 1944, after allied troops had broken into Hitler's *Festung Europa*, and the end of the European war seemed almost in sight. Already, a year earlier, Nelson had written to the President: "There is real need at this time to create confidence that the government is taking vigorous measures to assure an orderly and equitable reconversion of the economy to a peacetime footing, as and when military developments permit." In February, 1944, reporting to Byrnes as head of O. W. M., Bernard Baruch agreed with Nelson in principle: "Just as we prepare for war in time of peace, so we should prepare for peace in time of war." In March the Truman committee of the Senate, investigating war production, concluded that "plans for reconversion should be started immediately." Otherwise, there was danger of a postwar inflationary boom.

The War Department, however, launched a high-powered propaganda campaign against reconversion. The nation faced a "production crisis." War workers by the tens of thousands were leaving their jobs. Pampered stay-at-homes were betraying the fighting men at the front. The W. P. B. was demanding civilian luxuries and frills while the soldiers lacked adequate supplies of guns and ammunition. Such was the story, but the facts were quite different, according to Nelson. There was no production lag, except in a few isolated instances, and those were due to the earlier miscalculations of the Army itself. There was no shortage of munitions on the battlefields, except where transportation difficulties prevented their delivery, and that was a matter of logistics, not production.

The "ballyhoo campaign put on by the military people," as Nelson called it, did not solve any problems of production. But it did divert popular attention away from the mistakes of the War Department. It also stirred up bad feelings on the part of soldiers against their fellow citizens who were not in uniform. And it helped the Army defeat all plans for an early and gradual reconversion. President Roosevelt might have intervened to prevent defeat, but he did not do so. Men of lesser prestige and power hesitated to buck the Army and be accused of interfering with the war effort. "When it became apparent that a reconversion plan could be put into effect only by winning a knock-down fight with the military," Bruce Catton later explained, "most of the men who should have been making the fight discovered that they did not want to fight—not on that side, anyway."

Then, in December, 1944, came news of the Allied setback in the Battle of the Bulge. This news was irrelevant to the basic issue of military or civilian control of the economy, and yet it seemed to clinch the Army's case against reconversion. The Army made the most of it.

After the war we had inflation and skyrocketing prices, as the reconversionists had predicted. And the basic issue still remained. "The question of military control will confront us not only in war but in peace," Nelson said in 1946. "The lesson taught by these recent war years is clear: our whole economic and social system will be in peril if it is controlled by military men." [7]

[7] Donald M. Nelson, *Arsenal of Democracy: The Story of American War Production* (New York, 1946), 358-60, 388-94, 402-409; Catton, *War Lords of Washington*, 201-10, 240, 245-48, 291-92. Herman M. Somers, *Presidential Agency: OMWR, The Office of War Mobilization and Reconversion* (Cambridge, 1950), 28-29, 31, is more sympathetic with the military point of view and argues that Nelson's failures were due largely to his own faulty tactics. Eliot Janeway, *The Struggle for Survival: A Chronicle of Economic Mobilization in World War II* (New Haven, 1951), 354 ff., also places much of the blame on Nelson. But Janeway points out (pp. 51-52) another reason for Nelson's failure: "Ordinarily, Roosevelt's ranking appointees in any administrative area were rivals—witness Woodring and Johnson [in the War Department to 1940], Hull and Welles in the State Department, Hopkins and Ickes in the public works field. . . . Woodring and Johnson balanced the apparatus by working against one another; Stimson and Patterson upset it by working together. The civilian agencies were entrusted to the Assistant Secretary because he was counted upon to fight for his—and their—independence of the Secretary. But what started out as a scheme for balancing civilian against military power ended by producing a concentration of military power. Con-

Slave labor manned war plants in Nazi Germany and Soviet Russia, and conscript labor was available for war factories in Great Britain and the British dominions. Yet there was no labor draft in the United States.

This troubled Stimson, and he determined to do something about it. His efforts to get a "national service act" led to a controversy which coincided with that over reconversion and was closely related to it. In his attempt to assert complete Army control over civilian as well as military manpower, however, Stimson found the going much rougher than in his contest with Nelson and the W. P. B. Nelson and his board stood firm against labor conscription. So did Paul V. McNutt and the War Manpower Commission. So did organized labor and organized business. And President Roosevelt gave Stimson only halfhearted support.

Though eager for a labor draft from the outset, Stimson did not appeal directly to the President until December, 1943, when the nation's railroad workers were threatening to strike. Then Roosevelt, in his annual message to Congress in January, 1944, recommended a draft act. His own administration forces in Congress did not respond, but a couple of Republicans did, with the Austin-Wadsworth bill. This would have made liable to conscription for war work all males from the ages of eighteen to sixty-five and all females from eighteen to fifty. The Senate Military Affairs Committee opened hearings on the bill, and Stimson was the first and most important witness to testify in favor of it.

He argued that such a civilian draft was but the logical complement of a military draft: "The nation has no less right to require a man to make weapons than it has to require another man to fight with those weapons." And the measure was desperately needed, Stimson told the senators. He spoke darkly of "industrial unrest" and "irresponsibility"

---

fronted by the combination of the Secretary and the Assistant Secretary, the civilian agencies lost control of the home front to the military. . . ."

on the home front, which he said the men in uniform resented. "If it continues, it will surely affect the morale of the Army," he warned. "It is likely to prolong the war and endanger our ultimate success." The purpose of the bill, he explained, was to "get at this basic evil which produces the irresponsibility out of which stem strikes." With increasing gravity and emphasis he declared: "I say we have a situation of anarchy, and this is a step to cure that situation of anarchy and to restore law and order."

Stimson was speaking at a moment when most production goals were being reached and passed, when cutbacks were being ordered in various lines of war goods, when unemployment was rising in many parts of the country. Though shortages of certain kinds of skilled labor did exist, there was no general manpower shortage at all. The American people had performed miracles of production. Yet, as Bruce Catton has reported, "they were being told, on the highest authority, in a shrill voice that cracked with emotion, that they were in a state of anarchy, that their selfish irresponsibility was prolonging the war and endangering victory itself, and that the sternest of measures was needed to restore law and order." The labor draft—Stimson himself was saying as much—was intended not necessarily to make the people work as the Army wanted them to. This was, as Catton has put it, "psychological warfare directed at the American people themselves." [8]

The Washington commentator, I. F. Stone, writing in the *Nation*, agreed with Stimson that the government could as rightfully compel citizens to work as to fight. But Stone thought the real question was "*how the job can best be done*," and he thought the Secretary did not have the best answer. He said: "The men in charge of man-power—and the real authority has rested and will continue to rest with

[8] *On Active Service*, 481; *New York Times*, March 3, 10, 1942; Catton, *War Lords of Washington*, 211-25.

the War Department—have never shown the patience, the knowledge, or the organizing ability to work out an orderly and sensible program of total manpower mobilization, military and civilian." He charged, citing Baruch, that the War Department was to blame for labor hoarding by many industries—which gave the appearance of a labor shortage. He concluded that Stimson's bill, if enacted, would only "embitter labor by adding compulsion to confusion."

Union leaders agreed even less with Stimson. They pointed out a fundamental difference between drafting workers and drafting soldiers. The latter served only the government and people of the United States. The former, though they performed a public service in the war plants, also served a private employer who was in business for a profit. Therefore a so-called national service act would actually compel one man to labor for the benefit of another. It was, then, as labor spokesmen unanimously called it, something of a "slave labor" scheme. And on this point many spokesmen for business agreed. "Convert moral obligation into compulsion, take away the spontaneity of will," declared the Chicago *Journal of Commerce*, for example, "and you have a slave people—or a rebellious people!"

Labor's Monthly Survey, an A. F. L. publication, met Stimson on his own ground. It first disposed of the illusory manpower shortage and the exaggerated strike record. "Why then has this National Service Act been urged?" it finally asked. "The real reason has not been given us. If it was to impress the boys at the front, we can only say that the way to impress them is to tell them the truth about American labor's patriotic effort, sacrifice and achievement."

The Truman committee of the Senate came out strongly against a national service law. The committee found that the major battle of war production had already been won, largely through the "outstanding performance" of American labor. It condemned Stimson's plan as drastic yet unwieldy and ineffective as an antistrike measure. It felt that not only labor but also government and management must share responsibility for strikes that had occurred. Instead of adopting the draft, the committee concluded, the government should adopt a clear and consistent labor policy, to be administered by a single civilian agency with real powers.

None of these arguments made the slightest impression upon Stimson himself, who remained as sure as always that he was entirely right and his critics entirely wrong. He called in representatives of leading businesses and made a confidential appeal to them, but they were unmoved. Still he kept stubbornly at his campaign. In February, 1945, he appeared again before the Senate Military Affairs Committee, which was then considering the May-Bailey bill for limited national service. The committee members resented the fact that he had given a radio speech denouncing them for delaying the bill. They, in turn, denounced him for trying to "dictate" their legislation, giving soldiers and their families a misleading idea of what the country had produced under the voluntary system, and making statements which would not help the bill either in committee or in Congress.[9]

"Military necessity," as Stimson saw it, demanded drastic and unprecedented steps to secure the fullest and most efficient use of manpower. Yet he did not use the man and woman power of loyal Japanese-Americans quite as early and as extensively as he might have done. Yielding to pleas from their friends, he announced in January, 1943, that the Army would accept volunteers for a special combat team. Some of the Nisei felt that they should be distributed

9 I. F. Stone, "Some Facts for Mr. Stimson," in the *Nation*, 158: 123–24 (January 29, 1944); *Labor's Monthly Survey*, vol. 5, nos. 2, 4 (February, April, 1944); *United Automobile Worker*, Detroit, February 1, 1944; *Detroit Labor News*, March 10, 1944; *Chicago Journal of Commerce*, February 18, 1944; *New York Times*, April 23, December 7, 1944; February 7, 20, 1945; *On Active Service*, 481–88.

throughout the ranks, like men of any other ancestry, and some even feared that segregation was a plot to kill them off. Nevertheless, the Nisei volunteered eagerly for service to their country, and they performed valiantly on the field of battle.[10]

[10] Smith, *Americans from Japan*, 187, 306.

10 The Fateful Lightning

Imagine a city dump with its smells of wet ashes and rotting things, but one so large it extends almost as far as the eye can see. That was the ruins of Hiroshima, nearly half a year after an atom bomb had scorched and blasted it, killing seventy or eighty thousand people and burning and maiming many thousands more. That was Hiroshima as it appeared to Alexander Leighton, research leader of a team which the United States Strategic Bombing Survey sent to Japan after the war to study the feelings and attitudes of the survivors.

A widow, whose husband had died in the blast, told Leighton's team: "I only wonder why they didn't let the people know of this bomb and give us a chance before bombing us to give up."

"It was cruel," a businessman said, "to drop the bomb where ordinary people were living. I don't see why they didn't drop it in some army camp or something."

One woman asked: "If there is such a thing as ghosts, why don't they haunt the Americans?"

"Perhaps they do," Leighton reflected.[1]

Soon after we entered the war, a Yale professor, Nicholas J. Spykman, undertook to explain what we were fighting for, or what we ought to be fighting for. "If the foreign policy of a state is to be practical," the professor

[1] Alexander H. Leighton, *Human Relations in a Changing World: Observations on the Use of the Social Sciences* (New York, 1949), 18, 22, 33–35.

wrote, "it should be designed not in terms of some dream world but in terms of the realities of international relations, in terms of power politics." According to him, the continuing objectives of U. S. policy should be, in North and South America, predominance, and in Europe and Asia, a balance of power. We found ourselves at war because the balance on the opposite shores of both the Atlantic and the Pacific had been upset. So our war aim should be to restore the balance.

We must not annihilate either Germany or Japan, lest we leave Europe or the Far East open to domination by Russia. As for Europe: "A Russian state from the Urals to the North Sea can be no great improvement over a German state from the North Sea to the Urals." The same reasoning applied to the Far East: "The danger of another Japanese conquest of Asia must be removed, but this does not inevitably mean the elimination of the military strength of Japan and the surrender of the Western Pacific to China or Russia." Japan, as an insular power off the Asian continent, should be treated much like England, occupying a comparable position with relation to Europe. "It is illogical to insist that Japan accept a Chinese empire from Vladivostok to Canton and at the same time to support Great Britain in her wars for the preservation of buffer states across the North Sea." So argued Professor Spykman in 1942.[2]

But President Roosevelt proclaimed a rather different war aim in 1943. According to him, we were fighting to obtain the "unconditional surrender" of Germany and Japan, not to restore the European or Asian balance. Other official aims had been announced from time to time—the Atlantic Charter, the Four Freedoms, the Declaration of the United Nations—but no public spokesman explained very clearly how "unconditional surrender" would produce a

[2] Nicholas J. Spykman, *America's Strategy in World Politics: The United States and the Balance of Power* (New York, 1942), 446, 460, 469.

world in which these affirmative aims could be achieved. Stimson endorsed the "unconditional surrender" formula, and he did not concern himself seriously with the question of the postwar balance—until too late to do much about it. He agreed with Roosevelt not only on general aims but also on the main issues of the grand strategy for carrying them out. In the making and execution of war plans, however, he was relegated to a distinctly subordinate role, so long as Roosevelt remained alive. After Pearl Harbor he was included in few top-level conferences on strategy and seldom had access to the White House, except through such go-betweens as Harry Hopkins. Still, he endorsed Roosevelt's view that the European theater should have priority over the Pacific and that a firm alliance with Russia as well as Great Britain should be sedulously maintained. He thought that, in Europe, we should do all we could to "help the Russians kill Germans." On lesser questions concerning the most expeditious means of killing Germans—and Japanese—he sometimes disagreed with the President and was overruled by him.

From the beginning Stimson insisted, as did Stalin, that the Americans and the British should stage an early cross-channel assault on Hitler's European fortress. His planners in the Operations Division of the War Department prepared a strategy (BOLERO) for such an assault, starting with an immediate build-up of troops and supplies in the British Isles, and he quickly and enthusiastically adopted it. After they began to modify it in the light of changing circumstances, he continued stubbornly to adhere to their original plan. He opposed President Roosevelt's idea of a preliminary landing in North Africa, and he also opposed Prime Minister Churchill's scheme of campaigns in northern Italy, the eastern Mediterranean, and the Balkans. That Churchill's object was in part political—to forestall the postwar expansion of Russia into Western Europe—Stimson could never bring himself to believe. When he went to London in the summer of 1943, to discuss the problem of a second front with Churchill, no one there mentioned such a political argument to him.

He had a very serious difference with Roosevelt when the direct invasion of France from England (OVERLORD) was finally agreed upon. "I believe that Marshall's command of Overlord is imperative for its success," he then wrote to Hopkins, in the hope that Hopkins would take the message to the Chief. Not Marshall but Eisenhower got the assignment, and the operation nevertheless succeeded.[3]

Frustrated in his recommendations for the European theater, Stimson meanwhile gave close attention to strategy in the Far East, but here again he was to meet frustration. In China he saw two great objectives: to secure a base for operations against Japan, and to keep the Chinese in the war.

Early in 1942 he offered an assignment in China to Lieutenant General Hugh A. Drum, one of the few top-ranking officers in the U. S. Army who had combat experience. But he and Marshall gave Drum two different and contradictory impressions of what he was to do, the one implying that he was to open a main theater of war, and the other that he was only to head a military mission. Drum asked his superiors to clarify their ends and means, then sent them a statement of his own views. The upshot was a misunderstanding, from which Stimson angrily concluded that Drum "did not think the role in China which I had

[3] Henry L. Stimson and McGeorge Bundy, *On Active Service in Peace and War* (New York, 1948), 414–15, 429–38, 525–27; Robert E. Sherwood, *Roosevelt and Hopkins: An Intimate History* (New York, 1948), 202, 762, 766; Harry C. Butcher, *My Three Years with Eisenhower: The Personal Diary of Captain Harry C. Butcher, USNR, Naval Aide to General Eisenhower, 1942 to 1945* (New York, 1946), 373–74, 431; Ray S. Cline, *United States Army in World War II, The War Department, Washington Command Post: The Operations Division* (Washington, 1951), 145 n.

offered him was big enough for his capabilities." Though
Drum explained that he was eager to serve, whatever his
role, Stimson rebuked him for knocking down his plans
"like a house of cards," and refused to send him.

Marshall then recommended Lieutenant General Joseph
W. Stilwell, "Vinegar Joe," who had been a ringside observer of the war in China from 1937 to 1939. At first Stimson hesitated to consider Stilwell, because he once had
noticed him sitting with "his head down"—not militarily
erect. Marshall said that if Stilwell had his head down he
was probably getting ready to butt something. So Stimson
interviewed Stilwell, told him (more definitely than he had
told Drum) what he wanted done, gave him what Stilwell
called "the 'hand of destiny' stuff," and "God blessed" him
out.

As U. S. Army commander in the China-Burma-India
theater and chief of staff to Generalissimo Chiang Kai-shek,
Stilwell faced such odds that he scarcely had a chance of success without strong and united backing in Washington. He
had to fight the Japanese in the jungles of Burma, make good
soldiers out of poorly trained Chinese troops, and mediate
between the Chinese authorities and the British. He soon
concluded that the Generalissimo—the "Peanut"—was more
interested in holding power than in fighting the Japanese.
Finally, in 1943, Stilwell clashed with Major General Claire
L. Chennault, leader of the American Volunteer Group of
airmen in China, over a basic issue of strategy. Chennault
wanted to launch an immediate air offensive against Japan
from Chinese bases, while Stilwell thought it essential to
secure the Allied position in China and Burma first. Chiang
backed Chennault, and so did Roosevelt, overruling Stimson
and Marshall, who supported Stilwell throughout as best
they could.

Stimson, however, gave no indication that he shared Stilwell's growing concern over the postwar balance in the Far East. In the summer of 1944 the old jungle fighter jotted down in his private notes:

"The cure for China's trouble is the elimination of Chiang Kai-shek. The only thing that keeps the country split is his fear of losing control. He hates the [Chinese] Reds and will not take any chances on giving them a toehold in the government. The result is that each side watches the other and neither gives a damn about the war [against Japan]. If this condition persists, China will have civil war immediately after Japan is out. If Russia enters the war before a united front is formed in China, the Reds, being immediately accessible, will naturally gravitate to Russia's influence and control." [4]

Planning for the future of a defeated Germany began as early as March, 1943, when Roosevelt instructed Hull to consult about the matter with the British and with Stimson. The two Secretaries agreed upon a program, which Hull took to the Moscow conference in October, 1943. Their plan provided for unconditional surrender, occupation, denazification, disarmament, dismantling of war industries, etc. It evaded the question of Germany's political future—the question whether Germany should be dismembered—but it recommended a "tolerable standard of living" as necessary to "make democracy work."

To Secretary of the Treasury Henry Morgenthau, Jr., the Hull-Stimson recommendations seemed much too mild, as they did to Roosevelt also. Morgenthau believed that Germany should be deprived of industries, while Roosevelt insisted that the German people should be taught the lesson that they had lost the war. In August, 1944, after Stimson

[4] Theodore H. White, ed., *The Stilwell Papers* (New York, 1948), 25–27, 31, 155, 178, 321–22, 341; Charles F. Romans and Riley Sunderland, *United States Army in World War II, China-Burma-India Theater: Stilwell's Mission to China* (Washington, 1953), 63–76, 152, 186, 229, 263, 265–66, 321–22, and *passim*.

had approved a handbook for American occupation officials in Germany, Roosevelt rejected it as too lenient, then turned to Morgenthau and demanded that he and Hull and Stimson produce a more thorough plan.

The differences within this Cabinet committee came to a head when the three men met in Hull's office on September 5, 1944. Hull sponsored a State Department memorandum recommending the elimination of Germany as the dominant economic power in Europe, but also recommending the establishment of at least a subsistence standard of living. Stimson approved, except that he preferred a higher living standard. Morgenthau demanded the complete de-industrialization of the country, which would mean less than subsistence for the people.

Next day the three Secretaries presented their separate proposals to the President, Stimson agreeing on most points with Hull. The President withheld his decision. Later Stimson sent Roosevelt a memorandum protesting against Morgenthau's plan and insisting that the mines and mills of Germany should be conserved for the benefit of all Europe, especially Great Britain. Securing a luncheon date with Roosevelt, Stimson pressed his arguments upon him, but Roosevelt still declined to commit himself.

Then, on September 20, 1944, Stimson and Hull were amazed to learn from Morgenthau, just back from the conference of Roosevelt and Churchill at Quebec, that the President and the Prime Minister had initialed the Morgenthau plan. Hull and Stimson burned with rage and disgust.

Roosevelt, after his own return from Quebec, apparently began to have his doubts, for he again summoned his three Secretaries to the White House. The upshot was that the letter of the Morgenthau plan was dropped, though much of its spirit remained. Stimson approved a directive of the joint chiefs of staff, known as J. C. S. 1067, which ordered the American military governor to "take no steps (*a*) looking toward the economic rehabilitation of Germany or (*b*) to maintain or strengthen the German economy." That country was not going to be transformed into a goat pasture, after all. And yet Stimson, on re-reading J. C. S. 1067 a couple of years later, admitted that it was "a painfully negative document." [5]

As for the disposition of the Nazi leaders, Morgenthau had proposed that "war criminals" be shot as soon as captured, without ceremony. Stimson objected, preferring to have these men dealt with "in a dignified manner consistent with the advance of civilization."

He told the military lawyers in the War Department: "In many ways the task which we have to cope with now in the development of the Nazi scheme of terrorism is much like the development of big business" in the United States. As T. R.'s district attorney in the early 1900's he had found "conspiracy" a useful charge in prosecuting American businessmen. It would do as well, he thought, in the prosecution of Nazi war criminals.

At the Nuremberg trial the Nazi leaders were duly charged with various war crimes all linked together with the gravamen, as Stimson saw it, of conspiring to wage aggressive war. Stimson himself was the chief author of the putative law these men were thus accused of violating. This supposed law was not the Kellogg Pact itself but the Kellogg Pact with a Stimsonian gloss. The original pact, as signed by Germany and Japan among others, did not prohibit defensive war. As interpreted by Secretary Kellogg himself, it allowed each signatory to decide for itself what was necessary for its defense.

The chief American prosecutor at Nuremberg, Justice

---

[5] *On Active Service*, 582; *The Memoirs of Cordell Hull* (2 vols., New York, 1948), 2: 1284–86, 1602–15; *New York Times*, May 12, August 3, 1945.

Robert H. Jackson, based his brief on the Stimsonian ex-
egesis of the pact. "Unless this pact altered the legal status of
wars of aggression," Jackson declared, "it has no meaning
at all and comes close to being an act of deception." He
went on to say: "In 1932 Mr. Stimson, as Secretary of State,
gave voice to the American concept of its effect. He said:
'War between nations was renounced by the signatories of
the Briand-Kellogg Treaty. This means that it has become
illegal throughout practically the entire world.'"

Few Americans lamented the passing of the executed
Nazis, but some Americans, including able lawyers, criticized
the "victor's justice" as a gross violation of the great tradi-
tions of Anglo-American law. These critics maintained that
it violated the principle of equal responsibility (only the
losers were tried and punished); the principle that judges
and juries should have no direct interest in a case before
them; the principle of immunity for civilian and military
officials carrying out orders received from above; and, above
all, the principle that crimes could be punished only if they
were legally defined as crimes before they were committed.

Stimson himself denied that the Nuremberg trial was an
ex post facto proceeding, though he admitted that it was
"a new judicial process." According to him, it was the enforcement of a "moral judgment" that dated back a generation, to the Kellogg Pact. He wrote (in *Foreign Affairs*,
January, 1947): "It was of course quite true, as critics of
Nuremberg argued, that before 1945 there was little to indicate that the 'peoples of the world' were prepared to accept the capture and conviction of such aggressors as a legal
duty." But "a legal right is not lost because temporarily it is
not used." (Here Stimson seemed to be confusing a "moral
judgment" of his own with a "legal right" of the victorious
powers.) "With the judgment at Nuremberg," he proclaimed, "we at last reach to the very core of international

220   The Statecraft of Henry L. Stimson

strife, and we set a penalty not merely for war crimes, but for the very act of war itself, except in self-defense." [6]

There is, however, another way of looking at the Nuremberg achievement. Perhaps the lesson to be learned is not that the crime of aggressive war does not pay but that the crime of unsuccessful war does not pay. If, unfortunately, the Japanese had won the war, they might have tried Stimson himself as a war criminal according to his own concepts of international law.

Even before the surrender of Germany, a growing number of Japanese leaders realized that their country faced inevitable defeat. They set themselves to convincing other influential men, both in and out of office, and preparing the way for a government that would end the war. They gained a partial success in the summer of 1944 when, after a long string of losses in Pacific fighting, the cabinet of the warlike Hideki Tojo fell. His successor, Kuniaki Koiso, created a six-man Supreme War Direction Council, which for the first time brought the army and navy heads into a responsible relationship with the civilian authorities. The Koiso government could not cope with the worsening condition of Japan—the increasingly destructive American air raids, the progressive decline in stocks of aircraft, oil, steel, coal—and on April 8, 1945, after the Okinawa landings, Koiso resigned. Kantaro Suzuki, the new premier, assumed office with the

[6] *On Active Service*, 584–91; U. S. Congress, *Opening Address by Robert H. Jackson, Representative and Chief of Counsel for the United States of America, in the Trial of German War Criminals, together with a Copy of the Indictment* . . . (79 Congress, 1 session, Senate Document No. 129, Washington, 1946), 33–34. Lucius D. Clay, *Decision in Germany* (New York, 1950), 53–54, gathered from a conversation with Stimson in the summer of 1945 that he "believed that the arrest and trial of the Nazi leaders and war criminals were of utmost importance to future peace. He would have no part of a policy based on vindictiveness. . . ." Later, as reported in the *New York Times*, December 19, 1946, Stimson was distressed by criticisms of the Nuremberg proceedings as "lawless" from "many who should know better"—apparently including Senator Robert A. Taft, who had characterized the verdict as an act of vengeance and a blot on American justice.

aim of bringing about peace as quickly as he could. When Germany collapsed, early in May, the Supreme War Direction Council began to consider the question of ending the war.

The army heads now permitted the subject to be openly discussed in cabinet, though they insisted on continuing hostilities in the hope of obtaining terms more favorable to Japan than unconditional surrender. The navy leaders were divided. When the emperor, on June 20, told the council it was necessary to have a plan for closing the war at once, as well as a plan for defending the home islands, he got approval from the premier and the ministers of foreign affairs and the navy, but not from the army minister nor the army and navy chiefs of staff. In July the emperor and the peace-minded members of the council made overtures to the Soviet government with a view to Russian mediation between Japan and the United States. They intended to send Prince Konoye to Moscow as a special envoy with official instructions to seek terms short of unconditional surrender but with private instructions to agree to peace at any price.[7]

Meanwhile, from a quite different point of view, war planners in Washington also were considering ways of hastening the end of the Pacific war. They could depend on one or a combination of at least five approaches to their object. First, they could maintain and intensify the naval blockade and aerial bombardment of Japan. Second, they could threaten and ultimately launch an invasion of the home islands. Third, they could try psychological warfare by abandoning or softening their demand for *unconditional* surrender. Fourth, anticipating the active help of the Soviet Union, they could look to their Russian ally to smash the undefeated Japanese army on the Asian mainland. And,

[7] U. S. Strategic Bombing Survey, *Japan's Struggle to End the War* (Washington, 1946), 2–7.

finally, though only a handful among them were aware of this, they could perhaps paralyze the enemy's will to resist by means of an ultra secret weapon—the atom bomb.

This weapon did not enter into the calculations of the ordinary planning agencies of the War and Navy departments, since only a few of the chief officers had any advance knowledge of it, and they but little. In the spring of 1945 a member of the Operations Division happened innocently to raise the question in the War Department whether the Japanese might not be working on an atomic weapon and whether something should not be done about it. He was startled soon afterward by being subjected to an intense security check.

Lacking information about the bomb, Army and Navy planners considered only the more conventional strategies during the spring and early summer of 1945. The Air Forces came to the optimistic conclusion that Japan could be forced to surrender unconditionally as a result of a continued and intensified sea-air blockade alone, while the ground forces stuck to their more conservative and pessimistic view that an invasion also would be necessary. The question was largely one of time. A joint Army-Navy intelligence committee noted (April 18, 1945) that, according to various estimates, it might take anywhere from a few months to several years to win the war without an actual landing on the Japanese home islands. Air Force General Henry H. Arnold said (in July) that mass bombing was fast converting Japan into a nation without cities or industries and might destroy the enemy's resistance as soon as October, 1945. The War Department Operations Division, however, held to its schedule of two landings on the home islands—on Kyushu, November 1, 1945, and on Honshu (on the Tokyo plain), March 1, 1946.

These calculations, whether by the air or by the ground forces, assumed that the objective would remain simply unconditional surrender. The planners generally understood, of course, that a restatement of peace terms might change their estimates. The joint intelligence committee (in its paper of April 18, 1945) noted that a "clarification of allied intentions" might hasten Japan's desire to quit, that Japan might accept "a rationalized version of unconditional surrender" before the end of 1945—without an invasion but with continued bombing and blockade. Other government agencies in Washington looked much more deeply into the possibilities of this kind of psychological warfare. After warning for months against propaganda attacks on the emperor, the social scientists of the Foreign Morale Analysis Division reported to the Office of War Information (in May, 1945) their considered opinion that the Japanese might stop fighting soon if they were told that the emperor's fate was up to the Japanese people themselves. According to Captain Zacharias, an intelligence branch of the Navy Department designated as OP-16-W concluded that "by the end of June the plight of the Japanese had become desperate" and that "while Suzuki was talking of war, he was thinking of peace. Now, it was no longer a material consideration such as the retention of Manchuria or Korea which prevented him from saying in so many words that he would accept our terms. The only doubt which still forestalled a decision was the future status of the Emperor." [8]

This question of defining peace terms attracted the attention also of top policy makers in the administration— Secretary of War Stimson; Acting Secretary of State Joseph C. Grew, in place of the ailing Hull; Secretary of the Navy James V. Forrestal, successor of the dead Knox; and President Truman. To aid the three departments in integrating policy recommendations, the Assistant Secretaries had met

[8] Cline, *Operations Division*, 337-47; Leighton, *Human Relations*, 54–55, 58–75, 120–27; Ellis M. Zacharias, *Secret Missions: The Story of an Intelligence Officer* (New York, 1946), 334–35, 341–47, 367–70.

since 1944 as the State, War, and Navy Coordinating Committee (SWNCC or SWINK). One subcommittee concentrated on Germany and another on Japan. The chairman of the latter subcommittee was Eugene H. Dooman, a career diplomat widely experienced in Far Eastern affairs.

Early in the spring of 1945 Colonel Dana Johnson, chief of psychological warfare in Hawaii, called on Dooman and Grew in Washington. Colonel Johnson told them he had gathered, from his interrogations of high-ranking war prisoners, that the Japanese were on the point of giving up but were held back by a fear that the imperial institution would be abolished and the emperor himself punished as a war criminal. The colonel took the advent of the Suzuki government in early April as a sign that the enemy was ready to talk peace. Later Henry Luce, the magazine publisher, on his return from a Pacific visit, cautioned Grew that the failure of the United States to persuade Japan to surrender was damaging the morale of American troops who had fought the bloody battles of Saipan and Tarawa and were expecting even more fearful losses in an assault on Honshu or Kyushu. Grew, after telling Luce that the State Department was already working on that problem, speeded up the process by instructing Dooman to draft immediately, for ultimate presentation to the President, an outline of the policies to be followed if Japan surrendered. Dooman's paper included a clause specifically stating that the Japanese people's choice of a postwar government "may include a constitutional monarchy under the present dynasty if the peace-loving nations can be convinced of the genuine determination of such a government to follow policies of peace."

On May 29 representatives of the State, War, and Navy Departments met in Stimson's office in the Pentagon to consider Dooman's paper. Stimson, who presided at the meeting, said that he thoroughly endorsed the document. He added that Americans failed to give the Japanese enough credit for their capacity to produce such admirable statesmen as Shidehara and Wakatsuki. Forrestal agreed with Stimson. But Elmer Davis, Director of the Office of War Information, objected strongly to any definition of terms that might be construed as the basis for a negotiated surrender. And General Marshall, though approving the paper, warned that its early publication would be "premature." So it was laid aside for the time being.

Apparently Stimson was not satisfied with the disposition of it, for he promptly requested the Operations Division of the War Department to prepare for him two studies bearing on the subject. In the first of these the OPD concluded that the enemy's protracted resistance was based on the hope of obtaining a conditional surrender, and in the second, that a public declaration of war aims, amounting to a definition of unconditional surrender, would be advisable as a means of "political and psychological pressure" supplementing military preparations. A month or so later (July 12) the OPD recommended holding to the invasion plans, but added: "There is much to be gained by defining, as completely as possible, the detailed U. S. war aims in Japan."

Meanwhile Stimson continued to discuss surrender terms from time to time with Forrestal and Grew. He said, according to Forrestal's notes (June 12), that "our national objective was to secure the demilitarization of Japan" but that "no one desired the permanent subjugation of Japan, the enslavement of her people or any attempt to dictate what kind of government the country should have." He vigorously agreed with Grew (June 19) that something ought to be done "in the very near future to indicate to the Japanese what kind of surrender terms would be imposed upon them and particularly to indicate to them that they would be allowed to retain their own form of government and religious institutions while at the same time making it clear that we propose to eradicate completely all traces of Japanese militarism."

Then, in July, came information making the Japanese position very clear to the policy makers in Washington. They were still listening in on Tokyo by means of the same "Magic" as had given them access to Japan's confidential communications before Pearl Harbor. "The first real evidence of a Japanese desire to get out of the war," Forrestal recorded (July 13), "came today through intercepted messages from Togo, Foreign Minister, to Sato, Jap Ambassador in Moscow." Togo said that the Japanese "did not desire permanent annexation of any of the territories they had conquered in Manchuria." He said further that "the unconditional surrender terms of the Allies was about the only thing in the way of termination of the war." In reply Sato "strongly advised accepting any terms" (July 24). The Tokyo government answered that the "final judgment and decision" of the cabinet was that "the war must be fought with all the vigor and bitterness of which the nation was capable so long as the only alternative was the unconditional surrender." [9]

To enforce unconditional surrender within a reasonable time, the OPD had informed Stimson weeks earlier, would probably take not only an American landing in Japan, or at least the imminent threat of one, but also Russian participation in the Far Eastern war. In early 1945 most American military thinkers had shared this conviction that Russian aid was indispensable. To obtain it Stimson was then willing to postpone all the divergent issues between the Soviet Union

[9] U. S. Senate, *Hearings before the Subcommittee to Investigate the Administration of the Internal Security Act . . . on the Institute of Pacific Relations* (Washington, 1951), pt. 3, pp. 704, 727–30; Cline, *Operations Division*, 345; Walter Millis, ed., *The Forrestal Diaries* (New York, 1951), 68–70, 74–76. See also Joseph C. Grew, *Turbulent Era: A Diplomatic Record of Forty Years, 1904–1945* (2 vols., Boston, 1952), 2: 1421–24.

and the United States. In February, before the Yalta Conference, he prepared a memorandum for the Secretary of State in which he argued against raising the question of Russian buffer states in Europe, or the question of American bases in the Pacific, until the Russians had "clearly committed themselves" to fighting Japan.

He was slow to see in Soviet policy any potential threat to American interests in the postwar world. As late as April 23, when the State, War, and Navy Secretaries were discussing the insistence of the Russians on their own regime in Poland, Forrestal recorded: "The Secretary of War said that it was such a newly posed question so far as he was concerned he found great difficulty in making positive recommendations but he did feel that we had to remember that the Russian conception of freedom, democracy and independent voting was quite different from ours or the British and that he hoped we would go slowly and avoid any open break. He said that the Russians had carried out their military engagements quite faithfully and he was sorry to see this one incident project a break between the two countries." Forrestal replied "that this was not an isolated incident but was one of a pattern of unilateral action on the part of Russia, that they had taken similar positions vis-à-vis Bulgaria, Rumania, Turkey and Greece, and that . . . we might as well meet the issue now as later on."

On that same day, April 23, Stimson told Harry S. Truman, who had been President less than two weeks, that he doubted the wisdom of too "strong" a policy toward Russia, though he favored a "cold-blooded firmness."

Once the Russians should become, as expected, our active allies in the Pacific, there could be little doubt of the inevitability of Japan's surrender, unconditional if need be. But Forrestal, for one, doubted whether the United States would benefit from achieving such a negative and destructive aim. On May 1, at another meeting of the three Secretaries, he raised several questions: "How far and how thoroughly do we want to beat Japan?" Do we want to "Morgenthau" those islands? What about Russian influence in the Far East? "Do we desire a counterweight to that influence? And should it be China or should it be Japan?"

Much concerned about Roosevelt's secret agreement with Stalin at Yalta, Grew on May 12 raised questions similar to Forrestal's in a memorandum addressed to the Secretary of War. In the Yalta protocol Roosevelt had agreed that, as the price of Russian aid against Japan, Russia should resume the dominant position in the Far East she had held before the Russo-Japanese war. Now Grew asked Stimson whether the earliest possible entry of the Soviet Union into the Pacific war was of "such vital interest" to the United States as to preclude a reconsideration of the Yalta agreement, and whether the Soviet Union should be granted a share in the postwar occupation of the Japanese home islands. Stimson replied that Russian entry would "materially shorten the war and thus save American lives," that the Yalta concessions were "within the military power of Russia to obtain regardless of U. S. military action short of war," and that "our experiences with the Russians in the occupation of Germany" might "in the future lead to considerations which would point to the wisdom of exclusive occupation by our own forces." However, "The discussion of this subject prior to Russian entry into the Japanese war does not seem necessary at this time."

A military intelligence report of July 5 on the Chinese communist movement told Stimson: "With the total defeat of Japan, Russia will again emerge as the sole military land power of any account in Asia. But she will be vastly stronger than at any time in the past."

By this time Stimson himself was worrying about our prospective ally in the Far East. "But as the days passed," his memoirs recalled, "a new and important element entered

into his thinking about Russia, and by mid-summer it had
become almost dominant, dwarfing lesser aspects of the
problem." That new and important element—though his
memoirs did not specifically say so—was the atomic bomb.[10]

The development of the bomb itself, as well as the formation of policy for its use, owed a great deal to Stimson. In
the fall of 1941 President Roosevelt had put him on a committee to consider the military employment of nuclear
fission, and after May 1, 1943, he served as the President's
senior adviser in that field. Meanwhile he aided the work of
the atomic scientists by bringing about effective cooperation
between the War Department and the Office of Scientific
Research and Development. "Again and again," according
to the historian of the O. S. R. D., "he provided the impetus
which broke log jams and speeded major problems on their
way to solution."

According to the O. S. R. D. director, Vannevar Bush,
Congress appropriated funds for the so-called Manhattan
project, sight unseen, because of trust in Stimson. Immediately after the first use of the bomb, Prime Minister Churchill
paid a public tribute in which he declared that "the erection
of the immense plants was placed under the responsibility of
Mr. Stimson . . . whose wonderful work and marvelous
secrecy cannot be sufficiently admired." At the same time
President Truman publicly credited the development of
the new weapon largely to the persistence and determination of his Secretary of War.

By April, 1945, the Manhattan project had advanced to a
point where Stimson became concerned about "the various
questions raised by our apparently imminent success in developing an atomic weapon." He then appointed an "Interim
Committee" to advise him on these questions. It included

[10] *Hearings . . . on the Institute of Pacific Relations*, pt. 7A, p. 2309;
Forrestal Diaries, 28–29, 49–51; Grew, *Turbulent Era*, 2: 1455–59; *On Active
Service*, 605–11, 637–38.

two officers of the O. S. R. D., Vannevar Bush and Karl T. Compton, and was assisted by a panel of atomic scientists. The committee considered, among other things, the problem of the future control, domestic and international, of atomic energy. "But," as Stimson's memoirs said, "the first and greatest problem was the decision on the use of the bomb—should it be used against the Japanese, and if so, in what manner?"

On June 1 the committee recommended as follows: The bomb should be used against Japan as soon as possible. It should be used on a "dual target—that is, a military installation or war plant surrounded by or adjacent to houses and other buildings most susceptible to damage." And it should be used without advance warning as to its nature. These recommendations accorded with the opinions of Stimson's military advisers, among whom General Marshall in particular stressed the "shock value" of the new weapon.

Later in June another group of atomic scientists presented to Stimson a report containing very different advice. These scientists were represented by a "Committee on Social and Political Implications," appointed by the Metallurgical Laboratory in Chicago and headed by Professor James Franck. Here are excerpts from the Franck Report:

"The military advantages and the saving of American lives achieved by the sudden use of atomic bombs against Japan may be outweighted by a wave of horror and revulsion sweeping over the rest of the world." "From this point of view, a demonstration of the new weapon might be made, before the eyes of all the United Nations on the desert or a barren island." "After such a demonstration the weapon might perhaps be used against Japan if the sanction of the United Nations (and public opinion at home) was obtained after a preliminary ultimatum to Japan to surrender." "If the United States were to be the first to release this new means of indiscriminate destruction on mankind, she would sacrifice public support throughout the world, precipitate the race for armaments, and prejudice the possibility of reaching an international agreement on the future control of such weapons." "We believe that these considerations make the use of nuclear bombs for an early attack against Japan inadvisable."

Stimson's own Interim Committee discarded as impracticable such alternatives as a detailed warning or a demonstration in some uninhabited place. As Stimson later said: "Nothing would have been more damaging to our effort to obtain surrender than a warning of a demonstration followed by a dud—and this was a real possibility."

On June 18 he attended a White House meeting at which final plans for the contingency of an invasion of Japan were approved. He was pleased that President Truman was including him in conferences on strategic planning, as President Roosevelt had seldom done, and never after 1942.

On July 2 he gave Truman a memorandum containing his proposed program, to which Grew and Forrestal had agreed. In it Stimson said "the warning must be tendered before the actual invasion has occurred." "If Russia is a part of the threat, the Russian attack, if actual, must not have progressed too far." [11]

On July 16 an atomic bomb was successfully detonated, for the first time, on a tower above the sands of New Mexico.

Stimson received the news in Potsdam, Germany, where he had gone to counsel the President on atomic matters at the Big Three Conference. On his arrival there he had been

[11] *New York Times*, August 7, 1945; October 21, 1950; James P. Baxter, *Scientists against Time* (Boston, 1946), 32–33; Vannevar Bush, *Modern Arms and Free Men: A Discussion of the Role of Science in Preserving Democracy* (New York, 1949), 259; *On Active Service*, 616–24; "A Report to the Secretary of War, June 1945," in the *Bulletin of the Atomic Scientists*, vol. 1, no. 1, pp. 2–4, 16 (May 1, 1946). A poll of more than one hundred and fifty atomic scientists in the summer of 1945 showed that a majority favored a "preliminary demonstration on a military objective," about one-third preferred a "preliminary demonstration on an uninhabited locality," and small groups were for all-out use or were for no use at all.

surprised to meet Americans who still thought of getting the Soviet Union to help defeat Japan. The news from New Mexico, he later recalled with satisfaction, convinced all of them that it was "pointless" to go on trying to hurry up the Russians. "The Russians," he reflected, "may well have been disturbed to find that President Truman was rather losing his interest in knowing the exact date on which they would come into the war."

Stimson had taken with him a copy of Dooman's State Department paper defining the surrender terms, and at Potsdam he discussed this document with Churchill, then took it to Truman and James F. Byrnes, the new Secretary of State, and got their approval of it. On July 26 it was promulgated from Potsdam to Japan and to the world.

The proclamation contained—with one notable omission —essentially the same terms and threats as the original draft produced two months earlier and without knowledge of the atom bomb. Both that draft and the final document called in exactly the same words for "unconditional surrender of all Japanese armed forces" (but not of the Japanese nation) and concluded: "The alternative for Japan is prompt and utter destruction." Nothing had been added to hint that the source of this destruction was to be a new weapon of unprecedented frightfulness. But something had been taken away—the clause making clear that the Japanese, if they surrendered, could keep their emperor.

In Tokyo the six members of the inner cabinet, or Supreme War Direction Council, immediately began to consider the Potsdam declaration. Premier Suzuki and the minister of foreign affairs and of the navy felt that it must be accepted at once, but the war minister and the two chiefs of staff objected that the terms were "too dishonorable." They insisted on discussing the fate of the emperor, the disposition of "war criminals," and the future "national polity."

Suzuki informed his press conference, July 28, that his cabinet was taking, for the moment, a position of *mokusatsu*. This word has two meanings. By it Suzuki meant that his government would "withhold comment," but the Domei News Agency translated it so as to say his government would "ignore" the Potsdam declaration. Newspapers throughout the world announced that Japan was rejecting the terms.[12]

In Washington, after his return from Potsdam, Stimson's military staff brought him detailed plans for an atomic mission against Japan. He took the plans to President Truman, then with him eliminated from the list of proposed targets the city of Kyoto, which was to be spared as a shrine of Japanese culture. Stimson approved four other targets, among them Hiroshima and Nagasaki.

On August 6 the first bomb was let go over Hiroshima. On August 8 the Russians entered the war and began to over-run Manchuria. On August 9 a second nuclear bomb was exploded above Nagasaki. Meanwhile, in Tokyo, the three diehards on the Supreme War Direction council still held out against surrender on the Potsdam terms, but they finally agreed to refer the issue to the emperor's own decision. The emperor declared for peace, and then, on August 10, the full cabinet unanimously approved acceptance of the terms— on condition that these did not change the emperor's prerogatives!

When the Japanese reply reached Washington, by way of the Swiss government, American policy makers faced the

---

[12] *On Active Service*, 637–38; *Hearings . . . on the Institute of Pacific Relations*, pt. 3, p. 731; Department of State *Bulletin*, 13: 137–38, for text of the Potsdam declaration as released to the press, July 26, 1945; U. S. Strategic Bombing Survey, *Japan's Struggle to End the War*, 8; William J. Coughlin, "The Great *Mokusatsu* Mistake," in *Harper's Magazine*, 206: 31–40 (March, 1953). The importance of this mistake should not be exaggerated, since American officials already knew, through the "Magic" intercepts, of the Japanese government's growing disposition to talk peace. Regardless of broadcast ultimatums and replies, the United States could have approached Japan indirectly through diplomatic channels—if the object had been nothing more than to end the war promptly.

question of accepting the surrender with the string attached. Truman asked Stimson for his advice. Stimson said that "even if the question hadn't been raised by the Japanese we would have to continue the Emperor ourselves in order to get into surrender the many scattered armies of the Japanese who would own no other authority." The Japanese counter terms were accepted.[13]

And so the war ended—a little short of unconditional surrender.

Then the experts of the United States Strategic Bombing Survey visited Japan to study the effects of aerial warfare on that country. The Survey, in 1946, reported the following conclusions to the War Department: "Based on detailed investigation of all the facts, and supported by the testimony of the surviving Japanese leaders involved, it is the Survey's opinion that certainly prior to December 31, 1945, Japan would have surrendered even if the atomic bombs had not been dropped, even if Russia had not entered the war, and even if no invasion had been planned or contemplated."

These conclusions may be discounted, perhaps, as an effort of the Air Forces to justify the program of strategic bombing they had championed during the war. And yet there was certainly a strong possibility that Japan might have been brought to surrender, in 1945, by the pressure of the sea-air blockade alone. There was an even stronger possibility that Russian entry into the war, expected by the end of the first or second week in August, would quickly have applied the final coup to Japan. There was also the probability, not stressed in the Strategic Bombing Survey's report, that a modification or definition of the surrender terms would have hastened the end of the fighting, even without Russian participation in it.

These considerations soon after the peace began to arouse

[13] U. S. Strategic Bombing Survey, *Japan's Struggle to End the War*, 9; *On Active Service*, 627.

curiosity, at least in the minds of a few observers in Great Britain and the United States. They wondered why, if the object was simply to bring Japan to an early defeat, the terms were not more fully clarified, or the Russian attack not given a chance to show its effect. They wondered why the atom bomb was used. More particularly, they wondered why it was used so soon. Some of them began to make their own guesses.

In a magazine article in 1946 Norman Cousins and Thomas K. Finletter speculated that the real purpose of the sudden atom bombing was not merely to defeat Japan but to do it in such a way as to forestall the Soviet Union. Cousins and Finletter pointed out that, if Japan's early surrender had been the only consideration, the nature of the bomb could have been demonstrated under U. N. auspices at any time between July 16, 1945, the date of the first successful atomic explosion in New Mexico, and August 8, "the Russian deadline date." But not if the object was to head off Russia. "No; any test would have been impossible if the purpose was to knock Japan out before Russia came in—or at least before Russia could make anything other than a token of participation prior to a Japanese collapse." Cousins and Finletter suggested that the bombing could be defended on the grounds "that we avoided a struggle for authority in Japan similar to what we have experienced in Germany and Italy; that, unless we came out of the war with a decisive balance of power over Russia, we would be in no position to checkmate Russian expansion." [14]

Stimson, however, did not mention this as one of his

----

[14] U. S. Strategic Bombing Survey, *Japan's Struggle to End the War,* 13; Norman Cousins and Thomas K. Finletter, "A Beginning for Sanity," in the *Saturday Review of Literature,* vol. 29, no. 24, pp. 7–8 (June 15, 1946). Cousins and Finletter were reviewing *A Report on the International Control of Atomic Energy* by David E. Lilienthal and others. Regarding the problem of control, Cousins and Finletter said (p. 6), ". . . the first error may have been the biggest error. The first error was the atomic bombing of Hiroshima."

motives when, in *Harper's Magazine* for February, 1947, he published his own account of the decision to use the bombs. "The ultimate responsibility for the recommendation to the President rested upon me, and I have no desire to veil it," Stimson declared. "My chief purpose was to end the war in victory with the least possible cost in the lives of the men in the armies which I had helped to raise." He contended that, unless the bombs had been used, the Japanese would never have yielded without an invasion of their home islands. This invasion, planned to begin in November, 1945, would have resulted in millions of casualties on both sides. That is to say, the atomic bombing was quicker and cheaper—more humane! In this *apologia* Stimson ignored both the article by Cousins and Finletter and the report of the Strategic Bombing Survey.[15]

The Cousins-Finletter thesis was restated and elaborated in a book by a British atomic physicist, P. M. S. Blackett. Obviously more sympathetic with the Soviet Union than with the United States, Blackett called the bombing the first shot fired in an American cold war against Russia. The bombs, he implied, were really aimed at the Russians, though it was the Japanese who did the dying.

Stimson's memoirs repeated the argument of his *Harper's* piece. "The use of the bomb, in accelerating the surrender, saved many more lives than it cost," the memoirs said. "And yet to use the atomic bomb against cities populated mainly by civilians was to assume a . . . terrible responsibility. For

[15] Henry L. Stimson, "The Decision to Use the Atomic Bomb," in *Harper's Magazine*, 194: 99–107 (February, 1947). In a footnote (p. 105) Stimson cited the Bombing Survey's report on *Japan's Struggle to End the War* in support of his own statement that "all the evidence I have seen indicates that the controlling factor in the final Japanese decision to accept our terms of surrender was the atomic bomb." But the Bombing Survey's report had said (p. 12): "The Hiroshima and Nagasaki atomic bombs did not defeat Japan, nor by the testimony of the enemy leaders who ended the war did they persuade Japan to accept unconditional surrender."

thirty years Stimson had been a champion of international law and morality."

His memoirs also said that Japan's "vague proposals" for a conditional peace were "not considered seriously," and that he himself opposed negotiating with the Japanese in regard to the status of their Emperor or anything else. He thought it was no time for concession or compromise. War, he explained, is like a boxing match: a winning fighter would be foolish to let up when he finally had his opponent on the ropes.

War, he might better have said, is like a free-for-all: a winning fighter would be foolish to knock out a wiry scrapper whom he might need to help dispose of a bully lurking in the corner behind him.

Elsewhere the memoirs did indeed hint that Russia and not Japan was the real target of the atom bomb. By the time of the Potsdam conference, the memoirs said, Stimson had come to the view that the bomb would "give democratic diplomacy a badly needed 'equalizer'" as against the postwar power of the Communist colossus.[16]

If the purpose really was to check the Russians in the Far East, the destruction of their historic enemy in that area must seem, in retrospect, like a peculiar way to go about it. A quick peace with Japan, short of complete humiliation, might have been a more sensible expedient.

As the war drew to a close, Stimson did not look to the

---

[16] P. M. S. Blackett, *Fear, War, and the Bomb: Military and Political Consequences of Atomic Energy* (New York, 1949), 135–39; *On Active Service*, 617–18, 628–30, 637–38. In reply to a telegram from Senator B. B. Hickenlooper, June 25, 1951, Lieutenant General Leslie R. Groves, wartime director of the Manhattan project, said that he and Stimson had informed Roosevelt at the White House, just before the President left for Yalta in February, 1945, that the success of the A-bomb was "a 99 per cent certainty," that it "would probably be ready in August," and that it would be "extremely powerful." U. S. Senate, *Hearings . . . an Inquiry into the Military Situation in the Far East and . . . the Relief of General of the Army Douglas MacArthur from his Assignment in that Area* (Washington, 1951), pt. 4, p. 3119.

U. N. organization as a means of collective security and peace. True, he aided Hull in inducing both the Democratic and the Republican parties, in 1944, to adopt planks favoring American membership in the organization. And he continued to espouse the U. N. cause. But he advocated other things which conflicted with its original spirit and purpose.

He opposed President Roosevelt's idea that all colonies might well be made U. N. trusteeships. Most such territories, Stimson objected, were the "legal property" of various nations which felt tremendous "national pride and self-interest associated with colonialism." He was no more inclined than Winston Churchill himself to permit the liquidation of the British Empire, or any other empire for that matter, except the Japanese. He also opposed the idea of presenting conquered Pacific islands to the U. N. and then accepting them back as U. N. trusteeships. His own Pacific policy had stemmed from his imperial interest in the Philippines, and the war and the victory, he thought, had vindicated this interest. So the U. S. and not the U. N. must be the "principal guarantor" of peace in the Pacific, and "the policeman must be armed."

He renewed his old campaign for peacetime military training for all American youth. He contended that such training was essential for our "security," though he admitted he did not use the word in any literal sense. "I intend the broadest meaning of the term 'security,' " he told the House committee on postwar military policy, June 15, 1945. "I mean not merely protection against the physical invasion of our country. I mean the security . . . giving to that nation a leadership among the peoples of the world and a well-founded respect for it on their part which swells its power and influence." This was interesting: Americans should be forced to train for another war, not just to protect the United States against attack but to prepare it for "leadership" and "power and influence" over the rest of the world.

A high and noble aim, perhaps. One that Americans ought to be eager to fight and die for. Only they were being told that struggles for empire—for power and influence, for world leadership—were things of the past. The State Department was carrying on a campaign to educate the American public to the view that the U. N. was about to usher in a new day. For administration spokesmen, the problem was to reconcile the new internationalism with the new imperialism.

Stimson, for one, was equal to this challenge. The United States, he explained, "must retain her capacity effectively to discharge her obligations under the world peace organizations which are now in process of being formed." Force would be necessary "to prevent the depredations of an aggressor." U. M. T. would enable the United States to supply its share of force.

But "aggressors" in the language of the day meant Germany and Japan, for Russia along with Great Britain and the United States was officially defined as one of the "peace-loving" nations. With these three in concert, and with their late enemies in defeat and ruin, the U. N. would actually need only a very small force to take care of such insignificant tribes as might dare to disturb the *status quo*. It did not need a mass conscript army from the United States.

At a Cabinet meeting on September 7, 1945, according to Forrestal's notes, Leo Crowley "said that the assumption was that we had fought a war now to get rid of war, that we had the atomic bomb and we had the San Francisco Conference and all the various affirmations of faith in the possibilities of an organization to create the foundations of world peace, and that universal training would create the inference that we didn't have faith in our own platform." Stimson, according to Forrestal, "made an eloquent rejoinder, the substance of which was that the only way we could convince the world we *were* serious about preventing another war was to show that we took our responsibility in that direction with great seriousness."

If Stimson meant that we must convince the Russians we were serious, his argument for war preparation had a little more meaning. A couple of years later, in an article in *Foreign Affairs*, he spoke out somewhat more plainly. "We must no longer let the tide of Soviet expansion cheaply roll into the empty places left by the war," he then declared, "and yet we must make it perfectly clear that we are not ourselves expansionist."

The war had left "empty places"—vortices drawing the United States and the Soviet Union into conflict. The empty place in the Far East had resulted from the Stimson Doctrine, the diplomacy of Pearl Harbor, the Yalta agreement, "unconditional surrender," and the atom bomb. "It would be an irony indeed," Stimson thought in 1947, "if a new Manchurian crisis should one day develop because of arrangements made during a war whose origins were in that very area." [17]

It was an irony indeed.

[17] *New York Times*, June 16, 1945; Hull, *Memoirs*, 2: 1670; *Forrestal Diaries*, 93; *On Active Service*, 596–605, 637–38; Henry L. Stimson, "The Challenge to Americans," in *Foreign Affairs*, 26: 5–14 (October, 1947).

11 *War Is Peace*

At the end of his long career Henry L. Stimson was awarded a Distinguished Service Medal, the citation reading: "His steadfast purpose and unselfish devotion were an inspiration to men-at-arms in American forces throughout the world in their bitter fight to maintain moral right, freedom, justice, and civilization itself."

At his death Dean Acheson, then Secretary of State, declared: "He has served his country through a long life with the depth, the simplicity, the austerity of devotion of General Washington. Those who love and serve this republic will find his memory an ever present help in time of trouble."

At his funeral the Reverend Dr. Paul Austin Wolfe, of the Brick Presbyterian Church in New York, gave thanks for the life of "a son of Andover and Yale, a master of law, an officer in the Army, a servant of his God, a statesman of the world, a soldier of peace." [1]

Seemingly, the United States had been engaged in a crusade against the wicked nations of the world. The war had been fought for "moral right, freedom, justice, and civilization itself." It was a bitter struggle, but the forces of light had won their victory over the forces of darkness. The millenium should have arrived.

The fact was of course that the millenium was as far off as ever, maybe farther off than before the great crusade.

[1] *New York Times*, October 21, 1950; New York *Herald Tribune*, October 23, 1950.

There was no peace at the hour when Stimson, the soldier of peace, was praised and buried.

Americans were fighting and dying in Korea—within eighty-five miles of Manchuria. Russians and Americans were competing to revive and rearm the fragments of defeated and dismembered Germany. The United States was looking to Japan, the late enemy, as a future ally. "The door is open" for peace talks with the Soviet Union, John Foster Dulles told the political committee of the United Nations General Assembly, but in Washington Secretary Acheson warned there was no chance for "productive results" until the military might of the West was increased to match that of the Communist world.

All this was only a few years after the American people had been given the impression that once the "peace-loving nations" had prevailed in war a new day would dawn with universal concord and freedom multiplied by four. The people had responded with the most prodigious effort in the history of the republic. Then they were called upon to make huge sacrifices again—in order to undo what they so recently had done.

Having just fought their biggest war, presumably for peace and security and freedom, they still faced a dire threat to their freedom and security and peace.

Something had gone wrong.

Was anybody to blame?

Yes, according to a notion widely held in the United States. Foreign devils—Hitler, Tojo, Stalin—were responsible for the war and the frustrated peace.

But this answer, though it may contain a measure of truth, cannot entirely satisfy the citizens of a democracy. They possess a degree of control, at least potentially, over their own leadership but not over that of other countries. So they must concern themselves about the share of responsibility, if any, of their own statesmen. They can hardly exercise a wise influence upon them in the present and the future unless they look closely and critically at their performances in the past.

The standards for such criticism are difficult to set, if the criticism is to be fair. Some people, of course, easily apply the devil theory, blaming President Roosevelt and his advisers for all the evils of this country and the world. Others apply the opposite, the great-man theory, hailing Roosevelt and his advisers as heroes who rescued the nation from dread peril—even though a deadly peril remained after they had gone. Either of these views is too simple and undiscriminating to serve as a useful guide for the citizen in appraising the past, acting in the present, and taking thought for the future.

There is also the attitude that no one is to blame if things go wrong, that no alternatives existed, that statesmen in making their decisions had no real choice but took the only course they could. War with Japan, war with Russia, was bound to come, willy-nilly, according to this fatalistic view. It can be neither proved nor disproved. If it is true, policy makers deserve no more praise than blame, and citizens need not bother with public affairs, except perhaps for their cynical amusement.

Some people admit that alternatives may have existed but rule them out of consideration on the grounds that we cannot know what *might have* happened if different choices had been made. They say it is unhistorical even to raise the question *what if*. They say we must take into account only what actually was done and what actually happened.

Those who take this position are usually defenders and admirers of a particular statesman being criticized. They do not seem to realize that the argument cuts two ways. If it is true, it estops the defense as well as the attack, for admirers cannot praise a man without some guess, at least implied, as to the consequences that would have followed if he had *not* done what he did! For instance, to praise Roosevelt for his foreign policy is to predict that the consequences of a different policy would have been disastrous (or more disastrous) for the United States.

In truth, it is impossible to ignore "iffy" questions in history. History as a meaningful account of the past requires judgment about the wisdom of human actions, and such judgment requires assumptions (explicit or implicit) regarding the probable consequences of possible alternatives.

The objection arises that the historian views events with a time-perspective which the statesman, at the moment of decision, did not have. Such "hindsight" is said to give the historian an unfair advantage over the statesman. But history *is* hindsight. Its very function is to view events and their participants in the perspective of time. The historian is bound to trace events to their consequences and appraise the decisions of men in the light of what, unknown to them, was yet to come.

A justifiable caution is that, in doing so, the historian should not judge men by some abstract and absolute standard. Far from it. He should take into account the atmosphere of urgency and uncertainty in which they labored, and he should compare their policies and predictions with those of their contemporaries who labored under the same handicaps. The statesmen with the greatest foresight will suffer least from the hindsight of the historian.

While he should make allowance for the contemporary atmosphere, the historian cannot simply attribute the statesman's defects to the "contagion of the times"—to prevailing public opinion. This is a heads-I-win-tails-you-lose principle. According to it, the policy maker takes the credit if things turn out well; if not, the people take the blame. In a democracy there is or should be some degree of popular responsibility, of course. The more secret the policy, the less the public can be held to account for it. The more aloof the policy maker, the less the people are accountable for him, and if he is an unelected Olympian, their accountability approaches zero.

The adequacy of statesmanship is at bottom a moral or ethical matter. That is not to say, however, that the leader who thinks and talks in terms of righteous indignation is necessarily as right as he is indignant. There is a difference between moralizing and moral behavior, between legalistic rationalization and respect for law. It may be posited that the truly ethical and law-abiding leader applies the same set of standards to another as to himself and to other groups as to his own. It may be suggested that, in international affairs, a policy risking an increase of violence and instability in the world, though expressed in the language of a holy crusader, is not necessarily superior in ethics to another policy more modest in its pretensions and milder in its probable consequences.

Though Stimson prided himself on being prophetically right, the fact is that he misread the future again and again. For example, he predicted in 1940–41 (as in 1932–33) that economic pressure would cause Japan to yield. He prepared for a Japanese attack on Dutch or British possessions in the southwestern Pacific but not for the one that came—on Pearl Harbor. In 1945, he approved the use of atomic bombs against Japan, presumably as a means of redressing the postwar balance in the Far East against Russia. In every case there were alternatives and eloquent spokesmen for them.

Stimson was not solely responsible, of course, for any of the errors of his time. He was only one—and seldom a decisive one—among a whole blundering generation of American statesmen. Sometimes, indeed, he looked like nothing more than an intellectual chameleon. At one moment he reflected the progressivism of Theodore Roosevelt, and the next moment, that of Taft and Root. Under the influ-

ence of Root he denounced the idea of collective security
as contained in Wilson's covenant, then espoused the idea
as a friend of American friends of the League, and carried
it farther than the aging Root thought wise during the Manchurian crisis. Between President Hoover and the militant
pacifists, Stimson seemed to take an ambivalent attitude
toward the proposed European "consultative pact." In Latin
American affairs he followed Hoover's leadership and reversed the interventionism he had preached as T. R.'s dis-
ciple and practiced as Coolidge's agent. On the question of
the atom bomb and the surrender of Japan, he stifled his
own first impulse to define the peace terms so as to make
them more acceptable, deferring to General Marshall, who
considered a definition of terms premature and impressed
upon Stimson the shock value of the new weapon.

The twists and turns of his career, the ironical contradic-
tions, make it one of the most fascinating in the annals of
American statesmanship. Early in it he conspired to thwart
Woodrow Wilson's plans for international organization,
and at the end of it he accepted a Woodrow Wilson Award
for his "unremitting effort to establish a world of order
under law." He gained a reputation as a "soldier of peace,"
and a warlike pacifist he seemed indeed, one who sniffed
the battle from afar, like the warhorse of the Scriptures.
He preached crusades to destroy "Prussianism" and "militarism" in other countries while in his own country he demanded compulsory military service even in peace time
and, in war time, justified a wholesale violation of civil
liberties on the specious plea of military necessity. He first
contemplated force against the Chinese and sympathized
with the Japanese, then turned to champion the one and
harry the other. He expressed a sense of outrage when a
few hundred civilians died in the primitive and ineffectual
bombing of Chinchow or Shanghai, yet showed a remark-

able readiness to let many thousands perish in the vastly more efficient blasting of Hiroshima and Nagasaki.

Some of his changes may have been signs of growth and of adaptability to changing times. Anyhow, his career developed a basic consistency. Throughout, he played upon certain themes with increasing coherence and emphasis, until at the end he stood out as the great exponent of a widely accepted complex of ideas. Peace to him, as in his Nicaraguan mission and in his championship of the Kellogg Pact, was apparently something to be imposed upon other people by force or the threat of force. Empire, as in the Philippines, seemed a duty in itself, a debt of honor, a thing to be pursued without much regard to economic or even strategic needs and still less to popular wishes. It was the white America's burden, and its counterpart after the second World War was the high call of world responsibility and leadership. Not balance and stability but law and morality, as in Manchuria, appeared to be the guiding principles in the conduct of foreign affairs. Peace through force, imperial responsibility, law unilaterally interpreted and applied—these added up to the idea of an America policing the world, an idea inherent in the Stimson Doctrine.

Though Stimson himself did not originate any of the elements of the doctrine, he gave it authority and a name, and it lived on after him. True, in the years of appeasement from 1933 to 1939 the principle of nonrecognition ceased to be honored by the League powers, and in 1945 it was left out of the U. N. charter. But the United States remained faithful to it, and President Truman, listing the "fundamentals" of American policy, declared in a Navy Day speech in 1945: "We shall refuse to recognize any government imposed upon any nation by the force of any foreign power." In any event, nonrecognition was not the essence of the Stimson Doctrine. Its essence, a compound of

Wilson's covenant and the Kellogg Pact, was the notion of keeping the peace and maintaining international law and order by means of boycotts, threats, and violence—nonrecognition being but a preliminary step. Through Stimson's glosses on the Kellogg Pact an ideological link was forged to join the United States and the League. Its successor, the U. N., lacked an equivalent of Wilson's article ten, guaranteeing the integrity of every member, but the same spirit infused the new organization.[2] In the name of the U. N., American troops were fighting again only five years after the end of the second World War.

The United States was still following an essentially Stimsonian policy. "The history of the Nineteen Thirties is now influencing the approach of the United States to the aggressions of the Nineteen Fifties," James Reston observed in early 1951. "To Secretary of State Dean Acheson, Mr. Stimson was much more than an illustrious predecessor. He was a personal hero, carefully studied and perhaps unconsciously followed." Acheson was carrying on in the spirit of his hero. "Like Mr. Stimson, he is determined to punish the aggressors in Korea and China as much as possible."

But George Kennan, for one, thought this sort of thinking—this "legalistic-moralistic" approach to foreign policy —was itself a leading cause of the trouble we were in. "The Japanese," Kennan noted, "are finally out of China proper and out of Manchuria and Korea as well. The effects of their expulsion from these areas have been precisely what wise and realistic people warned us all along they would be. Today we have fallen heir to the problems and responsibilities the Japanese had faced and borne in the Korean-Manchurian area for nearly half a century, and there is a certain perverse justice in the pain we are suffering from

[2] Robert Langer, *Seizure of Territory: The Stimson Doctrine and Related Principles in Legal Theory and Diplomatic Practice* (Princeton, 1947), 285-90.

a burden which, when it was borne by others, we held in such low esteem." Kennan had been criticizing what constituted the Stimsonian approach to foreign affairs, though he averred that he would be "most unhappy" if any of his observations should be taken as "a mark of disrespect for such men as John Hay, Elihu Root, Charles Evans Hughes, or Henry Stimson."

Other commentators criticized the Korean peace-enforcement project as illusory, among them Dorothy Thompson. "The prevailing bi-partisan view is that peace is indivisible, and that it is the American duty to police the globe against aggression," Miss Thompson wrote. She herself believed, however, "that a universal system of collective security is impossible without agreement between the United States and the U. S. S. R., that an American attempt unilaterally to enforce peace—with whatever states can be persuaded to go along in secondary roles—has already involved us in war; that permanent political pacification as a result of it is quite unimaginable; and that the pursuit of this concept will bankrupt the United States and lead not to the strengthening of liberty and law, but straight into state socialism." ³

Stimson himself provided what are perhaps the most eloquent commentaries on the Stimsonian principle of imposing law and morality and peace upon the rest of the world. He wrote in 1936: "This world of ours is a growing, developing community. In such a world a reign of law, however desirable, cannot be used as a strait jacket to prevent growth and change and still less to protect injustice and perpetuate hardship. Any attempt to make use of such a system of war prevention will ultimately cause explosions which may well destroy the system itself. I fear Europe [and the world?] will never achieve a permanent system

³ *New York Times*, January 21, 1951; Dorothy Thompson, in the *Champaign-Urbana Courier*, May 16, 1951; George F. Kennan, *American Diplomacy, 1900–1950* (Chicago, 1951), 18–19, 37, 44–52, 92, 95, 100–101.

of war prevention, no matter how sound a judicial system she may devise, until she has provided methods of relieving fundamental causes of pressure resulting in discontent." And he wrote in 1947: ". . . we are forced to act in the world as it is, and not in the world as we wish it were, or as we would like it to become." [4]

[4] Henry L. Stimson, *The Far Eastern Crisis: Recollections and Observations* (New York, 1936), 248–49; "The Challenge to Americans," in *Foreign Affairs*, 26: 7 (October, 1947).

Bibliography

MANUSCRIPTS, OFFICIAL DOCUMENTS, AND
NEWSPAPERS

The most important source for any study of Henry L.
Stimson is his own diary. For the years from 1910 to 1930 it
consists of only scattered entries and memoranda. From September, 1930, to February, 1933, it contains an entry for almost every day, usually dictated on the same or the following
day, and usually rather extensive. From 1933 to 1940 it pro-
vides only a fragmentary record, but from 1940 to 1945 it is
again very full. To 1933 it is accessible on microfilm in the
Yale University Library. After 1933 it is not yet available as
a whole, though excerpts are given in Stimson's memoirs, in
Herbert Feis's *Road to Pearl Harbor,* and in the published
hearings of the joint congressional committee investigating
the Pearl Harbor attack.

Another diary important for the period when Stimson was
Secretary of State is that of William R. Castle, then Under
Secretary. It is contained in typewritten volumes in the pos-
session of Mr. Castle, in Washington, D. C.

These personal records have been supplemented by a conversation with Mr. Herbert Hoover in New York, December 28, 1951, and by conversations and correspondence with
others who were acquainted with Stimson but who prefer
not to be named.

Government documents used in the present study include
several published hearings and reports of congressional com-

mittees. These, more fully cited in the footnotes of this book, may be briefly listed here: supplement to the hearings on the establishment of a national budget system (1919), fourth interim report of the Tolan committee (1942), hearings and report of the joint committee investigating the Pearl Harbor attack (1946), and hearings on the Institute of Pacific Relations and on the relief of General MacArthur (both 1951). In addition, the opening address of Robert H. Jackson at the Nuremberg war crimes trials (79 Congress, 1 session, Senate Document No. 129, 1946) should be mentioned.

The *Foreign Relations* series of the State Department, containing representative items of diplomatic correspondence, have been consulted for the years 1927, 1930, 1931, 1932, and 1933. These also are fully cited in the footnotes. A special volume on Japan, 1931–1941 was published as a kind of wartime white paper in 1943. The Department of State *Bulletin*, vol. 13 (1946), gives the published text of the Potsdam declaration.

The United States Strategic Bombing Survey produced seventy-seven numbers of reports on the Pacific war alone (1945–47). No. 2 in this series, *Japan's Struggle to End the War* (July 1, 1946), is especially relevant to the question of American policy making with respect to the use of the atom bomb.

Two League of Nations publications have been used: the *Report of the* [Lytton]*Commission of Enquiry* (1932) and Special Supplement No. 112 of the *Official Journal* (1933).

Stimson's entire public life has been followed in the files of the *New York Times*, and certain phases of his career in the New York *Herald Tribune*. At occasional points a few other newspapers have been consulted, as indicated in the footnotes.

BOOKS AND ARTICLES

Baxter, James P., *Scientists against Time*. Boston, 1946.

Baylen, Joseph O., "Sandino: Patriot or Bandit." *Hispanic American Historical Review*, 31: 394-419 (August, 1951).

Beard, Charles A., *President Roosevelt and the Coming of the War, 1941: A Study in Appearances and Realities*. New Haven, 1948.

Bemis, Samuel F., *The Latin American Policy of the United States: An Historical Interpretation*. New York, 1943.

Blackett, P. M. S., *Fear, War, and the Bomb: Military and Political Consequences of Atomic Energy*. New York, 1948.

Bush, Vannevar, *Modern Arms and Free Men: A Discussion of the Role of Science in Preserving Democracy*. New York, 1949.

Butcher, Harry C., *My Three Years with Eisenhower: The Personal Diary of Captain Harry C. Butcher, USNR, Naval Aide to General Eisenhower, 1942 to 1945*. New York, 1946.

Catton, Bruce, *The War Lords of Washington*. New York, 1948.

Clay, Lucius D., *Decision in Germany*. New York, 1950.

Cline, Ray S., *United States Army in World War II, The War Department, Washington Command Post: The Operations Division*. Washington, 1951.

Clyde, Paul H., "The Diplomacy of 'Playing No Favorites': Secretary Stimson and Manchuria, 1931." *Mississippi Valley Historical Review*, 35: 187-202 (June, 1948).

Coughlin, William J., "The Great *Mokusatsu* Mistake." *Harper's Magazine*, 206: 31-40 (March, 1953).

Cousins, Norman, and Thomas K. Finletter, "A Beginning for Sanity." *The Saturday Review of Literature*, vol. 29, no. 24, pp. 5-9, 38-40 (June 15, 1946).

Creel, George, "Secretary of War." *Collier's*, 112: 17, 54 (August 7, 1943).

Current, Richard N., "How Stimson Meant to 'Maneuver' the Japanese." *Mississippi Valley Historical Review*, 40: 67-74 (June, 1953).

De Conde, Alexander, *Herbert Hoover's Latin American Policy*. Stanford, 1951.

Dembitz, Nanette, "Racial Discrimination and the Military Judgment." *Columbia Law Review*, March, 1945, pp. 175-239.

Dennis, Lawrence, "Nicaragua: In Again, Out Again." *Foreign Affairs*, 9: 496-500 (April, 1931).

———, "Revolution, Recognition and Intervention." *Foreign Affairs*, 9: 204-21 (January, 1931).

Farley, James A., *Jim Farley's Story: The Roosevelt Years*. New York, 1948.

Feis, Herbert, *The Road to Pearl Harbor: The Coming of the War between the United States and Japan.* Princeton, 1950.

Ferrell, Robert H., *Peace in Their Time: The Origins of the Kellogg-Briand Pact.* New Haven, 1952.

Fishel, Wesley R., *The End of Extraterritoriality in China.* Berkeley and Los Angeles, 1952.

Folliard, Edward T., and William Costello, "Secretary of War Stimson." *American Mercury,* 59: 270–82 (September, 1944).

Forrestal, James V., *The Forrestal Diaries,* edited by Walter Millis. New York, 1951.

[Franck, James], "A Report to the Secretary of War, June 1945." *Bulletin of the Atomic Scientists,* vol. 1, no. 10, pp. 2–4, 16 (May 1, 1946).

Freidel, Frank, *Franklin D. Roosevelt: The Apprenticeship.* Boston, 1952.

Fuess, Claude M., "Henry L. Stimson." *Atlantic Monthly,* 168: 335–42 (September, 1941).

Grew, Joseph C., *Turbulent Era: A Diplomatic Record of Forty Years, 1904–1945,* edited by Walter Johnson. 2 vols., Boston, 1952.

Grodzins, Morton, *Americans Betrayed: Politics and the Japanese Evacuation.* Chicago, 1949.

Grunder, Garel A., and William E. Livezey, *The Philippines and the United States.* Norman, Oklahoma, 1951.

Gunther, John, *Roosevelt in Retrospect: A Profile in History.* New York, 1950.

Hoover, Herbert, *The Memoirs of Herbert Hoover,* Vol. 2: *The Cabinet and the Presidency, 1920–1933;* Vol. 3: *The Great Depression, 1929–1941.* New York, 1952.

Hull, Cordell, *The Memoirs of Cordell Hull.* 2 vols., New York, 1948.

Janeway, Eliot, *The Struggle for Survival: A Chronicle of Economic Mobilization in World War II.* New Haven, 1951.

Jessup, Philip C., *Elihu Root.* 2 vols., New York, 1938.

Kalaw, Maximo M., "Governor Stimson in the Philippines." *Foreign Affairs,* 7: 372–83 (April, 1929).

———, "Why the Filipinos Expect Independence." *Foreign Affairs,* 10: 304–15 (January, 1932).

Kennan, George F., *American Diplomacy, 1900–1950.* Chicago, 1951.

Langer, Robert, *Seizure of Territory: The Stimson Doctrine and Related Principles in Legal Theory and Diplomatic Practice.* Princeton, 1947.

Leahy, William D., *I Was There: the Personal Story of the Chief of Staff to Presidents Roosevelt and Truman Based on His Notes and Diaries Made at the Time.* New York, 1950.

Leighton, Alexander H., *Human Relations in a Changing World: Observations on the Use of the Social Sciences*. New York, 1949.

McWilliams, Carey, *Prejudice: Japanese-Americans: Symbol of Racial Intolerance*. Boston, 1944.

Moley, Raymond, *After Seven Years*. New York, 1939.

Moore, John Bassett, "An Appeal to Reason." *Foreign Affairs*, 11: 547–88 (July, 1933).

Morgenthau, Henry, Jr., "The Morgenthau Diaries: IV—The Story behind Lend Lease." *Collier's*, October 18, 1947, pp. 16–17, 71–75.

Morse, Hosea B., and Harley F. MacNair, *Far Eastern International Relations*. Boston, 1931.

Muller, Edwin, "The Inside Story of Pearl Harbor." *Reader's Digest*, vol. 44, no. 264, pp. 25–27 (April, 1944).

Myers, William S., *The Foreign Policies of Herbert Hoover, 1929–1933*. New York, 1940.

——, ed., *The State Papers and Other Public Writings of Herbert Hoover*. 2 vols., New York, 1934.

Nelson, Donald M., *Arsenal of Democracy: The Story of American War Production*. New York, 1946.

Neumann, William L., "Franklin D. Roosevelt and Japan, 1913–1933." *Pacific Historical Review*, 22: 143–53 (May, 1953).

[Pearson, Drew, and Robert S. Allen], *Washington Merry-Go-'Round*. New York, 1931.

Pearson, Drew, and Constantine Brown, *The American Diplomatic Game*. New York, 1935.

Pringle, Henry F., "Henry L. Stimson: A Portrait." *Outlook and Independent*, 151: 409–11, 437–38 (March 13, 1929).

——, *Theodore Roosevelt: A Biography*. New York, 1931.

Quezón, Luis M., *The Good Fight*. New York, 1946.

Romans, Charles F., and Riley Sunderland, *United States Army in World War II, China-Burma-India Theater: Stilwell's Mission to China*. Washington, 1953.

Sherwood, Robert E., *Roosevelt and Hopkins: An Intimate History*. New York, 1948.

Smith, Bradford, *Americans from Japan*. Philadelphia, 1948.

Smith, Sara R., *The Manchurian Crisis, 1931–1932: A Tragedy in International Relations*. New York, 1948.

Somers, Herman M., *Presidential Agency: OWMR, the Office of War Mobilization and Reconversion*. Cambridge, 1950.

Spykman, Nicholas J., *America's Strategy in World Politics: The United States and the Balance of Power*. New York, 1942.

Stilwell, Joseph W., *The Stilwell Papers*, edited by Theodore H. White. New York, 1948.

Stimson, Henry L., *American Policy in Nicaragua*. New York, 1927.

Stimson, Henry L., "Artillery in a Quiet Sector." *Scribner's Magazine*, 65: 709–16 (June, 1919).

——, "Bases of American Policy during the Past Four Years." *Foreign Affairs*, 11: 383–96 (April, 1933).

——, "The Challenge to Americans." *Foreign Affairs*, 26: 5–14 (October, 1947).

——, "The Decision to Use the Atomic Bomb." *Harper's Magazine*, 194: 99–107 (February, 1947).

——, *The Far Eastern Crisis: Recollections and Observations.* New York, 1936.

——, "Future Philippine Policy under the Jones Act." *Foreign Affairs*, 5: 459–71 (April, 1927).

——, "The Pact of Paris: Three Years of Development." *Foreign Affairs*, 11, Special Supplement, i–ix, following p. 210 (October, 1932).

——, and McGeorge Bundy, *On Active Service in Peace and War.* New York, 1948.

Stone, I. F., "Facts for Mr. Stimson." *The Nation*, 158: 123–24 (January 29, 1944).

Tupper, Eleanor, and George E. McReynolds, *Japan in American Public Opinion.* New York, 1937.

Van Alstyne, Richard W., Review of *Foreign Relations, 1932. Pacific Historical Review*, 18: 505–9 (November, 1949).

Watson, Mark S., *United States Army in World War II, The War Department, Chief of Staff: Prewar Plans and Preparations.* Washington, 1950.

Williams, William A., *American Russian Relations, 1781–1947.* New York, 1952.

Wilson, Hugh, *Diplomat between Wars.* New York, 1941.

Young, C. Walter, *Japan's Special Position in Manchuria.* Baltimore, 1931.

Zacharias, Ellis M., *Secret Missions: The Story of an Intelligence Officer.* New York, 1946.

Index

257

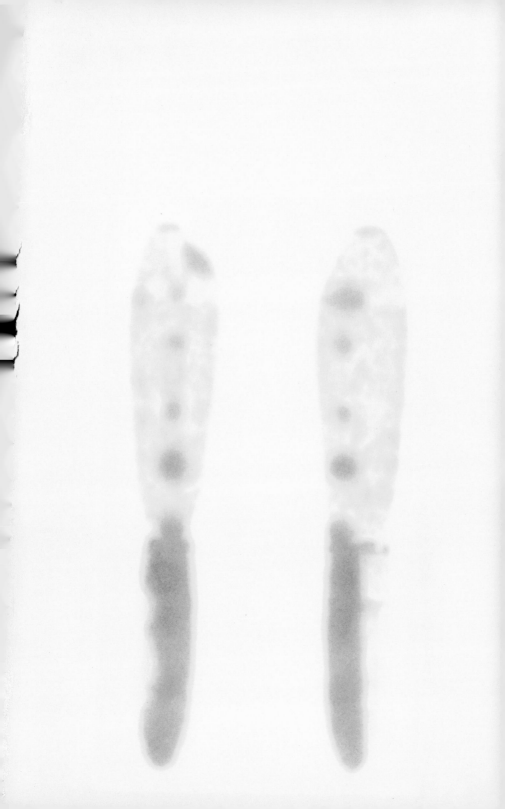